FINANCIAL INVESTIGATIONS

A Financial Approach to Detecting and Resolving Crimes

Acknowledgements

The men and women of Internal Revenue Service Criminal Investigation are proud to present this course to the colleges, universities and students who have expressed an interest in learning more about financial investigations.

The purpose of this course is twofold: first, to encourage young men and women to consider law enforcement as an enriching career and second, to bring to the reader's attention the serious and sometimes evil crimes that are motivated by money and greed.

We would like to thank the Internal Revenue Service Special Agents who instructed the pilot courses at the colleges and universities. We would also like to thank the colleges and universities that allowed the Internal Revenue Service Criminal Investigation to offer this new course at their institutions.

A special note of thanks goes to the National Association of Certified Fraud Examiners, and their Chairman, Joseph T. Wells, for their contributions to the text.

The following Internal Revenue Service Criminal Investigation Employees were involved in the research, development, writing, editing and publishing of the text:

Don Vogel	Cathy Pledger
Robert Pledger	Rich Tucker
Bob Wilson	Richard Ruffin
John Imhoff	Mike Spang
Robert Diffenderfer	Arnie Sitzmann
Ross Sutton	Diane Svoboda
Elliott Lieb	Diane Evans
Ed Federico	Patricia Reid
Douglas Gastorf	Sue Roderick
Paul Whitmore	Dennis Madden
Bill O'Connor	Vince Williams

Table of Contents

CHAPTER 1

Why Financial Investigation?

Early criminologists categorized criminal activity into two large groupings: crimes against people and crimes against property. Since the victims of crimes were either people (murder, robbery) or property (burglary, arson) it was natural to list criminal activity by victim. But today, criminal activities have evolved beyond merely "against people" and "against property." Criminal activity can now be classified by motivation factors: passion or greed. This textbook deals with crimes related to the latter, crimes motivated by money.

With this new view of crime comes the need for a new approach to dealing with criminal activity— the financial investigative approach. Gone are the days when the headlines read "James Gang Robs Bank." Today we are more likely to see a headline that reads "International Bank Implicated In Money Laundering Scheme." A special type of investigator is needed to deal with these crimes. This investigator must be able to use the investigative techniques of the past in combination with a new set of techniques. These new techniques focus on financial dealings. Throughout this textbook, you will learn about the techniques used by the financial investigator. But first, you will be provided with an introduction to the financial investigative approach. This chapter begins with a review of some of the more sensational headlines of the time. It will become clear that a new approach to criminal investigation is needed. You will then be provided with a general overview of the financial investigative approach and we will look into the types of crime where the approach is applicable.

The knowledges and skills required of a financial investigator will be identified and then the chapter concludes with a look at Federal government agencies that employ financial investigators.

After studying Chapter 1, you should be able to:

- State why there is a need for a new investigative approach.
- Provide a general overview of the financial investigative process.
- Identify the skills required of a financial investigator.

Today, the overwhelming majority of crimes committed in America are motivated by money. Criminal activity is directed toward making money in a way fashioned not to get caught. Although this is not a revolutionary concept to the experienced law enforcement officer, the importance of this fact is commonly disregarded. In today's law enforcement, a new investigative approach is emphasized along with a new type of investigator. This approach and this type of investigator are the focus of this chapter and this text.

A New Investigative Approach

It seems that we cannot pick up a newspaper, listen to a radio, or watch television without learning about some crime that has been alleged or committed. Crime is page-one news. It seems to be everywhere. Let's recall some of the major headlines and sensational stories that appeared in the news in the late 1980s and early 1990s. For example:

- Ten-term Congressman Mario Biaggi was sentenced to eight years in prison and fined $242,000 for 15 felony convictions ranging from racketeering to obstruction of justice and bribery. Biaggi was involved in the Wedtech scandal. Wedtech paid millions of dollars in bribes to public officials to obtain no-bid federal contracts.
- Hotel queen Leona Helmsley was convicted of tax evasion and sentenced to four years in prison. It seems she and her hus-

band avoided paying more than $1.7 million in federal and state taxes from 1983 through 1985.

- Ivan Boesky was sentenced to three years in prison and paid $100 million in fines for insider trading.

- Michael Milken, king of the junk bond, was indicted on 98 counts involving racketeering, insider trading, and assorted securities fraud. He pleaded guilty to six counts and the government dropped all other charges. Milken was sentenced to 10 years in prison and agreed to pay $600 million in penalties.

- Operation Ill Wind, an investigation into Pentagon procurement fraud, impacted individuals as well as corporations. Among the casualties of the probe were Unisys Corporation and Melvyn Paisley. Unisys agreed to pay $190 million in fines for having bribed its way to hundreds of millions of dollars worth of defense contracts. Paisley, a former assistant secretary of the Navy, admitted he sold his influence for bribes and leaked secret government information to defense firms bidding on weapons contracts.

- The savings and loan scandal rocked America. The collapse of the Lincoln Savings and Loan Association alone will cost the American taxpayers $2.6 billion.

The list could go on and on! And what do all of the crimes described above have in common? Money! It seems like most of today's criminal activity either involves money or money is its main motivator. And many of the crimes depicted by today's headlines are crimes that cannot be solved solely by the use of traditional investigative techniques.

In the past, police relied on investigative tools such as crime scene analysis, physical evidence, fingerprint identification, eye witness accounts, informants, and confessions of the offender to supply the understandable proof of the crime. These general investigative techniques work best in situations where a crime has been committed and then law enforcement tries to find the criminal. However, will these tools work when the criminal is known and authorities begin an investigation to prove the crime?

Infamous mobster Al Capone wasn't easy to catch. But when IRS Special Agents, who are trained accountants, stepped in and charged him with tax evasion, this crime czar's career came to an end. Proof that sometimes only the accountant can apprehend the criminal.

For example:

• Organized crime legends like Al Capone, Lucky Luciano, John Gotti, and Frank Balestrieri operated for years with relative impunity. How does law enforcement prove criminal activity when informants are killed, eye witnesses threatened, and confessions are nonexistent?

• Money launderers, tax evaders, and crooked politicians are for the most part respected pillars of society. How does law enforcement investigate the criminal activities of people like former Vice-President Spiro Agnew and rock and roll legend Chuck Berry? These are people whose power rivals that of law enforcement itself.

To answer these questions, it is necessary to go beyond the mere inclusion of a few new tools in law enforcement's investigative arsenal. A brand new approach is called for in light of the evolution of crime in America— *a financial investigative approach.* The growth of money-motivated crimes mandates the need for financial investigations. The future success of law enforcement is contingent upon its ability to conduct financial investigations in conjunction with general criminal investigations.

What's Involved in the Financial Investigative Approach?

The major goal of a financial investigator is to identify and document specific events involving the movement of money during the course of a crime. Suppose an accountant is suspected of embezzling money from her employer. A financial investigator would determine what accounts she is taking the money from, when she took it, and where she is putting it. If the investigator is able to identify these events and link them together, he or she will have the basis of proof indicating the commission of a crime. If the events cannot be identified and linked together, the investigation may support the determination to discontinue further inquiry into the matter.

Financial investigations by their very nature are record intensive; specifically, records pointing to the movement of money.

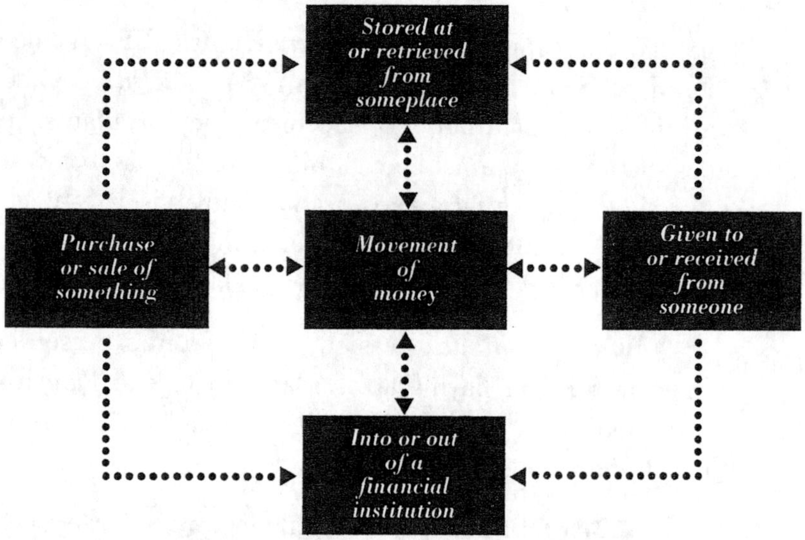

Bank account information (checking and savings account records), motor vehicle registrations (title, place of purchase, and lien-holder records), and real estate files (records showing mortgages and deeds records) are documents or records commonly found in this type of investigation. However, records such as computer disks, utility bills, divorce decrees, and credit card carbons can play important roles in financial investigations. Any record that pertains to or shows the *paper trail of events* is important to a financial investigation.

Crimes with a Financial Aspect

Now that you have a general understanding of what's involved in the financial investigative approach, let's identify some criminal activities where the application of the approach would be appropriate. The list below identifies and describes some crimes that are financial in nature.

- **Fraud.** Fraud is a generic term embracing all the ways one person can falsely represent a fact to another in order to induce that person to surrender something of value. Former television evangelist and PTL leader, Jim Bakker, was convicted of defrauding followers by offering $1,000 "partnerships" that promised a lifetime of lodging rights at his glitzy Heritage USA theme park in Fort Mill, South Carolina. Between 1984 and 1987, 153,000 partnerships were sold but only 258 rooms were available. It's obvious that there were not enough rooms for the number of partners that signed up. In fact, a reservations supervisor testified that in any month during Bakker's last year at the PTL, as many as 3,700 lifetime partners were denied accommodations at the theme park.

- **Tax evasion.** Tax evasion occurs when a person commits fraud in filing or paying taxes. Baseball legend Pete Rose was convicted of tax evasion. He failed to report $354,968 worth of income between 1984 and 1987.

- **Bribery.** Bribery occurs when money, goods, services, information, or anything else of value is offered with the intent to influence the actions, opinions, or decisions of the taker. You can be charged with bribery whether you offer the bribe or accept it. Jimmy Hoffa was convicted of bribing a juror who served at one of his trials.

- **Embezzlement.** Embezzlement occurs when a person who has been entrusted with money or property appropriates it for his or her own use and benefit. A former budget analyst with the U.S. Information Agency embezzled $16,234 from the agency by submitting bogus requests for cash advances which were supported by fake vendor receipts he created on an office computer. That budget analyst was in a position where he would be trusted with the agency's money. Instead, he decided to take some of the money for himself.

- **Larceny.** Larceny occurs when one person wrongfully takes another person's money or property with the intent to appropriate, convert, or steal it. If someone steals your car and then sells it, he or she has committed larceny.

- **Forgery.** Forgery occurs when a person passes a false or worthless instrument, such as a check or counterfeit security, with the intent to defraud or injure the recipient. An assistant bookkeeper with Real Estate Magazines, Inc. was convicted of stealing $54,000 from the company by cashing checks on which she forged the signature.

- **Counterfeiting.** Counterfeiting occurs when someone copies or imitates an item without having been authorized to do so and passes the copy off for the genuine or original item. We often hear of counterfeit money. But the next time you buy an item of designer clothing or pay for some prescription medication, make sure it's the real thing!

- **Blackmail.** Blackmail is a demand for money or other considerations under threat to do bodily harm, to injure property, to accuse of crime, or to expose disgraceful defects. Suppose a politician has a skeleton in his closet and he'd rather keep it there. Someone else knows the politician's secret and threatens to tell the world unless she receives $25,000. That's blackmail.

- **Extortion.** Extortion occurs when one person illegally obtains property from another by actual or threatened force, fear, or violence, or under cover of official right. A Washington, DC tax auditor was convicted of extortion when it was revealed that he threatened to assess high taxes against a small Ethiopian-owned business unless the owner gave him some money.

- **Kickback.** A company is awarded a contract to build a dormitory on a college campus. One day the president of the college receives a $3,000 payment from the company. The president calls the company's vice-president of finance, thanks him for the payment, and says he's glad the two parties were able to work out a deal— the contract for a few $3,000 payments. This is an example of a kickback scheme. A kickback occurs when the person who sells an item pays back a portion of the purchase price to the buyer (or a public official).

- **Racketeering.** Charges of racketeering can cover a wide range of things, but the bottom line is that racketeering is running an illegal business for personal profit.

- **Insider trading.** Insider trading occurs when a person uses "inside" or advance information to trade in shares of publicly held corporations.

- **Money laundering.** Money laundering is the investment or transfer of money from racketeering, drug transactions, and other illegal sources into legitimate channels so that its original source cannot be traced.

The crimes listed above are what we normally think of when we hear the term "financial crime." But financial evidence is also used to build cases against persons suspected of kidnapping, espionage, murder, and arson, to name a few.

Financial Investigation Skills

As you see, a financial investigator can be involved in all sorts of criminal investigations. This investigator brings a unique set of skills to any investigation. The successful financial investigator draws on different aspects from many professions to blend information in ways, shapes, and forms never imagined by his or her predecessors. Financial investigators need to be part cop, part investigator, part accountant, part sociologist, part computer operator, and part attorney in order to combat and resolve the major crimes of today and detect the crimes of the future. The ability to understand the interdependence between financial events and criminal activity is the essence of a successful financial investigator. Accordingly, a financial investigator needs to:

- Know the statute(s) that define the crime(s) under investigation
- Understand concepts relating to the collection and admissibility of evidence
- Locate and interpret records that contain financial information
- Trace the movement of money through a financial institution
- Use accounting and auditing techniques
- Use methods of proof to link financial events together
- Conduct financial interviews, record their findings, and summarize them in report form

- Use investigative techniques such as surveillance and undercover operations

Each of the items listed above is a topic in this textbook. When you complete this text, you will have a good understanding of what's involved in conducting a financial investigation, and, perhaps along the way, you will pick up a few financial investigative skills.

Today's Financial Investigators

The emergence of law enforcement's involvement in financial investigations is reflected in the evolution of the Internal Revenue Service's Criminal Investigation Division. Created in 1919 to investigate fraud and dishonesty among IRS employees, this Division has grown to over 2,800 agents and is the acknowledged leader in the fields of tax fraud and money laundering investigation. The ability of the special agents to trace financial transactions has taken them a long way from tax returns and into the middle of every major financial investigation in America— the Savings and Loan Scandal, junk bond frauds, the Iran Contra Affair, spy trials, and drug and organized crime prosecutions.

Many other federal agencies also employ financial investigators. These agencies expand in size, function, and authority as laws are developed and policies to emphasize enforcement of various crimes are devised. In the 1930s, emphasis was on bootlegging and the emerging Mafia. In the 1950s, organized crime's involvement in political corruption was the issue. The 1980s targeted the "War on Drugs." The 1990s are faced with the Savings and Loan and Wall Street scandals. For this reason, the size and employment needs of the agencies fluctuate to respond to current issues. The following is a list of those federal agencies and their major investigative authority which most commonly employ full-time financial investigators or utilize financial techniques in its investigations.

- **U.S. Customs Service.** The Customs Service has come to mean many things to many people. To the international traveler, Customs is the men and women who examine personal luggage and facilitate the entry of passengers upon their return to the United States. To the importer, Customs provides advice, and protection and control of merchandise shipped into the country. To the smuggler, Customs is the planes, vehicles, and vessels constantly monitoring the nation's perimeters to thwart attempts at illicit entries of merchandise, including narcotics and dangerous drugs. Within Customs, there is an increasing emphasis being placed on the investigation of schemes that defraud the U.S. Government of rightful revenue— the illicit transportation of currency, and export violations including the illegal shipment of arms and technologies.

- **U.S. Secret Service.** Along with their protection services, the Secret Service enforces the law against counterfeiting currency, coins, or securities of the United States. The agency also enforces the laws against fraud or forgery of government checks or bonds, and other securities and obligations of the United States. Other investigative responsibilities include credit and debit card fraud, computer fraud, and electronic fund transfer fraud.

- **U.S. Marshal Service.** The U.S. Marshal Service provides protection to the Federal courts, judges, jurors, and witnesses; apprehends Federal fugitives; executes court orders; manages and sells property seized from criminals; operates the Witness Security Program; and administers the National Asset Seizure and Forfeiture Program. Deputies assigned to the forfeiture program establish computer-assisted bookkeeping procedures and inventory control systems to account for receipt, storage, and disposition of seized assets.

- **Bureau of Alcohol, Tobacco, and Firearms.** The Bureau of Alcohol, Tobacco, and Firearms is an agency within the Treasury Department. The agency is made up of two sections: Compliance Operations and Law Enforcement. The Law Enforcement Section investigates tax evasion, operations carried on without a license or permit, and the illegal use of firearms, ammunition, and explosives.

- **Office of the Inspector General.** OIG agents investigate fraud, waste, and government abuses. The agency serves as the investigative watchdog for over fifty federal agencies. OIG agents, by their very nature, are financially-orientated. Making sure that government contracts, procurements, and payments are completed as designed requires financial analysis, accounting and auditing techniques, and the understanding of business principles.

• **Federal Bureau of Investigation.** The FBI has jurisdiction over 200 types of cases including white-collar crime, organized crime, foreign counter-intelligence, political corruption, civil rights violations, terrorism, Federal drug violations, kidnapping, bank robbery, and interstate criminal activity.

• **Internal Revenue Service.** The IRS is responsible for encouraging and achieving the highest voluntary compliance with tax laws and regulations. In addition to investigating violations of federal tax laws, special agents with the Internal Revenue Service's Criminal Investigation Division investigate money laundering offenses and conduct asset forfeiture investigations. On many occasions, special agents lend their expertise to multi-agency investigations.

• **Drug Enforcement Administration.** The DEA is the lead law enforcement agency having the responsibility of combating drug abuse. The agency enforces federal drug control laws and concentrates on high-level drug dealers, nationally and internationally.

• **Postal Inspection Service.** The United States Postal Service enforces the laws and regulations governing the mail system through its Inspection Service. The Inspection Service investigates all alleged violations of individuals suspected of mail fraud and mail theft. The Inspection Service is also involved in investigations concerning child pornography and the illegal transport of controlled substances through the mail.

• **Nonfederal Agencies.** State and local law enforcement agencies are beginning to approach criminal investigations from a financial perspective. Designations such as "White Collar Crimes Squad," "Financial Crimes Unit," and "Credit Card Fraud Team" are starting to join the traditional detective's classifications. Additionally, on-the-job training of local and state officers (including attorneys, investigators, and management officials) in financial investigative techniques is already taking place.

Summary

Today, gambling organizations, drug cartels, and "mom and pop grocery stores" are at ease with the personal computer and its capabilities. Corporate fraud, insider trading violations, and the savings and loan scandals have been completed by the creation of phony shell companies, ghost employees, and non-existent nominees. Sophisticated money launderers, large scale robbery rings, and embezzlement and kickback operations maintain elaborate accounting records that often are the envy of CPAs. *Big-time crime operates as a full-time business.* To resolve today's crimes and prepare for the challenges of tomorrow, law enforcement requires an understanding of financial information. Whether searching for leads in society's back alleys or board room suites, financial information is going to be discovered during the course of a criminal investigation. Consequently, law enforcement agencies are seeking officers with proficiency in financial analysis.

A major challenge for financial investigators is to provide investigative findings which present evidence of complex crimes in simple and understandable terms which are comprehensible by a jury. Consider the world of international high finance with its shell corporations, universal letters of credit, offshore banks, electronic transfers between numbered Swiss bank accounts, and interlocking reciprocal trade arrangements. To a juror, this is almost unfathomable. It's up to the prosecution team, of which an investigator is part, to dissect these complex ideas and translate them into simple thoughts that everyone can understand. It's pretty easy to understand "he was caught smuggling a suitcase full of $100 bills out of the country."

As you continue through this textbook, bear in mind that as law enforcement improves its techniques for detecting, combating, and resolving criminal activity, criminals will become more sophisticated and innovative in their endeavors. You can be sure that law enforcement practitioners will never work themselves out of a job.

CHAPTER 2

Laws Related to Financial Crimes

Chapter 1 provided a general overview of certain crimes that are normally thought of as financial in nature. In this chapter, we will identify some of the federal statutes, the formal written laws, that underlie particular financial crimes. Chapter 1 described embezzlement as the unlawful appropriation of money or property by a person who has been entrusted with those items. In Chapter 2, you'll see that there are several statutes related to embezzlement. As an investigator, you must be aware of what statute the accused is suspected of violating. Also, the commission of one crime could include the violation of several different statutes. For example, if someone is suspected of embezzlement from a bank, that person might also be suspected of tax evasion. Both of these violations are subjects of federal statutes.

You may be wondering why an investigator should be aware of the statutes that are related to a suspected criminal activity. After all, lawyers deal with things like statutes. So why does a financial investigator have to have knowledge of this area? Well, it's because statutes contain the elements of a crime— those parts of the crime that must be proven in order to gain a conviction. Once an investigator has identified the elements of a crime, he or she can focus evidence collection efforts on gathering relevant information to prove that the accused committed the crime in question.

After studying Chapter 2, you should be able to:

- Define or describe selected terms related to the field of law.

- Identify the statute(s) related to a particular crime.
- List the elements of a particular crime.

In Chapter 1, we stated that the successful financial investigator draws on knowledge from several professions. Among other things, an investigator must be part attorney. This chapter focuses on that part of a financial investigator.

Terms and Concepts

Before we begin a discussion of specific laws of interest to a financial investigator, we should review some basic concepts related to law. First, we will answer the question "What is law?" Next, different categories of law will be identified. Finally, some concepts related to crime will be discussed.

What is Law?

If you were to ask 10 people to define "law," you probably would get 10 different answers. Someone will see "law" as the police officer who hands out speeding tickets. Another person will see "law" as a judge sentencing a person to prison. And another will see "law" as a lawyer involved in a trial. As different as the 10 responses might be, they will all have one thing in common— a basic effort to place the affairs of society in order. And generally, that is what **law** is— a formal means of social control. It is intended to guide or direct human behavior toward ends that satisfy the common good. Laws embody moral principles and express the rights and obligations that members of society hold toward one another. They provide for individual protection and for the common well-being.

Categories of Law

In the legal world, there are many categories of law. There is **common law,** the system of law that originated in England and was the body of law carried by the earliest English settlers to the American colonies. There is **case law,** the practice of judges and lawyers looking into decisions from past cases to determine the state of the law for the case they are currently handling. The financial investigator is most interested in substantive law and two other categories of law derived from it: criminal and civil law. Each of these categories is described below.

- **Substantive law.** Substantive law is the body of law that creates, discovers, and defines the rights and obligations of each person in society. Substantive law is composed of the statutes and ordinances enacted by federal, state, and local legislative bodies and any regulations proclaimed thereunder, in addition to each state and federal constitution. Case law is part of the body of substantive law in the United States. *Criminal and civil laws are derived from substantive law.*

- **Civil law.** Civil law is the body of law that deals with conflicts and differences between individuals. These private wrongdoings are often referred to as **torts.** Remedies are usually in the form of money damages or court-ordered actions to do, or refrain from doing, certain specific things.

- **Criminal law.** Criminal law is that branch of the law that deals with offenses of a public nature, that is, wrongs committed against the state. Such laws may be imposed by federal or state statutes and usually provide penalties, fines, and/or incarceration for their breach.

Classifications of Crime

Crimes can be distinguished between those that are felonies and those that are misdemeanors. A **felony** is a serious crime punishable by incarceration for a period exceeding one year, a fine, and loss of certain civil rights (right to vote and to hold public office). **Misdemeanors** are crimes less serious than felonies and usually provide for incarceration periods of less than one year. Fines also may be imposed.

Crimes also can be classified as to those that are mala in se and those that are mala prohibita. Crimes that are **mala in se** are said to be evil or immoral in and of themselves. They are "offenses against human conscience." Common crimes of this type include felonies such as murder and rape. Crimes that are **mala prohibita** are offenses that are made criminal by statute but in and of themselves are not necessarily immoral. Mala prohibita crimes include most violations of government regulations, environmental laws, and even traffic offenses. Crimes that are mala in se often require proof of criminal intent, or, in legal terms, **mens rea.** Crimes that are mala prohibita don't usually require proof of criminal intent.

An Introduction to Statutes and the Elements of a Crime

Suppose you're an investigator for a federal agency and your boss asks you to investigate a case of alleged embezzlement. "Get right on it," she says. Where do you begin? Well, before you put your investigative skills into action, you've got to determine what law(s) the suspect is allegedly violating. But you're an investigator, not a lawyer. Why do you need to be familiar with the laws underlying a criminal violation? Because you need to be aware of the **elements of the crime.** The elements of a crime are those constituent parts that must be proven to sustain a conviction; that is, sufficient to make a prima facie case. With a criminal violation, a **prima facie case** is proven when evidence has been presented which proves, beyond a reasonable doubt, the elements of the crime. In Chapter 3, you'll read about collecting evidence and its admissibility in court. For now, we will key in on two other skills required of an investigator: interpreting the law(s) that underlie a crime and identifying the elements of the crime. But before you can do these two things, you must be able to locate the law(s) that define a crime.

United States Code

In 1925, Congress authorized the preparation of the United States Code, a multi-volume publication of the text of statutes enacted by Congress. The first set came out in 1926 and consisted four volumes. As of 1988, the United States Code consists of 19 volumes of statutes and several supplementary texts. The United

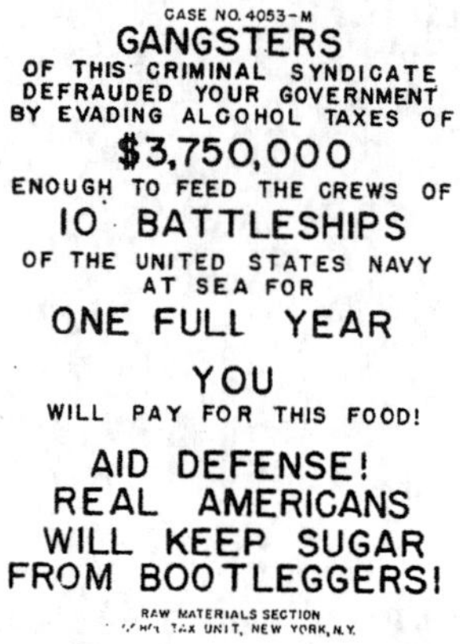

Financial investigations have been the most effective method of "following the money" to halt tax evasion since the United States Congress enacted the Revenue Act of 1913. The above poster, from the World War II era, solicits the support of American taxpayers in combatting tax evasion.

States Code is updated every six years with cumulative supplement volumes being issued during intervening years. You can usually find the United States Code in the reference section of any library.

The statutes are **codified** into 50 titles. Codification is the process of collecting and arranging laws by subject. For example, Title 2 is called "The Congress" and statutes relating to the election of senators and representatives, the organization of Congress, and the regulation of lobbying are found here. Titles may be further subdivided into parts, subchapters, and/or chapters.

Suppose you're reading a legal document and you came across the phrase "he was convicted of violating 26 U.S.C. § 7201." To find out what this person was convicted of, you need to be able to interpret what is meant by "26 U.S.C. § 7201." It's easy— U.S.C. stands for United States Code, 26 is the title number, and 7201 is the statute reference. You locate the volume of the United States Code that contains Title 26, turn to the statute referenced by the number 7201 and find the following:

§ 7201. Attempt to evade or defeat a tax or the payment thereof

Any person who willfully attempts in any manner to evade or defeat any tax imposed by this title or the payment thereof shall, in addition to other penalties provided by law, be guilty of a felony and, upon conviction thereof, shall be fined not more than $250,000 ($500,000 in the case of a corporation) or imprisoned not more than 5 years, or both, together with the costs of prosecution.

Upon reading the statute, you determine that the person previously referenced was convicted of tax evasion. But what did the investigator who worked on the case have to prove to show that the person committed tax evasion? In other words, what are the elements of the crime?

Elements of a Crime

Earlier, we stated that the elements of a crime are those constituent parts that must be proven to sustain a conviction. Well, to gain a conviction for evasion of taxes, there are three elements that must proven beyond a reasonable doubt. These elements are:

- The suspect owes additional taxes
- The suspect attempted to evade the taxes
- The suspect willfully attempted to evade the taxes

It is important that the financial investigator be able to use the United States Code to locate statutes, however, with the complex way statutes are written, it is not always easy to sort out the elements of the crime. If in doubt, discuss the elements with the prosecuting attorney. An understanding of these elements will enable an investigator to focus his of her evidence collection efforts on pertinent information.

Since criminal statutes may be enacted by any level of government— federal, state, and local— it is important to remember that the elements of any particular crime may vary between the three different jurisdictions. Investigators must be knowledgeable about the statute used for criminal prosecution so that the appropriate evidence can be collected.
The remainder of the chapter deals with statutes that are of interest to the financial investigator. Selected statutes from the following four United States Code titles will be discussed:

- Title 15, Commerce and Trade
- Title 18, Crimes and Criminal Procedure
- Title 26, Internal Revenue Code
- Title 31, Money and Finance

Federal Statutes: Title 18, Crimes and Criminal Procedure

Title 18 contains federal criminal laws that range from the trivial— a statute barring the unauthorized use of the Smokey the Bear emblem, to the monumental— the criminal provisions of the Antitrust laws. Selected statutes, along with the elements of the

§ 201. Bribery of public officials and witnesses

(b) Whoever—

(1) directly or indirectly, corruptly gives, offers or promises anything of value to any public official... or offers or promises any public official... to give anything of value to any other person or entity, with intent —

(A) to influence any official act; or

(B) to influence such public official... to commit or aid in committing, or collude in, or allow, any fraud, or make opportunity for the commission of any fraud, on the United States; or

(C) to induce such public official... to do or omit to do any act in violation of the lawful duty or such official...

shall be fined not more than three times the monetary equivalent of the thing of value, or imprisoned for not more than fifteen years, or both...

crime, are listed and described on the following pages. As was stated earlier, titles may be further subdivided into parts, subchapters, and/or chapters. Title 18 happens to be divided into 121 chapters. The Title 18 statutes described in this text are listed according to the chapter in which they are found in the United States Code. Keep in mind that chapters often contain multiple statutes, but this text lists just selected ones. So if you see only one statute listed under a chapter, chances are that other statutes exist in the chapter, but for purposes of this text they were not selected for inclusion.

Bribery, Graft, and Conflicts of Interest

Bribes are given to influence the taker's actions, opinions, or decisions. Title 18 U.S.C. § 201 makes it illegal for a public official or a witness to accept a bribe and for a person to offer a bribe to either of these parties. Section (b)(1), the part of the statute making it illegal to bribe a public official, is shown on the next page.

The elements of the crime of bribing a public official include the following:

- The suspect knowingly offered a bribe to a public official
- The bribe was intended to influence the public official's performance of an official act or lawful duty

§ 287. False, fictitious, or fraudulent claims
Whoever makes or presents to any person or officer in the civil... service of the United States, or to any department or agency thereof, any claim upon or against the United States, or any department or agency thereof, knowing such claim to be false, fictitious, or fraudulent shall be fined not more than $250,000, or imprisoned not more than five years, or both.

§ 371. Conspiracy to commit offense or to defraud the United States
If two or more persons conspire either to commit any offense against the United States, or to defraud the United States, or any agency thereof in any manner or for any purpose, and one or more of such persons do any act to effect the object of the conspiracy, each shall be fined not more than $250,000 or imprisoned not more than 5 years, or both.
If, however, the offense, the commission of which is the object of the conspiracy, is a misdemeanor only, the punishment for such conspiracy shall not exceed the maximum punishment provided for such misdemeanor.

Claims and Services in Matters Affecting Government

We must protect the funds and property of our government from fraudulent claims. Suppose someone is running a scheme where he or she files federal income tax returns for people who do not exist, and then pockets the refunds. This person is filing false claims against the Internal Revenue Service. Title 18 U.S.C. § 287 makes this illegal.

The elements of the crime include the following:

- The suspect made or presented a claim against the United States or any of its departments or agencies
- The suspect knew that the claim was false, fictitious, or fraudulent

Conspiracy

Sometimes, two or more people agree to join forces and carry out some illegal activity. Title 18 U.S.C. § 371 protects society from these mutual agreements. According to the statute, the illegal activity only has to be conspired to, it doesn't actually need to be accomplished. However, at least one of the co-conspirators must have carried out one "overt act" in furtherance of the conspiracy. The overt act need not be criminal in itself. It may be as innocuous as making a phone call or writing a letter.

Conspiracy counts are favored by the prosecution because they provide certain evidentiary and pleading advantages. If a conspiracy is shown, the acts and statements of one co-conspirator may be admitted into evidence against all, and each co-conspirator may be convicted for the underlying substantive offense.

A corporation cannot conspire with one of its own employees to commit an offense since the employee and employer are legally viewed as one. A corporation may, however, conspire with other business entities or third parties in violation of this statute.

The elements of the crime include the following:

- The conspiracy was willfully formed
- The suspect willfully became a member of it

- At least one of the conspirators knowingly committed at least one overt act in furtherance of the conspiracy

§471. Obligations or securities of the United States
Whoever, with intent to defraud, falsely makes, forges, counterfeits, or alters any obligation or other security of the United States, shall be fined not more than $250,000 or imprisoned not more than fifteen years, or both.

§ 641. Public money, property or records
Whoever embezzles, steals, purloins, or knowingly converts to his use or the use of another, or without authority sells, conveys or disposes of any record, voucher, money, or thing of value of the United States or any department or agency thereof, or any property made or being made under contract for the United States or any department or agency thereof; or
Whoever receives, conceals, or retains the same with the intent to convert it to his use or gain, knowing it to have been embezzled, stolen, purloined or converted—
Shall be fined not more than $250,000 or imprisoned not more than ten years, or both; but if the value of such property does not exceed the sum of $100, he shall be fined not more than $1,000 or imprisoned not more than one year, or both.
The word "value" means face, par, or market value, or cost price, either wholesale or retail, whichever is greater.

Counterfeiting and Forgery

Title 18 U.S.C. § 471 deals with the issue of committing fraud by doing things such as forging checks and making counterfeit money.

The elements of the crime include the following:

- A scheme to defraud
- The suspect willfully used a fake, forged, altered, or counterfeit U.S. obligation or security

Embezzlement and Theft

Chapter 31 of Title 18 contains several statutes related to embezzlement and theft. While the financial investigator will be interested in each of the statutes, only two are listed in this text.

Theft or Embezzlement From the Government

Title 18 U.S.C. § 641 states that it is illegal to embezzle, steal, illegally appropriate, or knowingly convert anything of value from the United States government. It is also illegal to receive, conceal, and retain these items.

The elements of the crime include the following:

- Intent
- Property belonged to the United States
- The suspect knew that property belonged to the United States

Theft or Embezzlement by Bank Employees

Title 18 U.S.C. § 656 focuses on theft, embezzlement, and misapplication of funds by employees and officers of banks. As you can see from the two statutes concerning embezzlement and theft, the value of the embezzled or stolen item impacts the punishment. If the value is less than $100, the fine does not exceed $1,000 and

§ 656. Theft, embezzlement, or misapplication by bank officer or employee
Whoever, being an officer, director, agent, or employee of, or connected in any capacity with any Federal Reserve bank... embezzles, abstracts, purloins, or willfully misapplies any of the moneys, funds, or credits of such bank... shall be fined not more than $1,000,000 or imprisoned not more than thirty years, or both; but if the amount embezzled, abstracted, purloined or misapplied, does not exceed $100, he shall be fined not more than $1,000 or imprisoned not more than one year, or both.

§ 872. Extortion by officers or employees of the United States
Whoever, being an officer or employee of the United States... under the color or pretense of office or employment commits or attempts an act of extortion, shall be fined not more than $250,000 or imprisoned not more than three years, or both; but if the amount extorted or demanded does not exceed $100, he shall be fined not more than $500 or imprisoned not more than one year, or both.

§ 873. Blackmail
Whoever, under threat of informing, or as a consideration for not informing, against any violation of any law of the United States, demands or receives any money or other valuable thing, shall be fined not more than $2,000 or imprisoned not more than one year, or both.

the prison time is less than one year. If the value is $100 or more, the fines and amount of prison time are much steeper.

The elements of the crime include the following:

- Intent
- The suspect is a bank employee or officer
- The suspect attempted to defraud the bank

Extortion and Threats

We have to protect ourselves from being forced to do things against our will. Chapter 41 of Title 18 contains statutes that prohibit the use of threats and force. Three of the statutes are listed below.

Extortion

Title 18 U.S.C. § 872 states that government employees and officers cannot use their employment status with the government to gain money or property through force or threats.

The elements of the crime include the following:

- Intent
- The suspect is an officer or employee of United States government
- The suspect used his or her employment with government as part of the extortion scheme
- Extortion is committed or attempted

Blackmail

Title 18 U.S.C. § 873 prohibits the use of blackmail to keep someone from informing of criminal violations. It also prohibits someone from blackmailing another by threatening to expose that person's criminal activities.

The elements of the crime include the following:

- Intent
- The suspect made threats

§ 874. Kickbacks from public works employees

Whoever, by force, intimidation, or threat of procuring dismissal from employment... induces any person employed in the construction, prosecution, completion or repair of any public work financed in whole or in part by loans or grants form the United States, to give up any part of the compensation to which he is entitled under his contract of employment, shall be fined not more than $250,000 or imprisoned not more than five years, or both.

§ 1001. False statements of entries generally

Whoever, in any matter within the jurisdiction of any department or agency of the United States knowingly and willfully falsifies, conceals or covers up by any trick, scheme, or device a material fact, or makes false, fictitious or fraudulent statements or representations, or makes or uses any false writing or document knowing the same to contain any false, fictitious or fraudulent statement or entry shall be fined not more than $250,000 or imprisoned not more than five years, or both.

Kickbacks

Title 18 U.S.C. § 874 prevents a worker on a governmental project from being compelled by force, threat, intimidation, or dismissal to give up part of the compensation he or she received or was entitled to receive.

The elements of the crime include the following:

- Intent
- The suspect made threats
- Compensation for threats would be from loans or grants provided by the government
- Public work financed, at least partially, by the government

Fraud and False Statements

Title 18 contains a number of related provisions which punish false or fraudulent statements, made either orally or in writing, to various federal agencies and departments. The principal statute is Title 18 U.S.C § 1001. It is most often used to prosecute false statements made to law enforcement or regulatory officials in the course of an official investigation, or on applications for federal employment, credit, visa, or passport applications, etc. This statute also pertains to violations relating to altered or false documents submitted to agencies of the federal government with the intent to defraud the United States.

A statement is "false" for the purposes of the statute if it was known to be untrue when made. A statement is"fraudulent" if it was known to be untrue and was made with the intent to deceive a government agency. The agency need not actually have been deceived, nor must the agency have in fact relied upon the false statement, for a violation to occur. The statement must have been "material," that is, capable of influencing the agency involved.

The elements of the crime include the following:

- Willfulness
- The suspect knew that the statement was false
- One or more of the following

— falsification or concealment of a material fact
— false statement
— false writing or entry

- Matter within jurisdiction of any U.S. agency

Mail Fraud

Chapter 63 of Title 18 contains statutes relating to the commission of fraud.

Mail Fraud

The mail fraud statute, Title 18 U.S.C. § 1341, is one of the most common criminal fraud statutes used by the financial investigator. This statute prevents the U.S. Postal Service from being used to carry out any scheme to defraud. The mailing itself does not need to contain the false and fraudulent representations, as long as it is an "integral" part of the scheme. What is considered integral or incidental depends on the facts of each case; generally any mailing which helps advance the scheme in any significant way will be considered sufficient.

The elements of the crime include the following:

- Intent
- Scheme to defraud
- Use of mails to further scheme

§ 1341. Frauds and swindles

Whoever, having devised or intending to devise any scheme or artifice to defraud, or for obtaining money or property by means of false or fraudulent pretenses, representations, or promises, or to sell, dispose of, loan, exchange, alter, give away, distribute, supply, or furnish or procure for unlawful use any counterfeit or spurious coin, obligation, security, or other article, or anything represented to be or intimated or held out to be such counterfeit or spurious article, for the purpose of executing such scheme or artifice or attempting to do so, places in any post office or authorized depository for mail matter, any matter or thing whatever to be sent or delivered by the Postal Service, or takes or received therefrom, any such matter or thing, or knowingly causes to be delivered by mail according to the direction thereon, or at the place at which it is directed to be delivered by the person to whom it is addressed, any such matter or thing, shall be fined not more than $250,000 or imprisoned not more than 5 years, or both. If the violation affects a financial institution, such person shall not be fined more than $1,000,000 or imprisoned more than 30 years, or both.

§ 1343. Fraud by wire, radio, or television

Whoever, having devised or intending to devise any scheme or artifice to defraud, or for obtaining money or property... by means of wire, radio, television communication and interstate or foreign commerce... shall be fined not more than $250,000 or imprisoned not more than 5 years, or both. If the violation affects a financial institution, such person shall not be fined more than $1,000,000 or imprisoned more than 30 years, or both.

Wire Fraud

Title 18 U.S.C. § 1343 prevents someone from using television and radio, or phone lines (computer modems included) to defraud the public.

The elements of the crime include the following:

- Intent
- Scheme to defraud
- Use of interstate communications to further scheme

§ 1344. Bank Fraud

(a) Whoever, knowingly executes, or attempts to execute, a scheme or artifice —
(1) to defraud a financial institution; or
(2) to obtain any of the moneys, funds, credits, assets, securities or other property owned by or under the control of, a financial institution by means of false or fraudulent pretenses, representations, or promises, shall be fined not more than $1,000,000 or imprisoned not more than 30 years, or both.

Bank Fraud

A relatively new federal statute makes it a crime to defraud, or attempt to defraud, a federally chartered or insured bank. Previously, such offenses were prosecuted under the more generic fraud statutes, such as mail or wire fraud. As in the mail and wire fraud statutes, the term "defraud" includes any misrepresentations or other conduct intended to deceive others in order to obtain something of value. The prosecution must prove only an attempt to execute this scheme, and need not show actual loss, or that the victim institution was actually deceived, or that the defendant personally benefitted from this scheme. The important aspect is the attempt.

The elements of the crime include the following:

- Intent
- Scheme to defraud a financial institution

Racketeering

Chapter 95 of Title 18 contains statutes related to money laundering. By definition, money laundering is the process by which one conceals the existence, illegal source, or legal application of income and then disguises that income to make it appear legitimate. This is taking "dirty money" and washing it to make it appear "clean". Through these laws, the mere moving of money known by an individual to be the proceeds from some illegal activity creates a substantive criminal offense separate from the illegal activity itself. For the financial investigator, these statutes provide criminal relief in investigations that involve the movement of money through financial institutions when that money is derived from an illegal activity. These money laundering statutes have forfeiture provisions which allow for seizure and forfeiture of money and assets that represent the proceeds of the substantive illegal activity. (Chapter 11 of this text deals with this topic).

§ 1956. Laundering of monetary instruments

(a)(1) Whoever, knowing that the property involved in a financial transaction represents the proceeds of some form of unlawful activity, conducts or attempts to conduct such a financial transaction which in fact involves the proceeds of specified unlawful activity— (A)(i) with the intent to promote the carrying on of specified unlawful activity; or (ii) with the intent to engage in conduct constituting a violation of section 7201 or 7206 of the Internal Revenue Code of 1986; or(B) knowing that the transaction is designed in whole or in part— (i) to conceal or disguise the nature, the location, the sources, the ownership, or the control of the proceeds of specified unlawful activity; or (ii) to avoid a transaction reporting requirement under State or Federal law, ...shall be sentenced to a fine of not more than $500,000 or twice the value of the property involved in the transaction, whichever is greater, or imprisonment for not more than twenty years or, both.

Money Laundering

Title 18 U.S.C. § 1956 makes it a federal crime to launder money known to be the proceeds of specified unlawful activities, as defined by federal statutes. Note that only part of the statute [(a)(1)] is displayed.

The elements of the crime include the following:

- The suspect must conduct or attempt to conduct a "financial transaction"
- The suspect must know that the property involved in the transaction represents the proceeds of some form of unlawful activity
- The transaction must involve property which, in fact, represents the proceeds of "specified unlawful activity"
- The suspect must engage in the transaction with either—
  — the intent of promoting the carrying on of the "specified unlawful activity," or—
  — the intent to engage in conduct constituting tax evasion under Title 26 U.S.C. § 7201 or tax fraud under Title 26 U.S.C. § 7206, or
  — knowledge that the purpose of the transaction, in whole or in part, was either to conceal or disguise the nature, location, source, ownership, or control of the proceeds of "specified unlawful activity;" or to avoid a transaction reporting requirement under State or Federal law

Transactions Involving Criminally Derived Property

Title 18 U.S.C. § 1957 states that it is unlawful to take part in, or attempt to take part in, monetary transactions involving criminally derived property that is of a value greater than $10,000 and is derived from a specified unlawful activity.

§ 1957. Engaging in monetary transactions in property derived from specified unlawful activity
(a) Whoever, in any of the circumstances set forth in subsection (d), knowingly engages or attempts to engage in a monetary transaction in criminally derived property that is of a value greater than $10,000 and is derived from specified unlawful activity, shall be punished as provided in subsection (b).
(b)(1) Except as provided in paragraph (2), the punishment for an offense under this section is a fine under title 18, United States Code, or imprisonment for not more than ten years or both.

The elements of the crime include the following:

- The suspect must knowingly engage in a "monetary transaction." A monetary transaction is any deposit, withdrawal, transfer, or exchange, in or affecting interstate or foreign commerce, of funds or a monetary instrument by, through, or to a financial institution. It excludes "any transaction necessary to preserve a person's right to representation as guaranteed by the sixth amendment to the Constitution"

- The value of funds or monetary instrument involved in the transaction or attempted transaction must exceed $10,000

- The suspect must know that the funds or monetary instruments involved in the transaction or attempted transaction constitute "criminally derived property"

- The property involved in the transaction must, in fact, constitute the proceeds of "specified unlawful activity"

- The offense must take place in the United States, in the special maritime and territorial jurisdiction of the United States, or, can take place outside the U.S. if the subject is a United States person— as defined in Title 18 U.S.C. § 3077, except for the class described in paragraph (2)(D) of that section

Racketeer Influenced and Corrupt Organizations (RICO)

RICO is probably the most well known and controversial federal statute in use today. Title 18 U.S.C. § 1961 was originally enacted in 1970 to fight organized crime's infiltration of legitimate business. Its powerful criminal and civil provisions have been used in a wide range of fraud cases. When applied in financial cases, the statute outlaws, in general, the investment of ill-gotten gains in another business enterprise, or the acquisition of an interest in an enterprise through certain specified unlawful activities. These unlawful activities include: illegal interstate gambling, trafficking in illegal substances, money laundering, prostitution, and other specific illegal activities delineated by Congress. Criminal penalties include stiff fines and jail terms, as well as forfeiture of all illegal proceeds or interests acquired. Civil remedies include treble damages, attorney's fees, dissolution of the offending enterprise, and other remedial measures.

RICO's complexity is due, in part, to efforts to avoid constitutional problems which voided attempted "anti-racketeer" legislation in the 1930s. The "1930 provisions" were found to be unconstitutional because they punished the mere "status" of being a gangster, rather than any particular wrongful conduct. RICO avoids this impediment by basing its definition of "racketeering" and enhanced penalties on "patterns" of conduct defined in the statute. The most controversial aspect of RICO is its civil provisions. Civil actions may be brought by the government or any private party injured by a defendant's business or property. Critics complain that private party suits have been used to reach "deep pocket" defendants, such as accounting firms who cannot be characterized as racketeers, and to coerce unwanted settlements from blameless defendants fearful of possible **treble damage judgments.** A treble damage judgment involves the payment of three times the amount of damages to the entity damaged by the defendant. Supporters contend that a plaintiff cannot recover unless he or she proves fraud or certain other identified criminal acts. Several bills to repeal or amend RICO, particularly these civil provisions, have been introduced in Congress in recent years.

Federal Statutes: Title 26, Internal Revenue Code

§ 7201. Attempt to evade or defeat a tax or the payment thereof

Any person who willfully attempts in any manner to evade or defeat any tax imposed by this title or the payment thereof shall, in addition to other penalties provided by law, be guilty of a felony and, upon conviction thereof, shall be fined not more than $250,000 ($500,000 in the case of a corporation) or imprisoned not more than 5 years, or both, together with the costs of prosecution.

§ 7203. Willful failure to file return, supply information, or pay tax

Any person required under this title to pay any estimated tax or tax, or required by this title or by regulations made under authority thereof to make a return, keep any records, or supply any information, who willfully fails to pay such estimated tax or tax, make such return, keep such records, or supply such information, at the time or times required by law or regulations, shall, in addition to other penalties provided by law, be guilty of a misdemeanor and, upon conviction thereof, shall be fined not more than $25,000 ($100,000 in the case of a corporation), or imprisoned not more than 1 year, or both, together with the costs of prosecution...

The Internal Revenue Code is the body of law which codifies all federal tax laws including income, estate, gift, excise, etc. taxes. Our focus is on Chapter 75; Crimes, Other Offenses, and Forfeitures.

Crimes, Other Offenses, And Forfeitures

The IRS is responsible for ensuring that we comply with tax laws and regulations. The statutes listed below deal with tax abuse and fraud.

Tax Evasion

Most individuals and corporations are required, by law, to pay taxes on earnings and other sources of income. Title 26 U.S.C. § 7201 states that it is illegal for any person to avoid paying taxes that they, or the corporation they represent, owe.

We covered the elements of this crime earlier; however, we shall revisit them here. The elements of the crime include the following:

- The suspect owes additional taxes
- The suspect attempted to evade the taxes
- The suspect willfully attempted to evade the taxes

Failing to File, Supply Information, or Pay Tax

Title 26 U.S.C. § 7203 basically states that if you are required to file a tax return, you must file it; if you are required to pay a tax, you must pay it; and if you are required to keep records or supply information concerning taxes, you must keep the records or supply the information.

If the suspect failed to file, the elements of the crime include the following:

- Duty to file
- Failure to file
- Willfulness

If the suspect failed to supply information, the elements of the crime include the following:

- Duty to supply information
- Failure to supply information
- Willfulness

If the suspect failed to pay taxes, the elements of the crime include the following:

- Duty to pay
- Failure to pay
- Willfulness

§ 7206. Fraud and false statement

Any person who— (1) Willfully makes and subscribes any return, statement, or other document, which contains or is verified by a written declaration that is made under penalties or perjury, and which he does not believe to be true and correct as to every material matter... shall be guilty of a felony and upon conviction, shall be fined not more than $250,000 ($500,000 in the case of a corporation) or imprisoned not more than 3 years, or both, together with the costs of prosecution.

Filing a False or Fraudulent Return

When you file your federal income tax form, you place your signature on it. In doing so, you state that the information presented on the form is accurate. Now, if you know that your return is not accurate, but you sign it anyway, you're filing a fraudulent return in violation of Title 26 U.S.C. § 7206.

The elements of the crime include the following:

- The suspect made and subscribed under penalty of perjury
- The suspect knew that the statement was false or fraudulent
- Willfulness

Federal Statutes: Title 15, Commerce and Trade

Title 15 contains statutes related to the exchange, buying, or selling of goods, productions, and properties of any kind. There are three "acts" contained in Title 15 that are of particular interest to the financial investigator. They are discussed below.

Securities Act of 1933

The Securities Act of 1933 (Title 15 U.S.C. § 77 et seq) provides for registration of securities which are to be sold to the public and for complete information as to the issuer and stock offering. A **security** is a stock, bond, note, or other document that represents a share in a company or a debt owed by a company or government entity.

Securities Exchange Act of 1934

The Securities Exchange Act of 1934 (Title 15 U.S.C. § 78 et seq) governs the operation of stock exchanges and over-the-counter trading. It requires, among other things, publication of information concerning stocks which are listed on these exchanges.

Title 15 contains numerous statutes which prohibit false statements and other fraudulent activity in connection with security transactions. These laws contain civil and administrative remedies, enforced by the Securities and Exchange Commission (SEC), as well as criminal sanctions enforced by the Department of Justice. Whether a particular violation is prosecuted civilly or criminally depends in large measure on the degree of willfulness that can be proven.

Electronic Funds Transfer Act

An **electronics fund transfer** is a transaction with a financial institution by means of a computer, telephone, or electronic instrument. The Electronic Funds Transfer Act provides a basic framework establishing the rights, liabilities, and responsibilities of participants in electronic funds transfer systems. The act addresses the provision of individual consumer rights.

"Computer crime" is a new term in law enforcement, and the Electronic Funds Transfer Act is one of several statutes that relates to this type of crime. In a computer crime, the computer can be the instrument of a crime or the object of one. As an instrument, a computer may be used to steal funds from a bank account. As the object of a crime, the information contained in a computer may be stolen, altered, or destroyed. Most computer crimes are still prosecuted under traditional fraud, theft, and embezzlement statutes. Generally, the elements of a computer crime include the following:

- Unauthorized access (or exceeding one's authority)
- An intent to defraud
- Obtaining anything of value

Federal Statutes: Title 31, Money and Finance

§ 5313. Reports on Domestic Coins and Currency Transactions
(a) When a domestic financial institution is involved in a transaction for the payment, receipt, or transfer of U.S. coins or currency (or other monetary instruments the Secretary of the Treasury prescribes), in an amount, denomination, or amount and denomination, or under circumstances the Secretary prescribes by regulation, the institution and any other participant in the transaction the Secretary may prescribe shall file a report on the transaction at the time and in the way the Secretary prescribes...

§ 5324. Structuring Transactions to Evade Reporting Requirement Prohibited
No person shall for the purpose of evading the report requirements of section 5313(a) with respect to such transaction —
(1) cause or attempt to cause a domestic financial institution to fail to file a report required under section 5313(a);
(2) cause or attempt to cause a domestic financial institution to file a report required under section 5313(a) that contains a material omission or misstatement of fact; or
(3) structure or assist in structuring, or attempt to structure or assist in structuring, any transaction with one or more domestic financial institutions.

Title 31 contains statutes governing the money and finances of the United States government. The two statutes listed below relate to the movement of money through a financial institution.

Financial transactions in excess of $10,000 in currency must be reported on a Currency Transaction Report (CTR). Title 31 U.S.C. § 5313 requires that financial institutions file this report. If a person takes actions to falsely or fraudulently stop a financial institution from filing the report with the federal government, a violation of criminal law has occurred.

Title 31 U.S.C. § 5324 makes it illegal for an individual to attempt to "structure transactions" in such a way as to evade the reporting requirements of Title 31 U.S.C. § 5313. Such structuring would include:

- breaking deposits into amounts less than $10,000
- withdrawing currency in amounts less than $10,000
- utilizing various financial documents (cashiers checks, certified checks, money orders)

Summary

This chapter has detailed important federal statutes relating to financial investigations. The successful financial investigator is one who can sort out the elements of a crime from the legalese of a statute so that he or she is in a position to gather the evidence needed to prove a violation and sustain a conviction.

Questions and Exercises

Answer the following questions then check your responses with those provided at the back of the book.

1. What are the differences between civil law and criminal law?

2. What are the differences between felonies and misdemeanors?

3. What is the difference between a crime that is "mala prohibita" and one that is "mala in se?"

4. Descriptions of criminal activities are listed below. For each description, identify all federal statutes that may have been violated and the elements of the crime. Refer only to those statutes contained in Chapter 2.

a. Jerry Wilson owns a clothing store in Chicago. He agreed to let a drug dealer buy thousands of dollars of clothes there, using $10, $20, and $50 bills that had been used to buy crack and cocaine on the streets.

b. Troy Avery is a high-ranking civil servant employed by the U.S. Navy. He has ties with a sports agent. One of the contractors who works with Avery has a son who is sure to be the first player selected in the college football draft. Avery tells this contractor that he had better convince his son to sign with Avery's sports agent friend or Avery will see to it that the contractor loses his job.

c. Jenny Lawrence cons unsuspecting victims into buying bogus vacation packages by placing adds offering inexpensive vacations in newspapers and listing an 800 number for potential victims to call.

d. David Stevens is employed by First National Bank and Trust. He is diverting money, via wire transfers, from the bank's general ledger account to a personal account at another bank.

e. Linda Carson is the president of a consulting firm that has fallen on hard times. But Linda has some dirt on a competitor and threatens to expose a kickback scheme that this person's company is involved in unless the competitor drops its pursuit of a contact that Linda's company is bidding on.

f. Susan Tompkins is required to pay estimated taxes four times a year. She has missed one payment and has no intention paying the other three.

5. Lance Gordon is a drug trafficker. Each week, he deposits his profits in several different banks and makes sure that each deposit is less than $10,000. What statute is he violating?

CHAPTER 3

Evidence

In Chapter 2, some of the federal statutes of interest to the financial investigator were identified. A corresponding list of the "elements of the crime" was provided for many of the statutes. These elements are of particular importance to the investigator because they direct the focus of the evidence gathering process. In this chapter we will discuss various concepts related to evidence. We will look at the differences between direct and circumstantial evidence. We will discuss various standards of proof and see how the standard of proof for a criminal case differs from the standards for a civil case. Selected "rules of evidence" also will be presented. The chapter begins with a discussion of the grand jury process, for it is here that initial evidence gathering efforts help determine whether a suspect in a criminal case goes to trial.

After studying Chapter 3, you should be able to:

- Describe the grand jury process.
- Describe the "investigative tools" used by the grand jury.
- Define evidence.
- Distinguish among the five standards of proof.
- Describe different classifications of evidence.
- Determine the admissibility of evidence by applying selected rules of evidence.

One of the major responsibilities of a financial investigator is to gather evidence. But there are many things the investigator must consider in his or her quest for evidence. Does the evidence bear directly upon a fact the prosecution wants to prove or must inferences be made to link the evidence to a fact? Is the person who supplied some relevant fact able to testify to that fact or are the communications between that person and the accused privileged? This chapter provides an introduction to many concepts surrounding the collection, strength, and admissibility of evidence. But before we get into a discussion of evidence, we will look at the grand jury process. It is here that the determination is made to charge someone with a violation of criminal law. The evidence an investigator collects plays a large role in determining whether there is sufficient cause to believe that the accused committed a crime.

The Grand Jury

The American system of justice is **adversarial** in nature. This means that both parties involved in the litigation (prosecution and accused) present evidence to a third party (judge or jury) for a determination of who is right or wrong (guilt or innocence). This differs dramatically from other systems of justice. For example, in an **inquisitional system,** defendants are presumed guilty and the evidence to convict them is extracted from their mouths.

One of the many legal concepts that the American colonists brought with them from England was that an individual accused of a high crime or major criminal violation should stand accountable to that accusation in front of his or her peers. Under our Constitution, a person cannot be **indicted,** receive a formal written complaint of criminal charges, without first having the facts and the reasons leading up to and contained within the indictment reviewed and approved by a jury of his or her peers— **a grand jury.**

At the federal level, a grand jury consists of 16 to 23 people chosen from the general population in a judicial district. The jurors investigate accusations against people and other entities. Upon a finding of probable cause, a grand jury returns an indictment which requires the accused to stand trial for a criminal violation.

Normally a grand jury "sits," or deliberates, for a period of eighteen months to perform its function. Grand jury proceedings are held in secrecy, and as such, only the jurors, government attorney, witness, and stenographer are present while the jury is in session. When the jury is deliberating or voting, no one else is allowed in the jury room.

The role of the grand jury is that of fact finder. The jury meets to gather information and documents, and to listen to witness testimony concerning alleged criminal violations. After the information, documents and testimony have been gathered, the grand jury decides, by voting, whether or not to return a criminal indictment. It takes 12 jurors to return an indictment, no matter how large the jury.

Tools of the Grand Jury

To accomplish their fact finding, the grand jury has the power to call witnesses to provide testimony, to issue orders that require the production of records, and to impose legal sanctions to ensure compliance with its powers. The primary investigative tool of the grand jury is the **subpoena** which requires a witness to appear before the grand jury. A subpoena can also require a witness to produce records and documents. A subpoena details the testimony or records to be supplied and the place and time for the witness' appearance before the grand jury. Subpoenaed witnesses that fail to comply can be cited for contempt of court and those that are dishonest while providing testimony may face perjury charges. Witnesses may not have their attorneys present with them during the grand jury proceeding, however, witnesses can confer with their attorneys outside the grand jury proceedings before answering questions.

Another grand jury investigative tool is the **grant of immunity.** Immunity is granted to convince or compel a witness to provide testimony or produce documents. By guaranteeing that the witness will not be prosecuted, the grand jury can obtain important information otherwise unavailable. There are two types of immunity grants: transactional and use.

Transactional Immunity

Transactional immunity completely protects the witness from prosecution for any criminal offenses about which he or she testifies during the grand jury proceedings. If a witness states that she has laundered money for a drug dealer, she cannot be charged for the offense if she has been provided transactional immunity. This form of immunity is rarely used.

Use Immunity

Use immunity protects witnesses from the prosecution's "use" of their testimony against them. Let's look at that same witness who laundered drug money. If she is granted use immunity, she cannot be prosecuted for money laundering unless the prosecuting attorney can develop independent information and evidence from a completely separate source of the witness' criminal wrongdoing.

Immunity can be given either formally or informally. **Formal immunity** is granted by the court. As part of a grand jury proceeding, the prosecuting attorney makes an application to a court (i.e. federal judge) requesting a grant of formal immunity for the witness. The court official reviews the application and bases his or her findings on:

- The importance of the information to the success of the investigation
- The availability of the information from other sources
- The culpability of the witness

If the court approves the application, a grant of formal immunity is issued to the witness.

Informal immunity is offered to grand jury witnesses by the prosecuting attorney via issuance of a "letter of immunity." Such a letter assures witnesses that their grand jury testimony will not be used against them in any subsequent criminal legal proceeding.

Immunity is a powerful tool and the investigator and prosecuting attorney must use it wisely. They must weigh the evidence they will receive from a witness against that witness' criminal wrong doings. The prosecutor will usually ask for a proffer. This is a statement from the witness which details his involvement and cannot be used against him. It is used to determine if immunity should be offered.

Role of the Financial Investigator in the Grand Jury Process

Financial investigators routinely work with grand juries. They serve subpoenas, gather information, take testimony from witnesses, and report their investigative findings to the grand jury. The cloak of secrecy applies to all information gathered by the agent during the grand jury proceedings.

The financial investigator also assists the prosecution in the investigative decision-making process. The investigator who has talked to witnesses and analyzed the financial information can advise the attorney on issues such as order of witness appearance, questions to ask the witness, and even whom to offer immunity grants.

A major advantage in conducting financial investigations through the grand jury process is the ability for various law enforcement agencies to work together. Allegations of criminal violations often impact various statutes for which numerous agencies hold investigative authority. Under the auspices of the grand jury, multiple violations can be simultaneously investigated and ultimately charged through a coordinated multi-agency effort.

One disadvantage to conducting an investigation through the grand jury process is related to the secrecy requirements of the grand jury. Grand jury information may not be used in non-grand jury investigations unless a court order is obtained permitting the release of the grand jury information. If a suspect is not indicted by the grand jury, the grand jury's investigative findings cannot be used in other investigative activities (i.e. intelligence sharing or other ongoing investigations) unless so authorized by a court order.

What Is Evidence?

From the discussion on the grand jury proceeding, you can see that the financial investigator's role as a gatherer of evidence is a vital one. In its simplest terms, **evidence** is anything that can make a person believe that a fact or proposition is true or false. Both parties involved in a lawsuit can submit evidence to prove their points. In a criminal case, the prosecution must present evidence to prove the commission of a crime. They do so by gathering information, documents, and other items that prove the elements of a crime. The defense presents evidence to show that allegations are invalid.

Standards of Proof

Evidence is collected to establish **proof.** In the world of law enforcement, the concept of proof varies according to the situation. In a criminal case, evidence must establish proof of a crime "beyond a reasonable doubt." In most civil cases, evidence must be strong enough to incline a person to believe one side over the other. Discussions concerning five standards of proof follow.

Beyond a Reasonable Doubt

A defendant charged with a criminal violation is presumed innocent until proven guilty. In a *criminal proceeding*, the government bears the burden of proving that the accused is guilty of the charges— the accused does not have to prove his or her innocence. To receive a guilty verdict, the government must prove each and every element of a crime beyond a reasonable doubt.

The concept of **beyond a reasonable doubt** is something that many of us talk about and, perhaps, struggle with. We do not have to be sitting on a jury to give our personal opinions about a case. We can read about a case in the newspaper. Some, we can watch on television. So, when we get ready to give our personal verdicts of guilt or innocence, we must measure the evidence presented and determine if the prosecution has proven its case beyond a

Video Spectral Comparator's are new technological tools used to clarify images and differentiate inks on documents. This technology was used to show conclusive proof that a check originally made payable to the IRS was altered through the use of different inks.

reasonable doubt. And then we ask ourselves— "What is meant by 'reasonable doubt'?"

Reasonable doubt is the degree of certainty that you have in accomplishing or transacting the more important concerns of your everyday life. For example, you are out for your nightly walk around the neighborhood and you stop at an intersection. At the same time, a car happens to pull up to a stop sign at the same intersection. You and the driver make eye contact and the driver waves at you to cross the street. You cross because you are convinced, beyond a reasonable doubt, that the car will not pull out and run over you.

We just described "reasonable doubt" in lay person's terms. Let's see how the court defines "reasonable doubt?" A recent court decision (U.S. v. Sunderland) defines the concept as follows:

> *A reasonable doubt, is a doubt founded upon a consideration of all the evidence and must be based on reason. Beyond a reasonable doubt does not mean to moral certainty or beyond a mere possible doubt or an imaginary doubt. It is such a doubt as would deter a reasonably prudent man or woman from acting or deciding in the more important matters involved in his or her own affairs. Doubts which are not based upon a reasonable and careful consideration of all the evidence, what are purely imaginary, or borne of sympathy alone, should not be considered and should not influence your verdict. It is only necessary that you should have certainty with which you transact the more important concerns in life. If you have that certainty, then you are convinced beyond a reasonable doubt.*

A defendant may not be convicted upon mere suspicion or conjecture. A defendant should be acquitted if the evidence is equally consistent with innocence as with guilt.[1]

Preponderance of Evidence

The degree of proof required in many *civil matters* is a **preponderance of evidence.** Let's say you are sitting on a jury in a case involving a lawsuit where one person is suing the other. You listen to the evidence presented by the defendant and then you listen to the evidence presented by the plaintiff. When it comes time to deliberate, you find that you happen to believe the plaintiff. Both sides presented evidence but the evidence presented by the plaintiff made you believe that person. This is proof by preponderance of evidence— evidence that inclines an impartial mind to one side rather than the other. And with preponderance of evidence, it is not the quantity of evidence that matters, it's the quality. For example:

> *...when it is said that the burden rest upon either party to establish any particular fact or proposition by preponderance or greater weight of evidence, it is meant that the evidence offered and introduced in support thereof to entitle said party to a verdict, should, when fully and thoroughly considered, produce the stronger impression upon the mind and be more convincing when weighed against the evidence introduced in opposition thereto. Such preponderances are not always to be determined by the number of witnesses on the respective sides, although it may be thus determined all of the things being equal.*[2]

Clear and Convincing Evidence

Another standard of proof used in certain *civil cases* where fraud may be involved is **clear and convincing evidence.** This type of proof is not proof beyond a reasonable doubt as required in a criminal case, but is stronger than a mere preponderance of evidence as normally required in a civil matter. For example:

> *A mere preponderance of the evidence, meaning merely the greater weight of the evidence, is not sufficient to prove fraud. This does not mean that you must be convinced of fraud beyond a reasonable doubt, because this is not a criminal case. However, an allegation of fraud does require a greater degree of proof than is required in most civil cases, and a mere preponderance of the evidence while enough to incline the mind of an impartial juror to one side of the issue*

rather than the other, is not enough to prove fraud. Fraud must be established by evidence which is clear, cogent, and convincing.[3]

Probable Cause

The three standards of proof just presented can be distinguished from **probable cause** which serves as the basis for arrest and search warrants. Probable cause is all the facts and circumstances within the knowledge of an investigator about a criminal activity that can be considered reasonable and trustworthy. For an arrest warrant to be issued, probable cause must be sufficient to cause a person of reasonable caution to believe that a crime has been committed and that the accused has committed it. To have a search warrant issued, probable cause must be sufficient to make a reasonable person believe that a crime has been or will be committed and that the evidence sought exists in the place to be searched. Probable cause requires more than mere suspicion or hunches but less than a preponderance of evidence.

Suspicious Situation

At the opposite end of the spectrum from "beyond a reasonable doubt" in the continuum of standards of proof is the **suspicious situation.** In Terry v. Ohio, 392 U.S. 1 (1968), the Supreme Court established case law stating that police may briefly detain and question a person for investigative purposes if there exists specific "articulable suspicions." Such a valid detainment of a suspect may yield evidence to effect arrest or provide evidence in support of a crime.

Classifications of Evidence

Now that you are familiar with the standards of proof, let's look at the types of evidence that can be presented. In legal terminology, evidence has various classifications. Evidence may be classified according to its proof results (direct or circumstantial) or according to its source (real, documentary, or testimonial). The following paragraphs describe the different classifications of evidence. Evidence admitted through a process called "judicial notice" is also discussed.

Direct Evidence

A person under investigation is suspected of accepting a $5,000 bribe. Another person states that he was with the suspect on November 12, 1992 and saw the suspect accept the bribe. This person has provided **direct evidence** of the crime. Direct evidence is evidence to the precise point at issue.[4] A person is suspected of accepting a bribe; another person says he saw the suspect accept a bribe. Nothing needs to be inferred or presumed.

Circumstantial Evidence

Now let's look at the same suspect, only this time let's look at some evidence that is not directly related to the point at issue. An investigator states that the suspect's bank statement reveals that the suspect deposited $5,000 on November 12, 1992. Another person testifies that on November 12, 1992, she saw the suspect having breakfast with the person suspected of offering the bribe. When looked at individually, neither of these pieces of evidence prove that the suspect accepted a bribe. However, viewed together, you get the feeling that the suspect could have accepted the bribe at breakfast and then deposited it in his bank.

The evidence presented in the previous paragraph is **circumstantial evidence.** Circumstantial evidence is evidence relating to a series of facts other than those at issue that tend, by inference, to establish the fact at issue.[5] Circumstantial evidence proves the existence of the fact indirectly and depends on the strength of the inferences raised by the evidence. The use of circumstantial evidence is recognized by the courts as a legitimate means of proof when it involves proving several material facts which, when considered in a relationship to each other, tend to establish the existence of the principle or ultimate fact.

Circumstantial evidence is the only type of evidence generally available to show certain elements of a crime, such as malice, willfulness, intent, or legal concepts which exist only in the mind of the perpetrator of the deed. Accordingly, the proof of most financial violations is based upon circumstantial evidence.

Real Evidence

Real evidence is evidence that is tangible; it can be presented to the jury for inspection. Material objects such as knives, bullets, guns, and jewelry are examples of real evidence.

Documentary Evidence

Documentary evidence consists of writings and documents, such as judicial or official records, contracts, deeds, and the less formal writings such as letters, memorandums, books, and records of private persons and organizations. Documentary evidence is primarily circumstantial in nature and must be introduced by a witness who can testify to the existence and authenticity of the evidence.

Testimonial Evidence

Testimonial evidence is evidence given by word of mouth. Witnesses under oath and affirmation provide testimonial evidence. A **witness** is a person who can testify as to what he or she knows from having seen, heard, or otherwise observed.

Judicial Notice

Not everything presented during a trial must be proved. There are matters so well known to the court that it would be a waste of time to compel a party to offer evidence of their truth. For example, it is a well known fact that the formula for water is $H_2 0$. There's no reason for a lawyer to call a witness to the stand to attest to that fact. The judge can allow the court to accept certain facts as evidence through a legal process known as **judicial notice.** However, if there is evidence which reasonably puts a fact in dispute, judicial notice will not be taken.

Rules of Evidence

The investigator is the one who gathers evidence during the investigative process. For the investigator, evidence of financial crimes includes the following:

- Admissions and confessions freely given by the suspect
- Statements made by witnesses who either observed the criminal event or were victimized by it
- Physical things which relate to the criminal activity (i.e. books and records, currency, bank account information, etc.)
- Analysis completed by the investigator

But even the best of evidence, that which would result in overwhelming indications of guilt, will mean nothing and will be inadmissible at trial if the investigator ignores the rules and procedures regarding the admissibility of evidence at trial. These rules directly impact on the financial investigator during the investigative process.

At the federal level, the rules governing criminal procedures and evidence have been codified and represent the benchmark to follow when gathering information during the investigative process. The following rules are relevant to financial investigations:

- Rule 401, Relevancy and Competency
- Rule 501, Privileged Communications
- Rule 801, Hearsay
- Rule 901(a), Chain of Custody
- Rules 1001 and 1002, Best Evidence and Requirement of Original

Relevancy and Competency (Rule 401)

To be admissible, evidence must be relevant and competent. These terms are not synonymous. If a fact offered in evidence relates in some logical way to the principle fact it is considered to be **relevant.** The **competency** of evidence means that the fact offered into evidence is adequately sufficient, reliable, and relevant to the case and is presented by a qualified and capable witness.

Relevancy implies a traceable and significant connection. A fact may not bear directly on the principle fact but it is considered relevant if it constitutes one link in a chain of evidence or if it relates to facts that would constitute circumstantial evidence. Some evidentiary matters that are considered relevant and therefore admissible are:[6]

- The motive for a crime
- The ability of the defendant to commit this specific crime
- The opportunity to commit the crime
- Threats or expressions of ill will by the suspect
- The means of committing the offense
- Physical evidence at the scene linking the accused to the crime
- The suspect's conduct and comments at the time of arrest
- The attempt to conceal and/or destroy evidence
- Valid confessions

Evidence, even if logically relevant, may be excluded by the Court if that evidence is likely to inflame or confuse a jury, or consume too much time. For example, testimony as to the statistical probability of guilt of the defendant, while logically relevant when based on prior testimony, may be considered too prejudicial and unreliable to be accepted by the Court.[7]

The issue of competency can relate to the witness presenting the evidence or the evidence itself. If a person is called to testify and does not understand the nature of the oath or is unable to narrate with understanding the facts that he or she is to testify to, that witness' competency will be questioned. Examples of incompetent evidence include confessions involuntarily obtained or unsigned carbon copies of a document which are offered into evidence without any explanation for the failure to produce the original.

Privileged Communications (Rule 501)

This rule is based on the belief that it is necessary to maintain the confidentiality of certain communications. However, it covers only those communications that are a "unique product" of a protective relationship. The one to whom the information has been given cannot divulge that information without the consent of the other party. Some of the more prevalent claims to privileged relationships are:

- Attorney/Client
- Husband/Wife
- Clergyman/Penitent
- Physician/Patient
- Accountant/Client
- Law Enforcement Officer/Informant

Attorney/Client

The attorney/client privilege must be strictly adhered to. However, this privileged relationship does not make every communication between a client to his attorney confidential. It applies only to those communications meant to be confidential and made to the attorney in his or her capacity as an attorney. When it does apply, the privilege covers corporate as well as individual clients.

For the investigator, the attorney/client privilege does not apply when a suspect's attorney is merely a conduit for handling funds or is involved in something like researching or recording the transfer of title to real estate (without consultation for legal advice). Similarly, if the attorney is acting as an accountant or tax return preparer, this privilege may not be applicable.

Husband/Wife

Communications between a husband and wife, privately made, are generally assumed to have been intended to be of a confidential nature, and therefore held to be privileged. These communications remain privileged even after a marriage terminates. However, if it is obvious from the circumstances or nature of a communication that no confidence was intended, there is no privilege. For example, communications between a husband and wife made in the presence of a friend are not privileged.

In addition to the confidential communication privilege, there exists an independent privilege— a testimonial privilege. A married person may refuse to testify against his or her spouse, at least when the latter is a defendant in a criminal prosecution.

Clergyman/Penitent

The privilege between clergyman and penitent has been recognized in the Federal courts, but this privilege has not been extended to financial matters, such as contributions made through a clergyman.

Physician/Patient

Many state courts recognize the physician/patient privilege, although Federal courts generally have not approved it.[8]

Accountant/Client

The accountant/client communication privilege is *not recognized* under common or Federal law. Workpapers belonging to an accountant are not privileged and must be produced if required. Similarly, a suspect may be required to produce an accountant's workpapers if they are in his or her possession.

An accountant employed by an attorney, or retained by a person at the attorney's request to perform services essential to the attorney/client relationship, may be covered by the attorney/client privilege.

Law Enforcement Officer/Informant

This privilege allows law enforcement agencies to withhold from disclosure the *identity* of persons who furnish information concerning violations of law. Unlike other privileges, it is the identity of the informant that is privileged, not the communication.

This privilege also differs from the others in that it can be waived only by the government, whereas the others are for the benefit of, and can be waived by, the accused individual. Where disclosure of an informant's identity or the content of the communication is relevant to a fair trial, the court may order disclosure. If the government withholds the information, the court could dismiss the charges.

Conversations in the known presence of third parties do not fall within the purview of privileged communications. The protected communications are those that are, in fact, intended to be confidential. Exceptions are recognized for those situations where third parties are indispensable to the communication itself (i.e., legal secretary, stenographer, or transcriber).

Hearsay (Rule 801)

Hearsay is evidence that does not come from the personal knowledge of the declarant but from the repetition of what the declarant has heard others say. For example, an investigator says that the suspect's business manager told him that checks written by the suspect were for personal expenses, not business expenses. This information would be considered hearsay and inadmissible in court. The information would be admissible if the business manager provided the testimony.

The major reason hearsay is inadmissible is the potential unreliability of the witness providing the hearsay. Witnesses must tell what they themselves know, not what they have heard from others. Testimony that merely repeats what another person said is not admitted as evidence because of the possibility of distortion or misunderstanding.[9]

The justice system recognizes that there are occasions when exceptions to the hearsay rule must be made. From a financial investigative standpoint, exceptions to the hearsay rule include the following:[10]

- Valid confession/tacit admission
- Prior statements
- Statement against interest

- *Res gestae* statement/excited utterance
- Dying declaration
- Official records rule
- Shop book rule
- Expert testimony

Valid Confession/Tacit Admission

A **valid confession** is a statement by the suspect acknowledging the facts and validity of those facts upon which a criminal conviction rests. Perhaps during an interview with the suspect, the suspect tells the investigator: "Yeah, I took the money. I got sick of my boss living the easy life off of all the hard work that I do so I forged his name to a couple of checks and tried to take off for South America." A **tacit admission** is less than a full acknowledgment by the suspect but is a statement of facts relative to his or her criminal activity. An investigator can offer into evidence a valid confession or tacit admission only if it was legally obtained during the course of an investigation.

Prior Statements

If a defendant takes the stand in his or her own defense, the prosecution can introduce, during cross-examination, statements made by the defendant at prior trials or hearings. This is done to show inconsistencies with the defendant's current testimony, or to reflect expressed or implied charges against the defendant relating to the current trial.

Statement Against Interest

A **statement against interest** is a prior acknowledgment of a material fact relevant to an issue now being litigated but this prior acknowledgment differs from what is now being claimed. For example, in a tax evasion prosecution, evidence in the form of a financial statement submitted for life insurance shows a defendant's net worth to be higher than she now claims. This prior statement can be used as evidence against the defendant.

Res Gestae Statement (Excited Utterance)

A **res gestae statement** is a spontaneous comment made at a time of great emotional strain (i.e., at the time of arrest or at the scene of an accident). The theory to allow this exception to the hearsay rule is that it is very likely that a statement made at such a time is a truthful response. For example, during a raid of a bookmaking establishment, one of the persons in the establishment, upon seeing the raiding officers enter the room says: "Burn the betting slips!" Even though the speaker is never identified and is not available as a witness, an investigator who heard the statement may be permitted to testify about it to prove that betting slips existed.

Dying Declarations

Dying declarations, either orally or in writing, are presumed to be forthright and honest statements. Since the witness is unavailable, an exception to the hearsay rule is made and the person who heard the dying declaration can testify to its validity.

Official Records Rule

The official records rule allows for the introduction of books, records, reports, and compilations kept as a regular and routine duty by a public official. Custodians of those records, even though they did not make the record per se, may introduce and act as witnesses for this type of official record at trial.

Shop Book Rule

The shop book rule states that books of original entry kept in the regular course of business can be introduced in court by the person who has custody of the books even though this person may not be the person who made the original entries to the books. In this instance, the "custodian" must authenticate the records, testify that he or she is the custodian, that the entries are original (not copies), and finally, that the entries were made contemporaneously with the transactions transcribed therein. For example, in attempting to prove a sales transaction between the defendant and Company ABC, the prosecution would call as a witness an employee of Company ABC who would bring the business's bookkeeping records to court. This employee, who is not the person who made the original entries into the books, would prove the sales transaction by showing how the funds paid to Company ABC by the defendant were recorded in the business's bookkeeping system.

Expert Testimony

In cases where the subject matter is too difficult or too technical for jurors to understand without assistance, expert testimony is permitted.

Chain of Custody (Rule 901(a))

This rule requires that when evidence is obtained during the course of an investigation, it should be marked, identified, inventoried, and preserved to maintain its original condition and to establish a clear chain of custody until it is introduced at trial. This rule applies to documentary evidence and any other objects acquired by the investigator. The term "acquired" means that the evidence was obtained as a result of a subpoena, search warrant, voluntary submission, or discovery during the course of the financial investigation. If gaps in possession or custody occur, the evidence itself may be challenged at trial on the theory that the document or object introduced may not be the original or is not in its original condition, and therefore is of doubtful authenticity.

For a document to be considered admissible as evidence, it is necessary to prove that it is the same document that was secured by the investigator and that it is in the same condition as it was when it was secured. An investigator who obtains original documents should immediately identify them by some type of marking so that he or she can later testify that they are the documents that were obtained and that they are in the same condition as they were when first obtained. Markings include an investigator's initials and the date the information was obtained, and could be placed in the margin, in the corner, or in some other inconspicuous place on the front or back of each document secured. If circumstances dictate that such markings would render the document subject to attack on the grounds that it has been defaced or that the document is not in the same condition as when it was obtained, the investigator may place the document into an envelope and write a description or any other identifying information relating to the document on the face of the envelope.

Best Evidence and Requirement of Original (Rules 1001 and 1002)

The Best Evidence Rule applies only to documentary evidence. It states that the best proof of the contents of a document is the document itself. However, if an original has been destroyed or is in the hands of another party *and* it is not subject to legal process by search warrant or subpoena, an authenticated copy of that original may be substituted as evidence.

Facts about a document, other than its contents, are provable without its production. For example, the fact that a sales contract was made is a fact separate from the actual terms of the contract and may be proved by testimony alone.

Certain documents such as leases, contracts, or even letters, which are signed in more than one copy are all considered originals and any one of the copies may be produced as an original. Production consists of either making the written document available to the judge and counsel for the adversary, or having it read aloud in open court.

All evidence falling short of the standard for best evidence is classified as **secondary evidence.** Secondary evidence may be either the testimony of witnesses or a copy of the writing. Before secondary evidence can be admitted, there must be satisfactory evidence showing the present or former existence of an original document. It must be established that the original has been destroyed, lost, stolen or otherwise unavailable. Further, it must be established that the party offering the document into evidence attempted all reasonable means to obtain the original. In each case, the sufficiency of the search for the original is a matter to be determined by the court. If a document is offered as secondary evidence, it must be shown to be a correct copy of the original.

For federal purposes, secondary evidence may be either a copy of the document or testimony of witnesses relating to the contents of the document itself. For example, the testimony of an investigator as to the contents of a sales invoice that is unavailable would be secondary evidence. The investigator's testimony is admissible even though the person who prepared the invoice is available to testify. The Best Evidence Rule will not be invoked to exclude oral testimony of one witness merely because another witness could give more conclusive testimony. However, in other jurisdictions, testimony will not be allowed to prove the contents of a document if there exists a secondary evidence to prove its contents. This is known as the **majority rule.**

If an original document is destroyed by the party attempting to prove its contents and who is offering it for evidence, secondary evidence will be admitted if the destruction was in the ordinary course of business or by mistake, or even intentionally, provided it was not done for any fraudulent purpose.

Summary

The rules of evidence and procedure establish the legal framework within which the financial investigator works. A full confession of guilt by the suspect becomes worthless if it was illegally obtained and therefore inadmissible in court. The investigative process requires the gathering of information, documents, and testimony from witnesses, victims, and subjects involved in criminal activities. Though the legal statutes institute the benchmarks of right and wrong, and the elements and degrees of proof necessary for criminal conviction, it is the rules of evidence and criminal procedure that control both the investigative process and the resultant judicial proceeding.

Questions and Exercises

Answer the following questions then check your responses with those provided at the back of the book.

1. a. How many jurors usually "sit" on a federal grand jury?

   b. How many jurors does it take to return an indictment?

2. Differentiate between transactional immunity and use immunity.

3. What is evidence?

4. What is the relationship between evidence and proof?

5. Differentiate between the following standards of proof: "beyond a reasonable doubt" and "preponderance of evidence."

6. You are investigating a mail fraud scheme. One of the elements of the crime is the use of mails to further the scheme. Provide an example of direct and circumstantial evidence that you could collect to prove this element of the crime.

7. What is judicial notice? Provide an example.

8. When an investigator gathers evidence, why is it important that he or she keep the terms "relevancy" and "competency" in mind?

9. Todd White is on trial in Federal court for drug trafficking and money laundering offenses. Read the following descriptions of proposed testimony and, based on the privileged communications rule, answer the following questions for each description: 1) Is the testimony admissible in court? and 2) Why or why not?

a. Todd White's wife, Kay, says that before they were married, Todd told her that he made a lot of money selling drugs.

1)

2)

b. While they were married, Kay White saw Todd measuring white powder on a set of scales. She saw him put the white powder into bags.

1)

2)

c. While they were married, Todd told Kay that the powder in the bags was cocaine. Kay was not involved in the distribution of drugs.

1)

2)

d. Todd's son, Joey, says his father asked him to sell some cocaine at school.

1)

2)

e. Leon Norton, Todd's accountant says that Todd told him that he had $25,000 in income from his auto repair business and $250,000 in income from an inheritance.

1)

2)

f. Kent Parks, Todd's attorney, says that he handled a real estate closing for a house Todd bought. Todd paid $250,000 for the house.

1)

2)

10. Why is hearsay evidence inadmissible?

11. What is the shop book rule?

12. What do the terms "best evidence" and "secondary evidence" mean to an investigator?

Endnotes

1 U.S. v. Sutherland, 56-2 USTC 9651 (D.D. Colo.)

2 Wissler v. U.S. 58-1 USTC par 9414 (So. Dist. of IA)

3 Gladden v. Self, 55-1 USTC 9227 (E.D. Ark.), Add'd 224 F2d 282 (CA-8)

4 John Evarts Tracy, *Handbook of the Law of Evidence,* (New York: Prentice-Hall, Inc., 1952), p. 6

5 *Handbook of the Law of Evidence,* p. 6

6 Jack T. Wells, W. Steve Albrecht, Jack Bologna, and Gilbert Geis, *Fraud Examiner's Manual,* (National Association of Certified Fraud Examiners, 1989), Section 11, p. 45

7 *Fraud Examiner's Manual,* Section 11, p. 44

8 Stephen A. Saltzburg and Michael M. Martin, *Federal Rules of Evidence Manual: A Complete Guide to the Federal Rules of Evidence, 5th Edition, Volume 1,* (Charlottesville, VA: The Michie Company, 1990), p. 423

9 *Fraud Examiner's Manual,* Section 11, p. 49

10 *Fraud Examiner's Manual,* Section 11, pp. 49, 50

CHAPTER 4

Sources of Information

Chapter 3 focused on concepts related to the collection and admissibility of evidence. This chapter addresses where to look for information that may ultimately be used as evidence against, or, on the other hand, in support of a suspect. As a financial investigation begins, questions concerning a suspect's finances are plentiful. Does the suspect own the home in which she lives or does she rent? If she owns the home, how much did she pay for it and how did she pay for it? If she rents, how much does she pay, and is she the one who pays or does some second party pay the rent? Does she have a criminal record? Does she own the car she drives? How did she pay for the trip to China she took last year? It all seems pretty simple— just ask her! Well, sometimes, if you have a cooperative suspect, it is that simple. But how cooperative would you be if you had the authorities investigating your actions— especially if you had something to hide?

This chapter begins with a discussion on selecting suspects to target for an investigation. The decision to target a suspect is not made lightly as both the suspect and the investigative team can be affected by a poor decision. The remainder of the chapter and a corresponding appendix (Appendix A) identify some of the many sources of information of interest to an investigator. For the investigator, the important thing to keep in mind is that most financial transactions, whether lawful or unlawful, are recorded and can be recreated if the investigator can piece together the correct "paper trail". The sources listed in this chapter and Appendix A provide a foundation for the initiation of that paper trail.

After studying Chapter 4, you should be able to:

- Discuss what factors influence the selection of a suspect to target in an investigation.
- Identify appropriate sources to obtain specific information.
- Analyze financial records for leads.

No matter how many computers, police cars, or Swat teams law enforcement may possess, not one criminal will be put behind bars unless the most precious of all commodities is available—information. Discovering, understanding, analyzing, and using information is one of the keys to successful law enforcement. When an investigator initiates an investigation, his or her knowledge of information sources is invaluable. This chapter and Appendix A provide you with many sources of information of interest to the financial investigator. These are selected sources and by no means should the listings provided be considered exhaustive. Remember, information is everywhere. The key is to focus on information that will resolve the allegation.

Initial Considerations

Before listing and describing various sources of information, we will explore some of the things that are considered when an investigation is initiated. What should be considered before targeting a suspect for investigation? How should an investigator deal with a suspect as a source of information? What happens when a suspect refuses to cooperate? Each of these issues will be addressed below.

Selecting Who to Target for Investigation

The role of a financial investigator is to gather evidence to support, or in the alternative, dispel allegations of financial criminal activity. Where to look and what to look for are two integral questions facing every investigator. In theory, neither question is difficult to answer— merely look everywhere for everything. But a problem surfaces when reality is thrown into the equation. Investigators cannot spend their whole careers working on only one investigation. Resources (personnel, equipment, time, and money) are scarce— but law enforcement's challenges are limitless. Available resources must be used wisely. Those who determine which investigations to pursue must deal with questions like: "Are we willing to commit 100 percent of our investigative resources for an extended period of time to investigate a high-level suspect when the probability of a conviction is only 40 percent? Would we be better served by dividing our work force and investigating three mid-level suspects with a probability of 65 percent success? How about initiating 10 financial investigations of low-level suspects with a success probability of 95 percent?"

The use of resources is only one factor to consider in determining which investigations to pursue. Suspects targeted for investigation also must be selected wisely. Determining which suspects to target is not a simple matter. Targeting priorities are determined through the interaction of judicial interpretation of law and jury appeal. The decision to target an individual for criminal investigation is a momentous decision. Whether it is called opening a file, numbering a case, initiating an investigation, or information gathering, it is going to change a person's life. When an investigator knocks on the door of a neighbor or shows his or her badge to a banker to ask questions about the now designated suspect, a chain of events is put into motion that cannot be stopped. Arguably, the worst nonphysical event that can occur to an individual is to have the authorities accuse him or her of criminal activity. Possibly even worse is to have the accusation circulated among business associates, friends, and family.

When confronted with allegations or investigative findings, suspects, in addition to telling the truth or lying, have suffered heart attacks, emotional breakdowns, and committed suicide. In 1985, the United States Attorney's Office, the arm of the Federal Government that handles criminal prosecutions, declined to prosecute 27 percent of the suspects under investigation.[1] In other words, in 1985 over one-fourth of the suspects investigated and subsequently recommended for criminal prosecution at the Federal level were in fact not prosecuted. Reputations, established professions, future business and financial prospects, and social and family relationships turn on the decision to start an investigation. The moral of the story is that by whatever means possible, choose suspects carefully.

The Suspect as a Source of Information

Once a suspect is targeted, the investigator must work the investigation effectively. He or she must identify the essence of the allegations and facts surrounding the crime, and address them early on in the investigative process. For example, a bank embezzlement scheme would quickly take the investigator to the institution's books and records. In an alleged tax evasion matter, the person who prepared the questionable return would be interviewed at the onset of the investigation.

Most often, the best source of information in an investigation is the suspect. The suspect has the answers to every allegation and the documents to support or corroborate those answers. By asking the suspect, the investigator may gain access to documents that summarize the suspect's personal income and expenditures. These documents could represent everything the investigator needs to complete the investigation. However, the response to that same question may vary depending on how the investigator asks it. There is a significant difference between asking (Would it be possible for me to take a look at your finance-related documents?) and commanding (I need to see those documents! Now!).

Law enforcement sometimes loses its objectivity when gathering information during the course of an investigation. It can get demanding and "badge heavy," assuming the answer before a question is asked. Particularly significant investigations or sensational crimes create intense media attention and public pressure. Sometimes, the investigator is tempted to go beyond the role of fact finder and becomes judge, jury, and executioner. The key is to be professional. An investigator must conduct every investigation in a fair and impartial manner using, as opposed to abusing, the tools of authority. Cooperation from witnesses and the suspect can be obtained much easier and more quickly with a fair and professional approach.

A suspect who says, "Get out of here! I'm not giving you anything. Talk to my attorney!" suggests another factor to consider when asking the suspect for investigative information. The United States Constitution, which establishes the ground rules for all levels of law enforcement, guarantees certain rights to the criminal, whether accused or convicted. The right to be secure in one's home, the right against self-incrimination, and the right to counsel are three important constitutional guarantees that directly impact financial investigations and the request for information from the accused.

What happens if the suspect in a financial investigation is unknown or, if known, refuses to talk or provide records? Is the investigation over, the matter dropped for lack of information? No, the search for information turns to other sources. Unlike investigations into crimes of passion where the only people directly involved in the crime are the criminal and the victim, financial crimes create "eye witnesses to the crime" every time a financial transaction occurs. Knowing where to find these witnesses, and what information they possess, is a key step toward a successful financial investigation.

When conducting a financial investigation, there are three things an investigator should keep in mind. They are:

- **Anyone may be a source of financial information.** It's possible that a suspect's relatives, friends, acquaintances, and business associates possess relevant documents. For example, ex-spouses may have kept records of bank accounts or financial statements, friends are often given financial documents for safe keeping, and business associates frequently compile their own files regarding the "suspect's" illegal activities.

- **Go to the source.** In Chapter 3, the "shop book rule" was described. This rule of evidence identifies the "custodian" of business records, that is, the individual who can introduce the records in court. A payroll clerk who works with and has knowledge of the information requested from a business may not be considered the legal custodian of those records. The legal custodian may be the company's comptroller or some other financial officer. Only the proper custodian can legally provide the information to the investigator.

- **Have authority.** Due to variations in statutory authority relating to law enforcement's ability to acquire information, an investigator should know, and follow, the legal requirements for obtaining, and if needed, compelling, the production of financial records from a custodian.

The key to any investigation is to know where to look or whom to ask to obtain knowledge about, or information on, anything. Sources of financial information can be obtained from:

- Public records
- Business records
- Government records
- Financial institution records
- Informants

The remainder of this chapter deals with information from public, business, and government records. Financial institution records are discussed in the next chapter. Using an informant as a source of financial information is discussed in Chapter 10.

Public Records

Laws and regulations require that records of certain financial transactions be disclosed and subject to review by anyone who wishes to inquire. These records are known as **public records** and they contain a tremendous amount of valuable financial information. The records not only provide answers to questions such as "What property does the suspect own?, Where is it located? and What did the suspect pay for it?," they can also be used to establish leads and corroborate or dispute the suspect's testimony.

Because of the wealth of information available from State, county, and municipal records, researching public records should be one of the first steps you take in an investigation. The secret, of course, is knowing where to look. The following pages list and describe various sources of public records.

Real Estate Records

Real estate records are normally maintained in the county where the real estate itself is located. Land ownership records such as **deeds of ownership** and **title certificates** are kept in the Register of Deeds or Land County Office. These records identify the current and previous owners of the real estate in question. Additionally, **property tax records** showing who pays the real estate taxes on a particular piece property are on file with the Tax Assessor's Office in the county where the land is located.

Corporate Records

All corporations must file documents in the state in which the incorporation occurred. If the incorporation occurred in one state and the corporation conducts business in another, it normally will have to file documents as a "foreign corporation" in the state in which business is conducted. Information concerning corporations varies somewhat by jurisdiction, but usually the articles of incorporation, annual reports on franchise taxes, and in some cases, bylaws, are available. This information can be valuable in tracing corporate ownership. Corporation documents will reflect names of the incorporators, the registered agent in the state (normally the attorney who prepared the documents), and the initial board of directors and officers. In a limited number of cases, financial statements are filed. If a company is publicly held, its financial statements and records of significant events must be filed with the Securities and Exchange Commission.

Partnerships

A partnership is the association of two or more persons to carry on as co-owners of a business for profit.[2] Partnership records may or may not be a matter of record in the state where the partnership was formed.

In the case of a **general partnership,** one in which the partners share in all profits and losses, there is normally no requirement to file agreements with licensing authorities. **Limited partnerships,** where a partner's liability is limited to his or her investment, are normally filed in the state in which the limited partnership is formed. This "Certificate of Limited Partnership," will usually list the general partners, limited partners, capital contributions of the partners, agreements regarding the divisions of profit and loss, and the powers and duties of the various partners.

Trusts

A **trust** is a legal entity in which a certain person or entity, known as the trustee, holds and administers property on behalf of others (the beneficiaries). Trusts commonly are used as vehicles for land transactions and other assets. Registration of a trust is required by some states; however, the beneficiaries of the trust are not always named.

Assumed Name Indexes

When a person or business conducts business in a name other than their own (via a name, commercial name, etc.), they must register their "assumed or fictitious name." An Assumed Name Certificate is filed in the county, city, or state where the business was organized. Although primarily used for legitimate purposes, the Assumed Name Certificate can be used to hide principals and the true nature of the business.

Better Business Bureau

The local Better Business Bureau maintains information concerning a business for one of the following reasons:

- The Bureau received a prior request for information
- The business has volunteered information
- A complaint has been lodged against the business

Chamber of Commerce

The role of a Chamber of Commerce is to promote the local area. It maintains information on commercial and industrial establishments within its vicinity as well as information on trade and travel. Many Chambers of Commerce publish extensive lists of business firms within the area and this list often includes the names of officers of the companies.

Uniform Commercial Code Filings (UCC)

Filings under the UCC are made at the state and county level and contain information regarding chattel (non-real estate) mortgages. The UCC filings normally record loans made to individuals or businesses for the purchase of equipment, furniture, automobiles, and other types of personal property.

Court Records

Transcripts and legal decisions in criminal and civil law suits are maintained at the Clerk of Court office. There are separate offices for the Federal, State, and local court systems. Information relating to divorce decrees, bankruptcy petitions, judgments, insurance, and property settlements are types of public records filled with financial information.

Other Public Records

The following financial information is maintained as a matter of public record by State, county, and municipal government offices. However, since no nationwide uniformity exists for retrieval, no specific source is cited.

Mortgages and releases	Conditional sales contracts
Change of name	Drivers' licenses
Hunting and fishing licenses	Building and other permits
Fictitious names index	School and voter registration
Professional registrations	State income tax returns
Personal property tax returns	Real estate tax payment
Inheritance and gift tax returns	Wills
Letters of administration	Inventories of estates

Welfare agency records	Civil Service applications
Public utility records	Health department records
Workmen's compensation file	Births, deaths, marriages, and divorces
Occupancy and business privilege licenses	Auto licenses, transfers, and sales of vehicles
Parole officers' and probation departments' file	Court records of civil and criminal cases
Registration of noncorporate business entities	Registration of corporate entities and annual reports
Minutes of board and agency proceedings	Bids, purchase orders, contracts, and warrants for payment
Judgments, garnishments, chattel mortgages, and other liens	State Unemployment Compensation records

Business Records

Business records are another source of financial information. Every business, large or small, legal or illegal, generates and maintains records. The array of records available to the investigator is as varied as the number of businesses in existence. Because of this, only two examples are presented in this chapter. Appendix A contains a number of other sources of business records.

Records from the Purchase of Real Estate

Let's say you are investigating Andrew Sinclair and you want to find out about the house in which he lives. Does he rent or own? If he rents, who owns the house? Your investigative research starts with the public real estate records found at the Register of Deeds or Land County Office in the county where the house is located. The records reveal that Mr. Sinclair owns the house and has an outstanding mortgage held by a lending company. The "warranty deed" indicates that the subject purchased the property for $120,000. The "Deed of Trust" (the mortgage document filed with the county recorder's office) reveals that an outstanding mortgage of $110,000 was obtained from ABC Mortgage Company.

You figure that Mr. Sinclair put the $110,000 mortgage loan toward the house and paid off the rest with a $10,000 downpayment. You contact ABC Mortgage Company and they confirm that the suspect has a $110,000 mortgage, but their information does not tell you *exactly* what Mr. Sinclair did with the $110,000. Mortgage loans are to be applied toward the house for which they are granted, but since you are investigating the guy because of some alleged shady business dealings, you decide to look further. You look to the business records surrounding the purchase of the house. Your investigation leads you to Mr. John Phillips, the real estate lawyer who handled the transaction.

Most real estate transactions are handled by a disinterested third party acting for both the seller and buyer. This third party is usually an escrow company or a real estate attorney. The mortgage company submits a cashier's check in the amount of the loan to the third party who ensures that all funds received are properly accounted for and that all disbursements are properly made in accordance with the sales contract.

A real estate sale may involve more than just a straight sale of the property. There are often additional fees to be paid: sales commissions to a real estate company, fees for appraisals, payoffs of existing mortgages, real estate taxes due, and the third party's service fee. Incoming monies received for the purchase may include the buyer's earnest money (money given by the buyer to the seller to bind the purchase agreement), downpayments, and the amount received from the mortgage company. After costs are allocated to the seller and buyer according to the sales contract, the third party collects and disburses any amounts due to the seller and buyer at the closing. Records of these financial transactions are business records and are retrievable by the investigator.

ABC Mortgage Company had made out the cashier's check for the mortgage loan to John Phillips, Esquire. Contact with Mr.

Phillips results in the acquisition of the document found on the next page. This document is the closing statement for the purchase of the house.

Closing Statement

	Due Seller	Buyer Credit
Sales price	$120,000	$(120,000)
Earnest money down		50,000
Appraisal	(800)	
Real estate commissions	(4,200)	
Escrow fees	(300)	(300)
Additional downpayment		60,000
Real estate taxes due	(5,000)	
New mortgage		$110,000
Balance due to OR (from)	$109,700	$99,700

Analysis of the closing statement reveals the following:

- The seller is to collect $120,000 for the house from the buyer. Of the $120,000, $10,300 is to be used to pay various fees ($800 to pay for the appraisal, $4,200 for real estate commissions, $300 for escrow fees, and $5,000 to pay outstanding real estate taxes).

- When all is said and done, the seller will leave the settlement with $109,700 ($120,000 minus $10,300).

- The buyer, Mr. Sinclair, must provide $120,300 at closing, $120,000 to pay for the house and $300 for his share of the escrow.

- Mr. Sinclair ends up having $220,000 at closing. He provided $50,000 in earnest money, $60,000 in an additional downpayment, and $110,000 from the mortgage company.

- The earnest money ($50,000) and additional downpayment ($60,000) are applied to the purchase price of the house ($120,000). This means that the buyer owes only $10,000 ($120,000 minus $110,000) toward the house.

- $10,000 of the loan supplied by ABC Mortgage ($110,000) will be used to cover the remaining $10,000 due to the seller. $300 will be used to pay the buyer's share of the escrow. $99,700 [$100,000 minus ($10,000 + $300)] remains. This money is provided back to Mr. Sinclair who initially brought the $220,000 to the closing. He can use the money to eventually pay off the mortgage, invest in other properties, etc.

Through this analysis, you realize that what you had originally thought (that the $110,000 mortgage was applied to the purchase price with the remaining $10,000 covered by a downpayment) is far from true. What you discover instead, is that Mr. Sinclair applied for and received a $110,000 mortgage loan when he really needed only $10,000. This discovery leads to other questions: Where did Andrew Sinclair get $50,000 earnest money and $60,000 for a downpayment? Did he falsify his application for the mortgage loan?

Your investigation into Andrew Sinclair's real estate deal may lead you to other business records pertaining to a real estate transaction. These records include:

- A sales contract
- Special instructions
- Photocopies of instruments used to make earnest money payments and downpayments
- Appraisals
- Receipts for currency received
- Existing mortgage loan payoff calculations (most often a statement from the existing mortgage company)
- A copy of new loan agreements, promissory notes, and related documents
- A copy of the instrument received from the new mortgage company who disbursed the new loan
- Copies of instruments received from buyer/seller at closing for amounts due

- Copies of all checks disbursed by the escrow company/real estate attorney at closing
- Correspondence with buyer and seller
- Broker's Worksheet, Buyer's Closing Statement, and Seller's Closing Statement

Records from the Purchase of a Vehicle

Similar to real estate information, both public and business records exist regarding motor vehicle transactions. State and/or county governments maintain comprehensive files listing vehicle ownership. The vehicle's identification number (VIN) can be cross-referenced to find the registered owner or vice versa. Finance companies or financial institutions that have an interest in the vehicle (lien holder) are recorded as a matter of public record.

The financial investigation into vehicle ownership should not stop after searching public records or lien holder information. Business records kept by automobile dealerships often provide detailed financial information and usually include:

- Various sales contracts/offers prepared by the salesman during negotiations
- The final sales contract or purchase agreement
- Loan documents if the customer obtained financing through the dealership's credit sources
- Carbons of receipts given to the customer for amounts received, usually denoting cash or check and the check number
- Photocopies of the checks or other instruments received in payment by the customer
- Appraisal of trade-ins prepared by the dealership service department
- Special instructions for registration of the vehicle

All requests for documents from an auto dealership should include the service department records. With the advent of computerized systems, the service department can usually provide a listing of all subsequent repairs and maintenance service performed on the vehicle at any authorized dealership. This can also be helpful in locating a subject who may have moved out of State.

Government Records

Information relating to financial transactions is maintained by numerous Federal, State, and local government agencies. From "information-gathering" activities like the FBI's National Crime Information Center (NCIC) to tax returns (IRS), records of financial transactions are compiled, stored, and retrievable from these sources of information. Several Federal intelligence networks are described below. Appendix A identifies other government sources and the information that they can provide.

National Crime Information Center (NCIC)

The National Crime Information Center is a repository of data relating to crime and criminals gathered by local, state, and Federal law enforcement agencies. The NCIC's computer equipment is located at FBI Headquarters in Washington, D.C. The present equipment is capable of accommodating nearly 2 million records on criminal activities. In a matter of seconds, stored information can be retrieved through equipment in the telecommunications network. Connecting terminals are located throughout the country in police departments, sheriff's offices, State Police facilities, and Federal law enforcement agencies. Dispatchers can respond quickly to requests. NCIC also furnishes computerized data in a matter of seconds to all agencies participating in the centralized State systems. The goal of NCIC is to serve as a national index to fifty statewide computer systems and heavily populated metropolitan area systems.

National Law Enforcement Telecommunications System (NLETS)

NLETS is a computerized communication network linking State and local enforcement agencies in all 50 States. It can provide information such as criminal history, driver's licenses, and vehicle registration.

El Paso Intelligence Center (EPIC)

EPIC is a multi-agency operation that collects, processes, and disseminates information on narcotics traffickers, gun smugglers, and alien smugglers in support of ongoing field investigations.

If a suspect is or has been engaged in any of the previously mentioned activities, it is possible that EPIC will have intelligence information on him or her. This information might include the name of the individual; and his or her known activities, significant events, associations among individuals or activities, aircraft or vessels used by the subject, observations of both foreign and domestic movements of the suspect, and his or her associates and their aircraft or vessels. EPIC also provides the name, agency, and telephone number of each investigator having expressed an interest in or having data regarding a subject. EPIC records often contain substantial *financial* information relative to the subject.

International Criminal Police Organization (Interpol)

Interpol is an international police agency with bureaus set up in member countries. In the United States, the National Central Bureau is under the direction and control of the Departments of Justice and Treasury.

The U.S. National Central Bureau can assist in such things as criminal history checks, license plate and driver's license checks, and the location of suspects, fugitives, and witnesses.

IRS National Computer Center

The National Computer Center is located in Martinsburg, West Virginia and it maintains the Master File, a tax record of all known taxpayers. The Master File is designed to accumulate all data pertaining to the tax liabilities of all taxpayers, regardless of location. The Master File is separated into several categories. Two of the categories are the Business Master File and the Individual Master File.

Summary

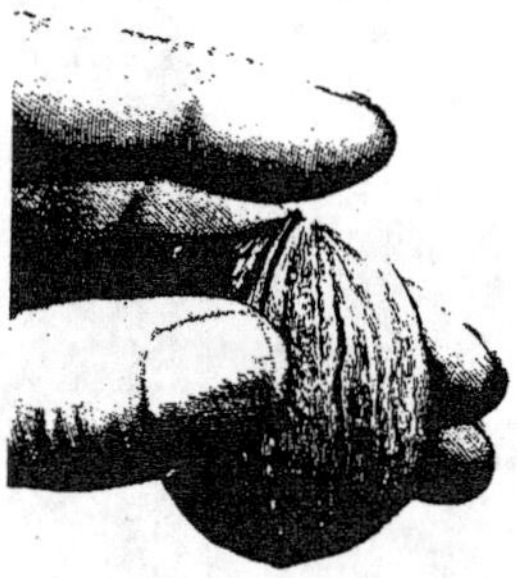

Selecting a suspect to target for investigation is not a decision that should be taken lightly. The probability of a conviction must be considered as well as the availability of resources and jury appeal. Once an investigation begins, information must be collected. Without information— an investigator's most valuable resource— no criminal will ever be put behind bars. The source of information with the most knowledge is the suspect. Some are cooperative, others are not. But no matter what type of suspect an investigator comes across, he or she must develop other sources of information to verify or contradict what a suspect says. There are all sorts of information available to an investigator, and the good ones know how to focus on what they need and where to go to get it.

Questions and Exercises

Answer the following questions using the information contained in this chapter and Appendix A. Once you have completed the questions, check your responses with those provided at the back of the book.

1. Your suspect's social security number is 421-00-0123. What lead does that provide?

2. You are investigating Base Ball, Inc. You wonder if any complaints have been lodged against the company. You know that Base Ball, Inc. does a lot of business with a ball glove manufacturing company in Raleigh, North Carolina. You do not know the name of the company in Raleigh, therefore, you want to get a list of companies in that geographic area.

a. Who would you contact regarding possible complaints against Base Ball, Inc?

b. Who would you contact for a list of businesses in the Raleigh, North Carolina area?

3. Your suspect admits to owning an American Express Card.

a. Who can provide you with information concerning the suspect's use of the credit card?

b. What leads might you obtain from analyzing a suspect's credit card activity?

4. What factors come into play when selecting a suspect to target for investigation?

5. What is the best source of information concerning a suspect? Why?

6. Your suspect recently became a naturalized American citizen. What Federal agencies maintain information concerning aliens and naturalized citizens?

7. You are investigating a forgery case. What Federal agency maintains records pertaining to forgery?

8. During the course of your investigation, you come across property you think is stolen. What Federal agency maintains the National Stolen Property Index?

Endnotes

1 *Compendium of Federal Justice Statistics, 1985,* (U.S. Department of Justice, Office of Justice Programs, Bureau of Justice Statistics, NCJ-123560, July 1990), p. 9

2 *Uniform Partnership Act,* Section 6

CHAPTER 5

Financial Institutions as Sources of Information

In Chapter 4, various sources of information were identified. Sources of public, business, and government records were provided. This chapter focuses on information that can be obtained from financial institutions. The chapter begins with a discussion of bank records. The term "bank records" refers to the records of banks, savings and loans, credit unions, and other similar types of institutions. These records are probably the single most important source of information available to the financial investigator. Banks handle two basic types of transactions: account and non-account. Account transactions involve actions such as depositing money to a savings account or withdrawing money from an account via a check. These actions directly affect the movement of money through a bank. Non-account transactions do not affect the flow of money through a bank. Receiving a bank loan is an example of a non-account transaction. All sorts of paperwork accompanies account transactions and most non-account transactions. An investigator must be aware of what records exist and must be able to interpret the information contained in the records.

Brokerage firms also maintain records involving financial transactions. Not only must an investigator be aware of what records exist, he or she must be familiar with the terminology of the securities and commodities markets. Banks and brokerage houses can provide a wealth of financial information, however, there are other financial institutions that maintain records related to financial transactions. This chapter concludes with a look at two of these sources: Western Union and casinos.

After studying Chapter 5, you should be able to:

- Describe terms related to banking and brokerage firms.
- State what records are available from banks and brokerage houses.
- Analyze bank and brokerage firm records.
- State what information is available from Western Union and casinos.

The financial investigator's main objective is to track the movement of money. This chapter examines the movement of money to and through banks and brokerage houses. While many criminal investigators view this ordeal as a "paper chase", financial investigators see financial institutions as road maps which lead directly to the perpetrator and resolution of the crime. These institutions are, in financial investigative terms, where the action is. After all, banks, brokerage houses, and other financial institutions were established to monitor the movement of money.

Banks as a Source of Information

Tracking the movement of money generated by criminal activity will normally involve tracing financial transactions to a bank and through its system. For the financial investigator, following the flow of transactions to and/or through a bank is comparable to any other asset tracing procedure. The investigator is looking for the ultimate source and disposition of funds, and one never knows what might turn up in the search— unknown witnesses, information, and documents; or, perhaps, new suspects.

The key to following the flow of money into and out of the banking system is an understanding of the inner workings of the system itself. From the tiniest rural community credit union to the international banking giants, they all take in, account for, pay out, and record the movement of money. The inner workings of the banking system can be divided into two types of transactions: account transactions and non-account transactions.

Account Transactions

Account transactions are financial events that directly affect the movement of money through a bank account. In this context, "directly affect" means deposits to, or withdrawals from, an account. Account transactions occur in checking, savings, and credit union accounts. Records of account transactions are maintained through the use of the following documents:

- Signature card
- Bank statements
- Deposit tickets/items
- Checks/withdrawal items
- Credit and debit memorandums

Signature Cards— Opening an Account

The first document prepared and maintained in a bank's system of recordkeeping is the **signature card.** Every financial institution requires that a customer (individuals, trusts, business organizations, etc.) fill out a signature card when opening an account. It indicates who owns the account and may require that the account owner(s) supply his or her address, occupation, employer, date/place of birth, and social security number. When a business organization opens an account, corporate resolutions, and partnership and trust agreements, if applicable, often are included as part of the background information requested by the bank. This type of information is kept with the signature card.

For the investigator, the signature card provides valuable leads to other witnesses or unknown co-conspirators. Since the card contains the signature of the account owner(s), it can serve as a sample of the owner's handwriting.

Bank Statements— Record of Transactions

Banks periodically reconcile the financial activity in each account. A record of this reconciliation is prepared and retained by the institution and a copy is sent to the account's owner. Details of all financial activity affecting the account for the period in question are shown on a **bank statement.** A portion of Anthony

Benidect's bank statement is shown on the next page. Mr. Benidect is a suspect in a drug trafficking investigation.

The financial investigator should retrieve all bank statements related to the time frame under investigative consideration, keeping in mind that some criminal activities are well underway prior to detection, therefore, bank statements must be retrieved for a period of time prior to the detection of criminal activity. Through bank statement analysis, the investigator will be able to reconstruct the financial transactions that occurred during the period of criminal activity, and identify sources of information or investigative leads to the movement of money. These sources or leads may include:

- Unusually high monthly balances in comparison to known sources of income
- Unusually large deposits, deposits in round numbers, or deposits in repeated amounts which are not attributable to legitimate sources of income
- The timing of deposits. This is particularly important when dates of illegal payments are known
- Checks written in unusually large amounts (in relation to the suspect's known practices)
- A lack of account activity. This may indicate transactions in currency or the existence of other unknown bank accounts

Checking Account Summary National Bank of the Nation

Customer Service-Operations Center
P.O. Box 0001, Washington, DC 20009

National Bank of the Nation

Anthony Benedict
1229 Springtide Pl, NW
Washington, DC 20001

Statement Period
03/20/92- 04/20/92

If you have questions about your account, please call 202-555-111 or toll free 800-222-9999

Checking summary for account 097405813

Beginning balance	1,532.46	Minimum Balance	1,040.33
3 Deposit(s) totaling	10,041.94+	Average Balance	4,304.59
Interest this period	0.00+		
8 Deduction(s) totalling	1,246.60-		
Other deductions	0.00-		
Service charges this period	0.00-		
Ending balance	10,327.80		

Description of Account Transactions		**Date**	**Amount**	**Balance**
Beginning balance				$1,532.46
Cash withdrawal	Trans #4552			
Landmark 1	Alexandria VA	03/22	100.00-	1,432.46
Check 546		03/23	67.25-	1,365.21
Check 547		03/27	234.63-	1,130.58
Purchase				
Mobil	Herndon VA	03/28	15.25-	1,115.33
Cash withdrawal	Trans #0849			
West Village	Washington DC	03/30	75.00-	1,040.33
Deposit		04/01	1,645.97+	2,686.30
Check 548		04/01	623.34-	2,062.96
Deposit		04/02	6,750.00+	8,812.96
Check 550		04/05	118.23-	8,694.73
549		04/12	12.90-	8,681.83
Deposit		04/15	1,645.97+	10,327.80
			Ending Balance	$10,327.80

Deposit Slips/Deposit Items

From the bank's point of view, the deposit function is the most important of all of the banking transactions. The majority of loans and investments made by the institution come from the depositors' dollars. When deposits cease, the institution ceases.

From the investigator's point of view, seeing a suspicious deposit on a bank statement does not in and of itself provide enough detail of the financial transaction. If a deposit appears to be suspicious, the investigator will want to examine the corresponding deposit slip. Upon reviewing Mr. Benidect's previously shown bank statement, the investigator wants to further examine the deposit made on April 2, 1992. That deposit slip is shown below and it reveals that the deposit was comprised of $4,500 in currency and a check for $2,250.

DEPOSIT TICKET

Anthony Benidect
1229 Springtide Place, NW
Washington, DC 20001

Date APRIL 2 19 92

DEPOSITS MAY NOT BE AVAILABLE FOR IMMEDIATE WITHDRAWAL

SIGN HERE FOR CASH RECEIVED (IF REQUIRED)

National Bank of the Nation

CASH	CURRENCY	4,500 —
	COIN	
LIST CHECKS SINGLY		2,250 —
TOTAL FROM OTHER SIDE		— —
TOTAL		6,750 —
LESS CASH RECEIVED		— —
NET DEPOSIT		6,750 —

15-099
540

USE OTHER SIDE FOR ADDITIONAL LISTING

⑆054000991⑆ 0974058 13⑈ 9987

Upon reviewing the deposit slip, the investigator has to wonder where Anthony Benidect got $4,500 in cash and who wrote the check that was deposited. Bank statements and deposit slips do not speak for themselves; they need to be interpreted by "financial witnesses"— the currency, checks, and other items that comprise the deposit. By retrieving and examining the items of deposit, the investigator may find additional leads to follow.

The original documents involved in a deposit are not retained by the bank. Currency is returned to circulation, checks go back to the bank of origin, and deposits made via an electronic transfer show up as mere bookkeeping entries. However, copies of each deposited item, except currency, are made. The bank organizes and maintains these copies on microfilm. By reviewing these records, the investigator may be able to locate other witnesses.

To successfully gather information from bank deposits, the investigator needs an understanding of the bank's system of maintenance, organization, and retrieval of deposit information. An overview of the system is shown on the next page and discussed below.

Transaction entry point

A deposit enters the banking system through a transaction entry point. There are three different types of transaction entry points:

- **Teller.** A teller receives deposits directly from the customer, or through the mail or automatic teller machine (ATM).

- **Cash Services Department.** High volume deposit customers such as major retail establishments, grocery stores, or governmental units make their deposits to the bank via armored cars or delivery services. The Cash Services Department handles these types of deposits.

- **Other Internal Departments of the Bank.** Deposit transactions can occur through intra-account activities (transfer of funds from a savings account into the same customer's checking account) or electronic transfers between financial institutions. Additionally, with the advent of direct deposit, businesses and companies can make deposit transactions into bank accounts from their own bookkeeping departments. Such services are handled by different departments inside the financial institution.

The transaction entry point is vital in the investigative process. It's even more than vital because at the point of deposit two undeniable events occur: money is moved from somewhere by someone *and* a permanent record is made.

Bank Operations

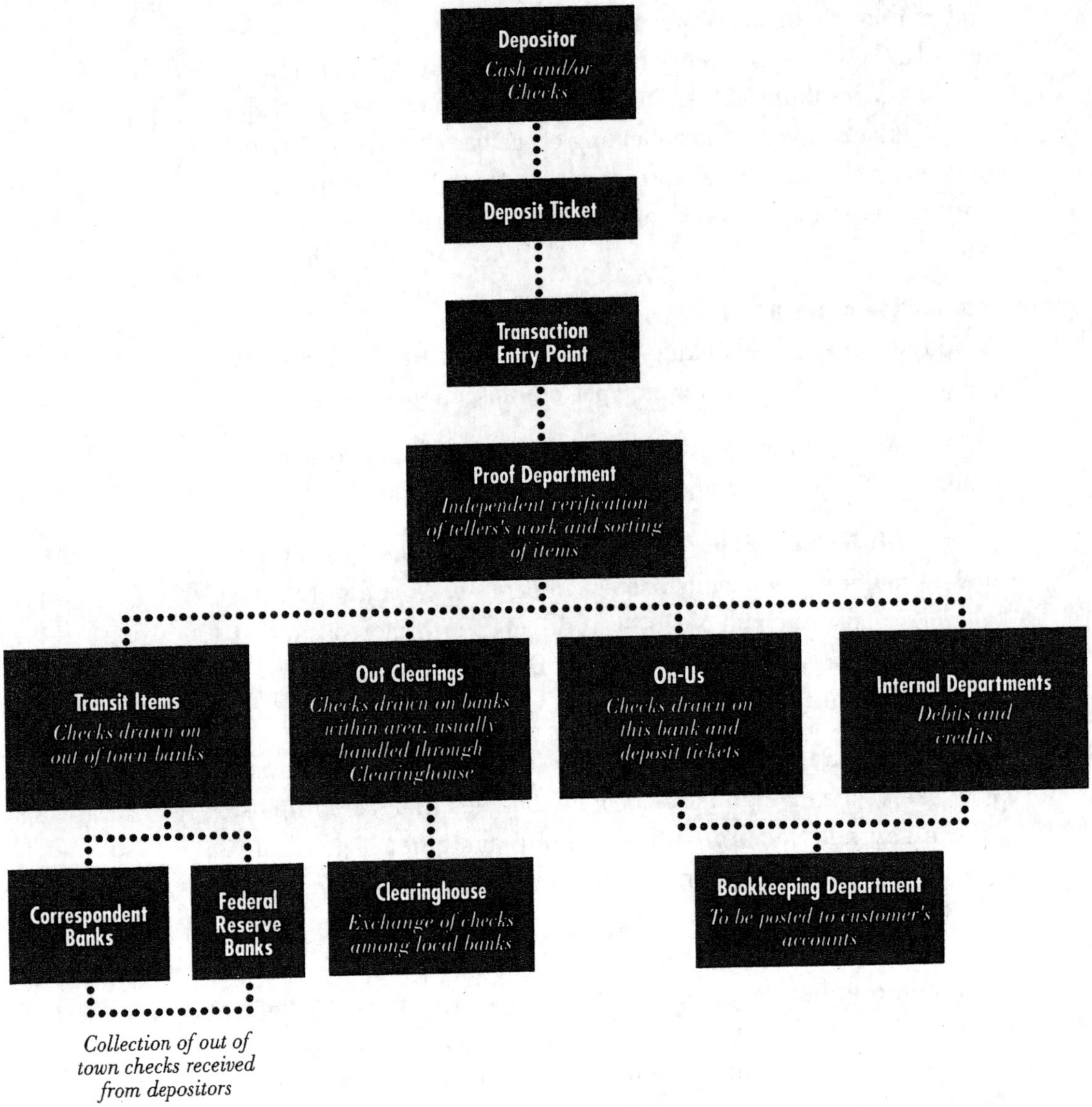

During the early stages of a financial investigation, books and records usually reveal nothing out of the ordinary and bank statements often seem inconclusive of any wrongdoing. The information collected by the investigator is sketchy and denials by the suspect are frequent :

"I don't even know that guy."

"My firm never did business with that company."

However, through deposit analysis, the investigator often finds:

- A photograph of the person who "didn't even know the guy" depositing currency into the "guy's" savings account. Financial institutions have security cameras that record teller window transactions.
- Checks from "that firm" going into "that company's" checking account.

In certain investigations, the transaction entry point can be critical to the investigation's success. In a counterfeiting investigation, for example, intervention by law enforcement at the point of entry is crucial. The same holds true for situations involving buy money (narcotics cases) or marked bills (extortion or blackmail cases). Investigators, perpetrators, and the currency in question must meet simultaneously at the transaction point of entry, in order to successfully defeat the criminal act. The importance of this is highlighted by the fact that all currency, once inside the banking system, is treated alike. Once past the point of entry, it is extremely difficult, if not entirely impossible, to reconstruct the source of the currency. Accordingly, in these situations the financial institution should be requested to separate and segregate the currency in question before it enters any further into the banking system.

The Proof Department

From the transaction entry point, deposits go to the Proof Department. Here, checks are encrypted with the bank's own numerical codes— **proof numbers.** Proof numbers establish the "location keys" for the bank's retrieval and bookkeeping system. Magnetic ink character recognition (MICR) encoding also occurs in the Proof Department. An MICR number enables a check to be read by high speed computers during the processing and clearing procedure. A portion of the MICR number is placed on checks when they are initially printed. After a check is deposited, the remainder of the MICR number is placed on the check in the bank of deposit's Proof Department. (The MICR number is discussed in greater detail later in this chapter.)

In addition to being encoded, the check is microfilmed. In the microfilming process, all checks shown on one deposit slip are microfilmed consecutively before proceeding to the next group of deposited items. The order of microfilming is generally determined by the transaction entry point. For example, all of Teller No. 1's transactions are microfilmed and then all of Teller No. 2's transactions are microfilmed, etc.

Currency is not microfilmed. Once it is inside the bank it is counted and, after the count has been verified, it goes its own separate way. Chapter 2 contains a discussion of Title 31 U.S.C. § 5313, that states financial institutions are required to file a report on currency transactions. One such report is the *Department of the Treasury Form 4789, Currency Transaction Report (CTR),* the first page of which is shown on the next page. When currency in excess of $10,000 is deposited, the CTR identifies the depositor by address, social security number, and date of birth, and the actual owner of the currency if he or she is someone other than the depositor. The CTR also records the total amount of the transaction, the types of bills involved in the transaction, and various other information.

Form **4789** (Rev. September 1991) Department of the Treasury Internal Revenue Service

Currency Transaction Report

▶ File a separate report for each transaction. ▶ Please type or print.
▶ For Paperwork Reduction Act Notice, see page 3.
(Complete all applicable parts—See instructions)

OMB No. 1545-0183
Expires: 9-30-94

1 Check appropriate boxes if: a ☐ amends prior report, b ☐ exemption limit exceeded, c ☐ suspicious transaction.

Part I Identity of individual who conducted this transaction with the financial institution

2 If more than one individual is involved, see instructions and check here . . . ▶ ☐

3 Reason items 4–15 below are not fully completed (check all applicable boxes): a ☐ Armored car service (name) ▶ ....
b ☐ Mail deposit/shipment c ☐ Night deposit or ATM transaction d ☐ Multiple transactions (see instructions)

4 Last name | 5 First name | 6 Middle initial | 7 Social security number

8 Address (number, street, and apt. or suite no.) | 9 Occupation, profession, or business

10 City | 11 State | 12 ZIP code | 13 Country (if not U.S.) | 14 Date of birth (see instructions)

15 Method used to verify identity: a Describe identification ▶ ....
b Issued by ▶ c Number ▶

Part II Person (see General Instructions) on whose behalf this transaction was conducted

16 If this transaction was conducted on behalf of more than one person, see instructions and check here . . . ▶ ☐

17 This person is an: ☐ individual or ☐ organization | 18 If trust, escrow, brokerage, or other 3rd party account, see instructions and check here . ▶ ☐

19 Individual's last name or Organization's name | 20 First name | 21 Middle initial | 22 Social security number

23 Alien identification: a Describe identification ▶ ....
b Issued by ▶ c Number ▶ | Employer identification number

24 Address (number, street, and apt. or suite no.) | 25 Occupation, profession, or business

26 City | 27 State | 28 ZIP code | 29 Country (if not U.S.) | 30 Date of birth (see instructions)

Part III Types of accounts and numbers affected by transaction (If more than one of the same type, use additional spaces provided below)

31 S ☐ Savings ▶ .... T ☐ Securities ▶ .... H ☐ CD/Money market ▶ ....
C ☐ Checking ▶ .... L ☐ Loan ▶ .... O ☐ Other (specify) ▶ ....
☐ ▶ ☐ ▶ ☐ ▶

Part IV Type of transaction. Check applicable boxes to describe transaction

32 E ☐ Currency exchange (currency for currency)

33 CASH IN:
D ☐ Deposit
G ☐ Security purchased
P ☐ Check purchased
F ☐ CD/Money market purchased
H ☐ For wire transfer
A ☐ Receipt from abroad
K ☐ Other (specify) ▶

34 CASH OUT:
C ☐ Check cashed
T ☐ Security redeemed
W ☐ Withdrawal
R ☐ CD/Money market redeemed
U ☐ From wire transfer
B ☐ Shipment abroad
Y ☐ Other (specify) ▶

35 Total amount of currency transaction (in U.S. dollar equivalent) (always round up)
Cash in $ .... .00
Cash out $ .... .00

36 Amount in Item 35 in U.S. $100 bills or higher
Cash in $ .... .00
Cash out $ .... .00 ☐ Unknown

37 Date of transaction (see instructions)

38 If other than U.S. currency is involved, please furnish the following information: a Exchange made ☐ for or ☐ from U.S. currency
b Country .... c Amount of currency (in U.S. dollar equivalent) $ .... .00
b Country .... c Amount of currency (in U.S. dollar equivalent) $ .... .00

39 If a negotiable instrument or wire transfer was involved in this transaction, please furnish the following information and check this box (see instructions) . ▶ ☐
a Number of negotiable instruments involved.......... c Total amount of all negotiable instruments and all wire transfers
b Number of wire transfers involved (in U.S. dollar equivalent) ▶ $ .00

Part V Financial institution where transaction took place

40 a ☐ Bank (enter code number from instructions here) ▶ [ ]
b ☐ Savings and loan association c ☐ Credit union d ☐ Securities broker/dealer e ☐ Other (specify) ▶

41 Name of financial institution | 42 Address where the transaction occurred (see instructions) | 43 Employer identification number

44 City | 45 State | 46 ZIP code | 47 MICR number | Social security number

48 If this is a multiple transaction, please indicate: a Number of transactions ▶ .... c ZIP codes ▶
b Number of branches ▶

Sign Here ▶
49 Signature (preparer) | 50 Title | 51 Date
52 Type or print preparer's name | 53 Approving official (signature) | 54 Date | 55 Telephone number ( )

Cat. No. 42004W

Government regulations allow financial institutions to exempt certain customers from the CTR filing requirements. High volume cash businesses, payroll account holders, and other commercial companies that are routinely involved in transactions which exceed $10,000 may be exempt. However, the bank must maintain a record of these exempted customers.

When an investigator searches the bank's proof tapes (microfilm), he or she must be particularly careful when tracing a currency deposit. For example, investigative findings indicate that a suspect received $18,000 in illegal payments on May 1, 1992. A review of the target's bank statement for that period reveals that on May 1, the suspect deposited only $9,000. By using the bank's proof tape system, the investigator finds a deposit slip and it shows a $9,000 currency deposit. (Note that the suspect kept the deposit under $10,000 so he or she would not have to file a CTR form.) The investigator has located half of the illegal payment, but where did the other $9,000 go? A continued search of the proof tape locates a similar $9,000 currency deposit to another account which, unknown to the investigator, is also owned to the target. Often, this type of extended search will uncover split currency deposits and/or multiple transactions.

From the Proof Department, deposited items take different routes through the bank of deposit's system. The path that an item takes is dependent upon the bank of origin's (bank upon which the item is drawn) relationship to the bank of deposit. Let's look at the four paths an item of deposit may take by looking at four items deposited into Bank A. The four types of items and their paths are shown and described on the following pages.

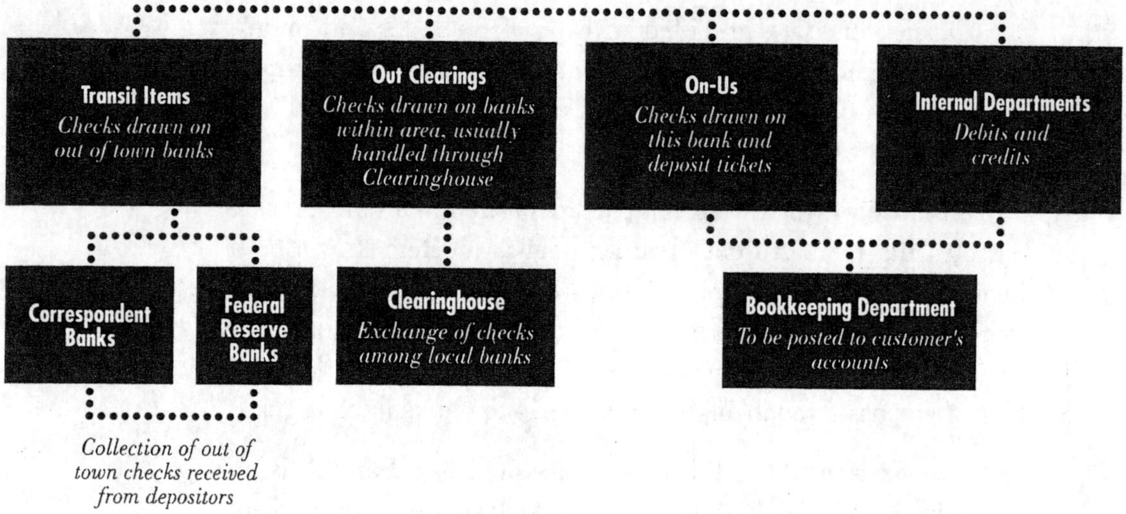

• **Transit items.** The first of our four items deposited into Bank A is a transit item. Transit items are checks and other items (money orders and travelers' checks) drawn on financial institutions other than the bank of deposit. In the case of a check, the bank of deposit ships the check back to the bank of origin. The bank of origin, in turn, normally sends the check back to the customer by including it in his or her bank statement. This happens after the bank of deposit sends the check to an intermediary bank that was established to assist in the clearing process.

Certain banks act as clearing houses for transit items. These banks, known as **correspondent and clearing house banks,** receive items from banks all over the country and process them back to the bank of origin located in their particular area. Major banks in metropolitan areas act as correspondent banks. Also, the Federal Reserve Bank is a clearing house bank.

Actually, there are 12 Federal Reserve Banks (and some have branch banks) located throughout the country. The role of each is to monitor the commercial and savings banks in its region to ensure that they follow Federal Reserve Board regulations. Each Federal Reserve Bank is a separate corporation, its stock owned by commercial banks that are members of the Federal Reserve System. The Federal Reserve System is made up of all nationally chartered banks and any State chartered bank that is accepted for membership.

Transit items are provided with proof numbers and microfilmed by each bank they pass through during their return trip to the bank of origin. This establishes a retrieval "audit trail" for each item.

- **Out clearings.** The second item deposited into Bank A is an out clearing item. An out clearing item is an item drawn on a bank in the same geographic area as the bank of deposit. These items are handled in the same way as transit items and, like transit items, they are given proof numbers and microfilmed by each bank they pass through on their return trip to the bank of origin.

- **On-us items.** The third item deposited into Bank A is an on-us item. An on-us item is a check drawn on the bank of deposit. Certain on-us items require special handling during the clearing process and are sent to a particular internal department for final processing. All on-us items eventually flow into the bookkeeping department.

- **Items from a bank's internal departments.** The fourth item that Bank A deals with is an item from one of its internal deposits. This item might be a transfer between intrabank accounts, loan proceeds, a certificate of deposit, or an electronic transfer into an account.

Checks/Withdrawal Items

Funds normally are withdrawn from a bank account through the issuance of a check. Withdrawal slips and automatic teller machines are also used to withdraw funds. The face of a check contains information that is of interest to an investigator. It shows the bank of origin, date and amount of the check, name of the payee (the entity to whom the check was made payable), and the authorized signature of the owner of the account on which the check is drawn. The following information also appears on the face of a check:

- **American Banker's Association (ABA) Transit Number and Federal Reserve Routing Code.** Have you ever noticed the number on the upper right side of a check that looks something like a fraction? It provides several pieces of information. The numerator contains the ABA transit number; the denominator is the bank of origin's check routing symbol.

An ABA transit number is a two-part code assigned to banks and savings institutions by the American Banker's Association. The first part shows a two- or three-digit number that corresponds to the city, state, or territory where the bank of origin is located. (A complete list of these two- or three-digit numbers is found in Appendix B.) The second part of the ABA transit number identifies the bank itself. The ABA transit number on the check shown below tells an investigator that the bank is located in Washington, DC and that "099" is the code for the National Bank of the Nation.

The bank of origin's check routing symbol is a three- or four-digit number that provides the following three pieces of information:

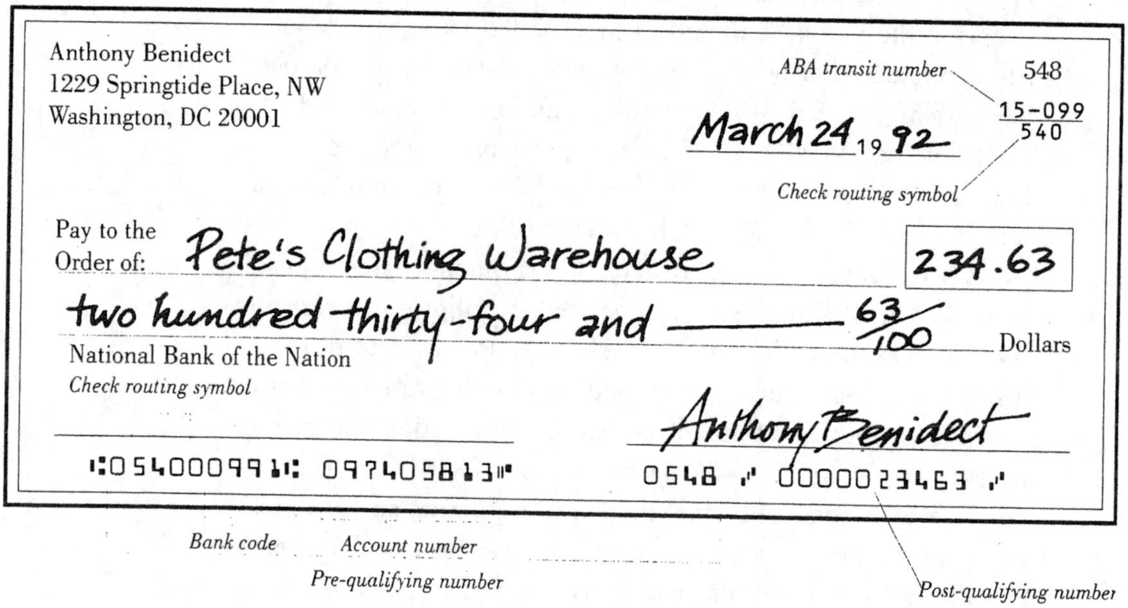

- The bank of origin's Federal Reserve district (These districts are listed in Appendix B)

- The federal reserve facility through which the check is collected

- The funds availability assigned to the check. Funds availability is either immediate or deferred. If "0" is the last digit, immediate availability is indicated. A digit of 1 through 9 indicates a deferred payment.

- **Pre-Qualifying Numbers.** The portion of the MICR number that comes printed on a check. The pre-qualifying number indicates bank of origin information (paying bank's number and check routing symbol), customer account number, and the check's number.

- **Post-Qualifying Number.** The portion of the MICR number entered by the bank of deposit's Proof Department. It shows the dollar amount of the check.

When investigators request a copy of a check, they should ask for copies of both sides because the back side of a check also contains valuable information. For one thing, it will show who endorsed the check. If the check was issued to an individual, it should contain that person's signature; if it was issued to a business organization, it will probably contain a stamped endorsement. The back of a check will also contain information related to the movement of money. Proof numbers from all of the banks that the check passed through will be available.

When a payee receives a check, he or she may either deposit it or cash it. If the check is deposited, it follows the clearing process previously discussed. Checks that are cashed are recognizable by teller stamps or "cashed" codes that are encoded or stamped on the face of the check itself. These codes can lead an investigator to the teller who cashed the check and who therefore needs to be interviewed about the specific transaction. A teller's stamp or "cashed" code also can be a possible link between a specific teller and the suspect. Many times a suspect will go to the same teller and develop a relationship with that person. Conversations between these people may reveal leads to the crime. Whether knowingly or unknowingly, the teller may possess valuable information.

From an investigator's standpoint, checks are of equal or greater importance than deposits. Checks establish a strong financial link that cannot be overcome by verbal denials. Checks may identify other bank accounts, credit cards, the purchase or location of major assets, and loan transactions which directly impact on financial investigations. A $25 check for a utility hookup may identify a $250,000 hidden condo.

Checks can be organized to reveal patterns of financial activity through an investigative technique known as check spread analysis. To perform **check spread analysis,** the investigator lists a suspect's checks by payee. A sample check spread analysis, using checks obtained from our suspect, Mr. Anthony Benidect, is shown below.

Check by Payee Analysis

Date	Virginia Electric	Date	Franklin Gardens
1/23	$101.79	1/3	$650
2/21	$121.32	2/2	$650
3/21	$92.56	3/1	$650
4/25	$87.87		
5/21	$59.12	5/2	$650
6/27	$63.45	6/2	$650
7/22	$79.73	7/1	$650
8/20	$98.92	8/3	$650
9/23	$92.83	9/2	$650
10/21	$64.55	10/1	$650
11/24	$58.52		
12/28	$87.62	12/2	$650

In the sample check analysis, the investigator listed all of Mr. Benidect's checks payable to the Virginia Electric Company for one calendar year. From this list, the investigator is able to determine that Mr. Benidect paid his electric bill every month. The investigator then listed all checks payable to "Franklin Garden Apartments," the complex where Mr. Benidect rents an apartment. The investigator finds that checks for rental payments are missing for the months of April and November. The investigator will want to find out how Mr. Benidect paid his rent for those months. The absence of a check may indicate a currency payment which can lead to possible undisclosed sources of illegal income.

Credit and Debit Memos— Special Transactions

Any transaction that affects an account but does not involve a deposit ticket or check withdrawal requires special handling. A record of these "unusual transactions" is listed on the customer's bank statement through memorandum entries. These entries are shown to report the movement of money that takes place without going through the normal transaction points of entry or withdrawals through checks. **Credit memos** or **"CM"** indicate an **increase** in the account funds, a flow of funds into the account. A **debit memo** or **"DM"** indicates a **decrease** in the account funds, a flow of funds out of the account.

Credit and Debit Memos

CM (+)	DM (-)
Interest earned	Interest payment
Loan proceeds	Loan payment
Wire transfer in	Wire transfer out
Special collection of funds	Check printing fees
Transfer between accounts	Transfer between accounts
Electronic deposit	Electronic withdrawal

Non-Account Transactions

Non-account transactions are financial transactions that occur at a financial institution but *do not* flow through an account. Examples of non-account transactions include loans; purchase or negotiation of cashier's checks, money orders, travelers checks; and currency transactions such as exchanging currency for currency and cashing third-party checks. For investigative purposes, wire transfers, entries into a safe-deposit box, and the purchase or sale of securities are also considered non-account transactions.

Loans

Loan applications, loan repayment ledgers, and loan correspondence files are usually maintained by financial institutions. A loan application usually requires a financial statement completed by the individual requesting a loan. It represents a good "financial lead document" for the investigator. If an investigator is looking to identify a suspect's assets and accounts, he or she should turn to any available loan applications, since the suspect, eager to impress the bank with his or her solvency, will identify assets and other accounts more candidly on that document than in an investigative interview. Furthermore, loan applications most often contain a statement that the applicant is aware, by signing the document, that it is a federal crime to knowingly make false statements when applying for a loan.

The loan repayment schedule and correspondence files can be used by the investigator to detect:

- **Repayment methods.** Lump sum, accelerated, or unusual repayments can be traced through the bank's proof system
- **Final disposition of loan proceeds.** The disposition may be within the bank (on-us items) or elsewhere. Either situation is traceable through the bank's recordkeeping system
- **Loan collateral.** The security pledged for the loan, if any, may be an unknown asset
- **Downpayment.** The loan proceeds may have been used to finance an asset, the downpayment for which came from illegal funds
- **Credit checks and internal memoranda.** The investigations done by the credit department to determine the risk for the bank may lead the investigator to additional assets, loans, bank accounts, etc.

In any case, loan information leads to other people and other assets. For example, loan proceeds may have been deposited into hidden accounts or these accounts may have been used to repay a loan. Loan documents may have been co-signed by a previously unknown associate or the suspect may have taken a loan out for someone else. Loan repayments could be traced to previously unknown accounts or associates. Tracing the ultimate disposition of the loan proceeds and the ultimate source of the loan repayments is a vital technique for the trained investigator.

Cashier's Checks, Certified Checks, Traveler's Checks, and Money Orders

These financial instruments require special handling by a bank because they involve various departments inside the bank.

Cashier's checks are checks drawn by the bank on its own funds and are issued by an authorized officer of the bank. The bank employee will ask the customer to designate a remitter (person purchasing the check) and a payee in order to fill in these lines on the check. A **certified check** is a check where the bank guarantees that there are sufficient funds on deposit for that particular check. A **money order** is a negotiable instrument that serves as a substitute for a check. The money order is issued for a specific amount of payment and the customer fills in the name of the purchaser and payee. The bank employee imprints only the amount of payment. A **traveler's check** is an internationally redeemable draft. It is purchased in various denominations, such as $20.00, $50.00, and $100.00, and is only valid with the holder's own endorsement against his or her original signature.

Investigative analysis of the bank checks described above follow the "proof process" if they were deposited into or purchased by withdrawal from a known account. If these documents were purchased with currency or checks drawn on an unknown account, locating them is significantly more difficult. In most situations, retrieval requires a hand search of each bank check written, which is a very labor intensive process. In the alternative, *interviewing bank employees* in an attempt to pinpoint the transaction date and the amount may prove more successful. If the suspect goes to the same bank and uses the same bank officer or teller to complete his or her bank transactions, these people may be able to assist in narrowing the search for the retrieval of the bank checks at issue.

Currency Transactions— Currency Exchanges and the Cashing of Third-Party Checks

Documenting the movement of money involved in a pure currency exchange is difficult. Currency-for-currency exchange transactions generally leave no paper trail inside the bank system unless the amount exceeds the $10,000 and then a CTR must be filed. The best source of information is the testimonial recollections of bank personnel.

A **third-party check** is a check that the payee endorses to another party. It can be traced by the bank's "proof system" *if* the third party is a legitimate entity. Financial institutions routinely require two forms of identification to cash a check, but if the check is made payable to a fictitious third party and is cashed using false identification, the proof system is unworkable. When this situation occurs, the only alternative is to contact the entity who originated the check.

Wire Transfers— Electronic Transfers

There is nothing mysterious about a wire transfer. Records detailing both ends of the transaction should be available either from the bank of origin or destination, or both. Out-of-the-country (off shore) wire transfers can create a retrieval problem depending on the country involved. Various **"haven countries"** are known to offer a legal and/or economic climate for laundering money or hiding illegally gotten profits. These are often located in the Caribbean and other areas, and restrict dissemination of this type of financial information. When money is moved by a wire transfer and neither the source of the funds nor the date of the transfer is known, retrieval of any identifying information is very difficult.

Safe-Deposit Boxes

Financial institutions rent or lease storage facilities in secured areas of the bank to its customers. The safe-deposit box rental agreement indicates the date the box was first rented and the identity of the renter, however, bank records will not reveal the contents of the box. An entry log maintained by the bank shows the date and times of visits to the box and also reports the identity of the visitor. This information may have significant investigatory importance. For example, records of entry into a safe-deposit box can corroborate testimony relating to the receipt of illegal currency or the proceeds from illegal activities.

Bank Credit Cards

Since many banks offer credit cards to their customers, charge slips and repayment information relating to these cards might be available. The financial investigator may find leads to purchases of jewelry, cars, furs, etc. through these records.

Questions about Bank Records

Before discussing other types of financial institutions as sources of information, the following two items concerning the retrieval of financial records should be addressed:

How easy is it for an investigator obtain to financial records from a financial institution?

As was stated in Chapter 4, the most knowledgeable source of financial information are the suspects targeted for investigation. Just as they have the answers to questions relating to guilt or innocence, they also have custody of financial records of importance to the investigator. Suspects are the customers of banks, the applicants for loans, and the purchasers of the securities. Therefore, they possess the original records relating to the money movement. By asking for these records, the investigator can gain access to this otherwise restricted information.

Financial institutions restrict access to records of money movement. The Bank Secrecy Act and the Right To Financial Privacy Provisions of Federal law restrict open dissemination of financial information to law enforcement. Accordingly, without the individual customer's permission, banks are forbidden to provide financial records to anyone, except when they are legally compelled to do so. Banks are also required to notify the customer of any request unless legally told not to. Such legal compulsion can take the form of subpoenas, summonses, or court orders.

While financial institutions cannot provide documents or access to information in the customer's account, except in accordance with the law, they can notify the Government of the existence of relevant information in those records. The law states, "nothing in this chapter shall preclude any financial institution, or any officer, employee, or agent of a financial institution from notifying a Government authority that such institution or officer, employee, or agent has information which may be relevant to a possible violation of any statute or regulation."[1]

In other words, if a financial institution has information or a belief that information exists relating to a violation of a Federal statute or regulation, they can contact the Government (or agency charged with responsibility for compliance) and tell them that such information exists. It is up to the Federal agency to go through the hoops to get the proper authority for dissemination of the records.

How long is a financial institution required to maintain customer records?

The Bank Secrecy Act requires financial institutions to keep certain records of customer transactions. United States Treasury Regulations implementing the Bank Secrecy Act provide, in part, that an original, microfilm, or other copy or reproduction of most checking account deposits and savings accounts records must be retained for 5 years.[2] The records must include the following:

- Signature card
- Statements, ledger cards, or other records disclosing all deposits and withdrawals
- Copies of both sides of customer checks, bank draft money orders, and cashier's checks drawn on the bank or issued and payable by it

In addition, banks must retain, for a 2-year period, all records necessary to:

- Reconstruct a customer's checking account. These records must include copies of customers' deposit tickets.
- Trace and supply a description of a check deposited to a customer's checking account.

The requirements listed above apply only to checks and deposits in excess of $100. Most banks, however, find it cheaper to microfilm all such records including checks and deposits of less than $100 rather than sort their records. The Bank Secrecy Act also requires financial institutions to retain a record of any extension of credit over $5,000 as well as every transfer of more than $10,000 outside the United States.

Brokerage Firms as a Source of Information

To analyze stock accounts, an investigator must possess a knowledge of the different types of brokerage transactions and terminology related to the field. There are two basic types of brokerage markets: securities and commodities. The **securities market** involves buying and selling of stocks and bonds. The **commodities market** involves buying and selling of produced goods, such as grain, livestock, gold, or timber. Both markets operate under similar structures, but the terminologies may differ somewhat.

Fundamentals of Securities

People who own **stock** own part of the corporation issuing the stock. A person's ownership is represented by the number of shares that he or she owns. The shares are a claim on the corporation's assets and earnings. A **bond** is any interest bearing or discounted government or corporate security that obligates the issuer to pay the bondholder a specified sum of money, usually at specific intervals, and to repay the amount of the loan at maturity.

Stocks

When a corporation is formed, **capital stock** may be issued. Capital stock is stock that is authorized by the company's charter and represents ownership of the corporation. Each stockholder is entitled to a stock certificate showing ownership of a specified number of shares of stock in the corporation. There are two principal classes of stock, common and preferred. **Common stock** are units of ownership that allow the owner to receive dividends on his or her holdings. A **dividend** is a distribution of earnings. **Preferred stock** is so called because of the preferences granted to its owners. One preference concerns dividends. If a corporation declares dividends, the preferred stockholders will receive their dividend before common stockholders. Preferred stock does not ordinarily carry voting rights. If a corporation is authorized to issue only one class of stock, it is common stock that is authorized. The number of shares authorized by a company's charter can be changed by formal approval of the stockholders.

Shares issued and subsequently reacquired by the corporation through purchase or donation are referred to as **treasury stock.** Treasury stock cannot be voted and it pays or accrues no dividends. The number of shares of stock that a corporation has outstanding will always equal the number of shares issued, less the number of shares of treasury stock.

If a stockholder desires to buy more stock, it is not necessary to obtain the permission of the corporation. The stockholder acquires it privately or by purchase in the open market. Conversely, if a stockholder desires to sell shares, he or she cannot demand that the corporation buy back the stock. Instead, the stockholder is free to seek a buyer for the stock either in the open market or by private sale.

After the sale terms have been agreed upon, the mechanics are simple. The seller signs his or her name on the back of the stock certificate and delivers it to the buyer or the buyer's broker. A record of all outstanding stock certificates is kept by the corporation or by its duly appointed **transfer agent,** usually a commercial bank appointed by the corporation. The transfer agent records the names and addresses of the stockholders and the number of shares owned by each. After determining that an old stock certificate is in proper form for transfer, the transfer agent issues a new certificate to the new owner. Most companies have a **registrar** whose duty is to double check the actions of the transfer agent to prevent improper issue of stock or fraudulent transfer.

Dividends

A corporation may pay a dividend in cash, stock, or property. When **cash dividends** are paid, the company or its dividend disbursing agent (usually a bank), sends checks to all stockholders whose names appear on the books of the company. When cash dividends are distributed they are paid in terms of so much per share.

Some companies, in order to conserve cash, pay a dividend in their own stock. A **stock dividend** is usually stated as a percentage of the outstanding shares, up to a maximum of 25 percent.

When a corporation pays a **property dividend** it is usually in the form of stock of another corporation which has been acquired for investment or some other purpose.

Bonds

When a corporation or governmental unit wishes to borrow money for some period, usually for more than 5 years, it will sell a bond issue. Each bond is generally of $1,000 denomination and the certificate issued serves as evidence of a loan from the bondholder to the corporation or governmental unit. A bond pays a stated rate of interest and matures on a stated date. On that date, a fixed sum of money will be repaid to the bondholder. Bondholders do not have corporate ownership privileges as stockholders do.

There are several different types of bonds. Some are described below.

- **Corporate Bond.** A corporate bond is issued by private corporations such as railroads, public utilities, and industrial corporations. They are registered bonds, that is, they are bonds registered in the name of the holder on the books of the issuer or the issuer's registrar and can be transferred to another owner only when endorsed by the registered owner.

- **Municipal Bond.** A municipal bond is an obligation of a state, county, municipality or any agency thereof. By statute, all municipal bonds issued after July 1, 1983, are registered. The interest accrued on a municipal bond is free from Federal taxes.

- **U.S. Government Obligations:**

T-Bills: *Short-term*
T-Notes: *Intermediate*
T-Bonds: *Long-Term*

Treasury Bills. T-Bills are short term securities with maturities of one year or less (13 weeks, 26 weeks, and 52 weeks). They do not pay a fixed rate of interest and they are issued, and subsequently traded, at a discount from face-value. No certificate is issued; the purchase and payment are strictly accounting entries. T-Bills are issued in minimum denominations of $10,000 with $5,000 increments.

Treasury Notes. T-Notes are intermediate securities with maturities from one to ten years and are issued in denominations ranging from $1,000 to $1 million, or more. They carry a fixed interest rate and are issued and traded at face value or at a percentage of their face value.

- **Treasury Bonds.** T-Bonds are long-term bonds with maturities of 10 years or longer (usually 25-40 years). They carry a fixed interest rate and are issued and traded as a percentage of their face value. Minimum denomination is $1,000.

Not only are there different types of bonds, there are also the following classifications:

- **Registered Bond.** The name of the owner of a registered bond appears on the bond certificate. The owner's name is also recorded on the proper corporate records (usually maintained by a registrar and/or transfer agent). Interest on the bond is paid by check directly to the registered holder. While a registered bond possesses limited negotiability, it has the advantage of protecting the owner in the event of its loss.

- **Coupon Bond.** A coupon bond has coupons attached to the bond certificate, one coupon for each interest payment due during the life of the bond. The interest is payable to whoever turns in the coupon, whether or not that person initially bought the bond. The holder of the coupons is the bond's legal owner, hence the term "bearer bond."

- **Registered Coupon Bond.** With a registered coupon bond, the name of the owner appears on records maintained by a registrar and/or transfer agent. The interest coupons attached to the bond certificate do not contain the name of the owner and are payable to the bearer. Registered coupon bonds are registered for the principal only, not for interest.

Organized Securities Exchanges

Securities exchanges or stock exchanges neither buy nor sell securities themselves. An exchange functions as a central marketplace and provides facilities for executing orders. Member brokers representing buyers and sellers carry out these transactions.

The two major exchanges are the New York Stock Exchange (NYSE) and the American Stock Exchange (AMEX), both located in New York City. While there are approximately a dozen additional regional exchanges (Midwest, Pacific Coast, Philadelphia-

Baltimore-Washington, etc.), the NYSE and AMEX together handle more than 90 percent of the trading done through organized exchanges.

If a security is to be traded on an exchange, the issue must be approved for listing by that exchange. Securities traded on the NYSE or AMEX may also be listed and traded on a regional exchange, however, no security is listed on both the NYSE and AMEX.

Over-the-Counter Market

The over-the-counter securities market handles most of the securities transactions that take place in the United States. In fact, its operations are so extensive that the easiest way to describe it is to indicate what it does not do in securities transactions. The over-the-counter market does not handle the purchase or sale of securities that are listed on securities exchanges, but it handles everything else in the way of securities transactions. Thus, securities not listed on a securities exchange are "unlisted," that is, traded over-the-counter.

Many different types of securities are traded over-the-counter. They include the following:

- Bank stocks
- Insurance company stocks
- U.S. Government securities
- Municipal bonds
- Open-end investment company shares (mutual funds)
- Most corporate bonds
- Stocks of a large number of industrial and utility corporations, including nearly all new issues
- Securities of many foreign corporations

The over-the-counter market is not located in any one central place. Rather, it consists of thousands of securities houses located in hundreds of different cities and towns all over the United States. These securities houses are called brokers or dealers and are engaged in buying and selling securities usually for their own account.

Ownership of Securities

There are two principal ways securities are held, in the **name of the account holder** or in **street name.** In the first instance, the securities owned simply reflect the name of the customer who maintains the account. When securities are held in a street name, they are registered in the name of the broker.

Fundamentals of Commodities

Where the stock market is involved with the buying and selling of shares in corporations, the commodities market is generally involved with buying and selling commonly accepted quantities of marketable materials. Things sold on the commodities market include soy beans, wheat, corn, pork bellies, rice, gold, silver, and many more too numerous to mention. In the commodities market, the basic instrument of exchange is called the **futures contract.** A futures contract is a legally binding commitment to make delivery (sell) or take delivery (buy) of a given quantity and quality of a commodity at a contracted price and date. Virtually every type of marketable item is sold on the commodities market.

Organized Commodity Exchanges

In general, futures contracts are bought and sold on commodities exchanges. Commodities exchanges are similar to stock exchanges in that they function as central marketplaces and provide facilities for executing buy and sell orders. Two major commodities exchanges are the Chicago Board of Trade and the Chicago Mercantile Exchange. Other U.S. commodities exchanges are located in New York, Minneapolis, and Kansas City. The exchanges do not enter into the trading of contracts or establishment of contract prices.

Actual trading of futures contracts is done "on the floor" of the exchange by exchange members. There are specific rules governing the trading of futures. All contracts are standardized regarding size, date, and delivery terms. Basically, the price of the contract is the sole variable, and this is negotiated at the exchange. Buying or selling a futures contract does not mean that an investor necessarily accepts or makes delivery of the actual commodity (although legally obligated to do so). The primary means of fulfilling one's obligation under the contract is to enter into an offsetting contract. This legally cancels the outstanding obligation.

Available Documentation

A broker is an agent who handles the public's orders to buy and sell securities and commodities, usually for a commission. A broker may be a corporation, partnership, or individual and is often a member of a stock exchange or a member of a stock exchange securities firm. A registered representative, also known as a securities salesperson, account executive, or just plain broker, personally places customers' orders and maintains their accounts. While commonly referred to as a broker, a registered representative is usually an employee of a brokerage firm rather than a member.

The broker or brokerage firm can furnish virtually all source documents relating to securities and/or commodities account activity. The principal documents available are:

- **An application for an account.** This document is prepared by the customer when opening of an account. It includes personal data and some financial information such as bank reference, credit checks performed, etc.

- **Customer account cards.** This card is kept in the broker's personal files for reference. The broker records all transactions conducted for the customer on this card. A sample card is shown on the next page.

Client	Anthony Benidect	Account number	40-3801
Home address	1229 Springtide Place, NW Washington, DC 20001	Home telephone	(202) 555-7896
Business address	94 West Avenue Sterling, VA 22170	Business telephone	(703) 555-3654
Investment objective	Growth		
Special interests	None		

Description	Bought			Sold			Approximate	
	Date	#Share	Price	Date	#Share	Price	Profit	Loss
Kingman	6/4	10	22 5/8	6/20	10	17 1/4		$54
"	6/17	12	23 1/4					
"	8/1	20	17 1/8					
Dane Ind.	10/2	40	16 3/8	10/15	40	23 1/2	$280	
Kingman	10/4	6	19 7/8					
Bremer Co.	11/7	22	20 3/4					

- **Signature card.** A signature card shows who has authority to conduct transactions on the account.

- **Securities receipts.** These receipts are issued to a customer when he or she delivers securities to the broker for sale.

- **Cash receipts.** These receipts are issued to a customer when he or she delivers currency to the broker.

- **Confirmation slips.** Confirmation slips are issued to a customer to show the type of transaction (buy or sell) and the amount involved in the transaction.

- **Securities delivered receipt.** This receipt is signed by the customer when a securities purchase is actually delivered to the customer.

- **Brokerage account statement.** The brokerage account statement is usually issued on a monthly basis and provides information on all transactions conducted during the period. It lists all purchases and sales, the name of the security, the number of units, the amount per unit, the total amount of the transaction, the account balance, payments received from the customer, disbursements to the customer (usually with the check number issued), and the customer's position (securities that are held by the brokerage firm for the customer). A sample statement is shown below.

Roberts and Company Incorporated

Member New York Stock Exchange— American Stock Exchange
1485 I Street, NW, Washington, DC 20006
(202) 555-4500

Entry Date	Bought or Received	Sold or Delivered	Description	Price or Entry Description	Amount Debited	Amount Credited
02/12	100		Overton Airlines	Sec Rec		
02/12		100	Overton Airlines	9 5/8		$936.30
02/14		100	Polk Corp.	41 5/8		$4,098.20
02/15			Funds	Cash Dsb	$5,034.50	
02/15		100	Weber Corp.	36 7/8		$3,624.60
02/15	100		Weber Corp.	Sec Rec		
02/15	100		Dare, Inc.	Sec Rec		
02/23		100	Dare, Inc.	84 3/4		$8,412.50
02/28			Closing Balance			$12,037.10
			Position			
			None			

Mr. Anthony Benidect 1229 Springtide Place, NW Washington, DC 20001	02/28/92 Period Ending	40-3801 Account Number	1 Page

When a subject purchases stock, he or she usually has the option of taking **"delivery"** of the certificates from the broker or leaving them in the broker's custody for possible future sale. A person active in trading usually keeps all stock with his or her broker. If the customer takes delivery of the certificates, the number of shares would be noted in the **"sold or delivered"** column, and the **"date"** column would show the date of delivery. The same holds true if a customer delivers stock certificates to the broker for sale, except the number of shares would be placed the **"bought or received"** column.

Other Financial Institutions

Banks and brokerage firms are not the only financial institutions where financial transactions occur. Let's take a look at two other types of financial institutions and see what information they can provide to the financial investigator.

Western Union

A financial transaction conducted with a Western Union money order creates the following three documents:

- The original application prepared by the purchaser or sender
- The original request for payment prepared by the recipient of the funds
- The bank draft drawn by Western Union payable to the person receiving the money

The canceled drafts, after clearing through banking channels, are united with the original telegram applications and sent to the St. Louis, Missouri office for storage under the jurisdiction of the money order auditor. These records (except for money orders over $1,000) are destroyed after three years.

Casinos

Casino operations maintain extensive financial information concerning the movement of money. Their records represent a blend of information— bank account statements, credit card and loan applications, and hotel/room service documentation. Since the casino industry is Government regulated, currency movements in excess of $10,000 (purchase of chips or redemption of winnings) must be reported to the U.S. Treasury Department via a *Currency Transaction Report by Casinos, Form 8362*. A sample Form 8362 is found on the next page.

Form **8362** (Rev. May 1992) Department of the Treasury Internal Revenue Service

Currency Transaction Report by Casinos

File a separate Form 8362 for each transaction. Please type or print.

(Complete all applicable parts—see instructions)

OMB No. 1545-0906

Part I Individual or Organization for Whom This Transaction Was Completed

Individual's last name	First name	Middle initial	Social security number	
Organization's name	Employer identification number (EIN)		Passport number	Country
Address (number, street, and apt. or suite no.)	Occupation, profession, or business		Alien registration number	Country
City / State	ZIP code	Country (if not U.S.)	Driver's license (number and state)	

Part II Identity of Individual Conducting the Transaction (Complete only if an agent conducts a transaction for the person in Part I)

Last name	First name	Middle initial	Social security number	
Address (number, street, and apt. or suite no.)	Passport number	Country	Alien registration number	Country
City / State	ZIP code	Country (if not U.S.)	Driver's license (number and state)	

Part III Patron's Account or Receipt Number ▶

Part IV Description of Transaction

If more space is needed, attach a separate schedule and check this box . . . . ▶ ☐

1 Type of transaction. Check the applicable boxes to describe transaction.

a ☐ Currency exchange (currency for currency)

b CASH IN:

(1) ☐ Deposit (front and safekeeping) (3) ☐ Check purchased (see item 6 below) (5) ☐ Collection on account

(2) ☐ Chips purchased (4) ☐ Wire transfer of funds (6) ☐ Other cash in .... (specify)

c CASH OUT:

(1) ☐ Withdrawal of deposit (front and safekeeping) (3) ☐ Chips redeemed (5) ☐ Other cash out .... (specify)

(2) ☐ Check cashed (see item 6 below) (4) ☐ Credit advance

2 Total amount of currency transaction (in U.S. dollars) $ .00	3 Amount in item 2 in $100 bills or higher $ .00	4 Date of transaction (month, day, and year)

5 If other than U.S. currency is involved, please furnish the following information:

Currency name	Country	Total amount of each foreign currency (in U.S. dollars) $ .00

6 If a check was involved in this transaction, please furnish the following information (see instructions):

Date of check	Amount of check (in U.S. dollars) $ .00	Payee of check
Maker of check		Drawee bank and city

Part V Casino Reporting the Financial Transaction

Name	Employer identification number (EIN)
Address (number, street, and apt. or suite no.) where transaction occurred	
City / State / ZIP code	

Sign Here

▶ .... (Casino employee who handled the transaction) .... (Title) .... (Date)

▶ .... (Casino official reviewing and approving the Form 8362) .... (Title) .... (Date)

For Paperwork Reduction Act Notice, see back of form. Cat. No. 62291Z Form **8362** (Rev. 5-92)

Summary

This chapter describes the types of financial information available from banks, brokerage houses, casinos, and Western Union. The key is to know what information is available and how to interpret it. Seemingly insignificant details, such as charges for interest on a bank statement, have resulted in resolving major financial crimes. Securities held in a "street name" have lead to the discovery of information that has put criminals behind bars. High rollers at "the tables" have been defeated by financial documents revealing their activities. Tracing financial records to and through financial institutions is much more than a mere paper chase. Whether it is a check, a wire transfer, a deposit, a sale of a stock or bond, a purchase of a marketable security, the movement of money and the paper trail which it leaves behind is, for the financial investigator, "where the action is" and the road map of criminal activity.

Questions and Exercises

Answer the following questions then check your responses with those provided at the back of the book.

1. What information does the following check provide?

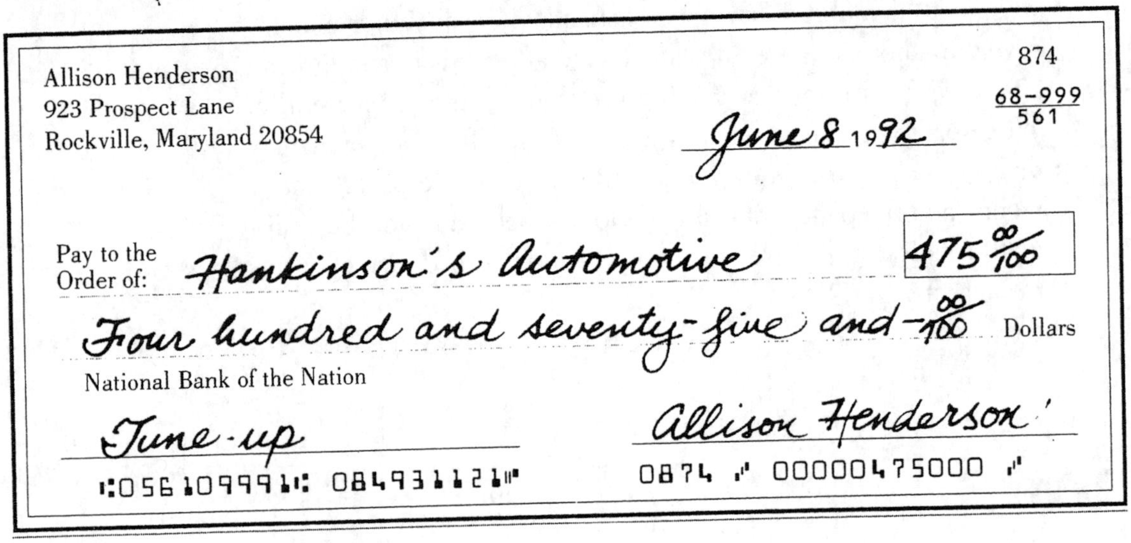

Allison Henderson
923 Prospect Lane
Rockville, Maryland 20854

874

68-999
561

June 8 1992

Pay to the Order of: Hankinson's Automotive 475 00/100

Four hundred and seventy-five and 00/100 Dollars

National Bank of the Nation

Tune-up

Allison Henderson

⑆0561099910⑆ 084931121⑈ 0874 ⑇ 0000047500 ⑇

2. Why is check spread analysis a useful investigative tool?

3. What information surrounding a safe-deposit box is useful in a financial investigation?

4. For a checking account, what records are banks required to retain for 5 years?

5. Why is it difficult to trace a currency-for-currency transaction?

6. What must an investigator do to gain access to a suspect's bank records?

7. What are "haven countries" and what role do they play in financial investigations?

8. Why is a loan application a good source of financial information?

9. What financial information is available from the following:

a. Western Union

b. A casino

10. Distinguish between the following:

a. Securities and commodities

b. Stock and bond

c. Common stock and preferred stock

d. Transfer agent and registrar

e. Corporate bond and municipal bond

f. Treasury bill and treasury bond

g. Securities held in owner's name and securities held in street name

11. Analyze the following three bank statements and identify four things an investigator will want to follow up on.

Checking Account Summary Conewango Bank

Account Number 65432198

David Davids
8 Mockingbird Lane
Herndon, Virginia 22070

Statement Period
05/01/92- 05/31/92

Transaction	**Date**	**Amount**	**Balance**
Beginning Balance			$2,145.98
Check 176	05/02	745.00-	1,400.98
Deposit	05/02	1,534.56+	2,935.54
Check 177	05/09	57.23-	2,878.31
Check 178	05/13	152.61-	2,725.70
Deposit	05/15	1,534.56+	4,260.26
Check 179	05/22	19.56-	4,240.70
Check 180	05/25	198.21-	4,042.49
Check 181	05/28	234.34-	3,808.15
Ending Balance			$3,808.15

Checking Account Summary Conewango Bank

Account Number 65432198

David Davids
8 Mockingbird Lane
Herndon, Virginia 22070

Statement Period
06/01/92- 06/30/92

Transaction	**Date**	**Amount**	**Balance**
Beginning Balance			$3,808.15
Check 182	06/02	745.00-	3,063.15
Deposit	06/02	1,534.56+	4,597.71
Check 183	06/06	2,000.00-	2,597.71
Deposit	06/10	5,000.00+	7,597.71
Deposit	06/15	1,534.56+	9,132.27
Check 184	06/20	22.03-	9,110.24
Check 185	06/23	189.13-	8,921.11
Check 186	06/29	429.84-	8,491.27
Ending Balance			$8,491.27

Checking Account Summary Conewango Bank

Account Number 65432198

David Davids
8 Mockingbird Lane
Herndon, Virginia 22070

Statement Period
07/1/92- 07/31/92

Beginning Balance $8,491.27

Transaction	**Date**	**Amount**	**Balance**
Deposit	07/01	1,534.56+	10,025.83
Check 187	07/04	5,000.00-	5,025.83
Check 188	07/14	54.11-	4,971.72
Check 189	07/14	156.21-	4,815.51
Deposit	07/15	1,534.56+	6,350.07
Check 190	07/20	22.46-	6,327.61
Check 191	07/28	141.69-	6,185.92
Check 192	07/30	533.37-	5,652.55
Ending Balance			$5,652.55

a.

b.

c.

d.

12. Why would you be suspicious if you located the following deposit slips?

DEPOSIT TICKET

Larry Fox
12 Mountain Drive
Barrington, Illinois 60005

Date July 14 1992

DEPOSITS MAY NOT BE AVAILABLE FOR IMMEDIATE WITHDRAWAL

SIGN HERE FOR CASH RECEIVED (IF REQUIRED)

Bank of the Loop

:071009991: 089217406" 1212

CASH		
	CURRENCY	7,500 00
	COIN	
LIST CHECKS SINGLY		
TOTAL FROM OTHER SIDE		0 00
TOTAL		7,500 00
LESS CASH RECEIVED		
NET DEPOSIT		7,500 00

2-999
710

USE OTHER SIDE FOR ADDITIONAL LISTING

DEPOSIT TICKET

Larry Fox
12 Mountain Drive
Barrington, Illinois 60005

Date July 14 1992

DEPOSITS MAY NOT BE AVAILABLE FOR IMMEDIATE WITHDRAWAL

SIGN HERE FOR CASH RECEIVED (IF REQUIRED)

White Sox Bank

:071000011: 042529807" 7212

CASH		
	CURRENCY	6,000 00
	COIN	
LIST CHECKS SINGLY		
TOTAL FROM OTHER SIDE		0 00
TOTAL		6,000 00
LESS CASH RECEIVED		
NET DEPOSIT		6,000 00

2-001
710

USE OTHER SIDE FOR ADDITIONAL LISTING

13. Interpret the following brokerage account statement.

Henry and Sons, Inc.

Member New York Stock Exchange— Washington Stock Exchange
920 H Street, NW, Washington, DC 20006
(202) 555-9700

Entry Date	Bought or Received	Sold or Delivered	Description	Price or Entry Description	Amount Debited	Amount Credited
07/18	250		Lakewood, Inc.	5 ½	$1,375.00	
07/22	1000		K Engines	Sec Rec		
07/22		100	Lake/wood, Inc	6		$600.00
07/22	100		Smith, Inc.	17 ⅜	$1,737.50	
07/24		50	Lakewood. Inc.	6 ⅝		$1,031.25
07/30	200		Warren Inc.	10	$2,000.00	
07/31			Closing Balance		$5,112.50	$1,631.25
			Position			
			None			

Nancy Garrity 25 Chelsea Lane, N.E. Washington, D.C. 20007	7/31/92 Period Ending	72-8072 Account Number	1 Page

Endnotes

1 United States Code, Title 12, Section 3403(c), "Right to Financial Privacy Act," (Washington, DC: U.S. Government Printing Office, Superintendent of Documents)

2 United States Code, Title 31, Section 103.31 through 103.37, inclusive, as stated in Title 12, Section 1829b, (Washington, DC: U.S. Government Printing Office, Superintendent of Documents)

CHAPTER 6

Tracing the Movement of Money through a Business

Chapter 5 dealt with tracing the movement of money through financial institutions. In this chapter, you'll see how an investigator traces the movement of money through a business. This skill requires an understanding of business organizations and a working knowledge of the principles of accounting. The proprietorship, partnership, and corporation are the predominate forms of business organization found in the American economy. The composition and fundamentals of each will be addressed in this chapter.

Accounting is the language of business. It reports, classifies, and summarizes the effects of financial transactions upon a business. From the writing of a check for the purchase of raw materials, to the receipt of currency for the sale of a finished product, accounting maintains a record of all business financial events. Illegal events such as embezzlement, insider trading, tax evasion and money laundering can often be detected through the analysis of accounting records. Accordingly, a familiarity with business books and records, accounting systems and methods, financial reports, and auditing techniques becomes important to the financial investigator.

After studying Chapter 6, you should be able to:

- Describe the basic forms of business organization.
- Explain why a knowledge of accounting is important to the financial investigator.
- Define or describe basic accounting terms.

- Journalize transactions.
- Post journal entries to a general ledger.
- Prepare a balance sheet and an income statement.

The discussion in Chapter 5 focused on tracing the movement of money to and through financial institutions. The focus of this chapter is tracing the movement of money through the financial records maintained by a business. But before we get into that, a discussion on the different types of business organizations is necessary. It is important that the financial investigator be aware of the "form" of the business organization he or she is investigating. A business organization's form can be manipulated to conceal true ownership or financial interest, or to hide illegal activities. Also, the type and complexity of a business's accounting system can be affected by the business's form of organization.

Types of Business Organizations

Consider the different types of businesses that make up today's economy: fast food restaurants, gas stations, video stores, hospitals, construction companies, government agencies, etc. There are literally hundreds of thousands of businesses. Luckily, for both the accountant and the financial investigator, there are not hundreds of thousands of different types of recordkeeping and organization systems. Standards for recordkeeping have been established and our legal system recognizes the following three primary types of business organizations:

- Proprietorship
- Partnership
- Corporation

Proprietorship

Generally speaking, a **proprietorship** (also known as the single or sole proprietorship) is a business owned by one person who is usually both the manager and the owner. Historically, proprietorships have been small scale or localized operations, however, there is no legal or theoretical limit to the scope, complexity, or size of this type of operation.

A proprietorship is the most common form of business operation and, as such, it is the most frequent type of business the financial investigator will encounter. *Anyone who enters into a business without designating an organizational type is considered a sole proprietor.* There are no special legal requirements to be met in starting a proprietorship.

The sole proprietor has the advantage of making all decisions and collecting all profits, but he or she also shoulders all responsibilities and suffers all losses.

Partnership

In order to become successful, a business may require more resources than are available to a single person. Specific knowledge, skills, or management capabilities may be required that one person alone cannot supply. In these situations, and in many others, two or more people combine assets and skills and become joint owners in a single business— a **partnership.** A partner can be a person, another partnership, or a corporation and, like a proprietorship, there are no special legal requirements to be met in starting a partnership.

Partnerships have been in existence for a long time. The English common law of partnership, from which the American system is derived, began as Roman law. The Uniform Partnership Act (UPA) codified the majority of the common-law rules relating to partnership actions and is acknowledged as the controlling document for partnership activity. Section 6 of the UPA defines a partnership as "an association of two or more persons to carry on as co-owners of a business for profit."[1] Because partners are co-owners, each:

- Has a right to share in the business profits (and losses)
- Has a voice in management affairs
- Is a co-owner of the partnership property

Since a partnership involves two or more persons, it requires more structure than a proprietorship. A partnership agreement is essential, although it is not a legal requirement. This agreement will prevent (hopefully) future misunderstandings. An agreement of this type, generally known as the **Articles of Partnership** (see page 129), contains all the terms pertinent to the formation, operation, and dissolution of the partnership, including:

- The names of the partners and the partnership
- The name, location, and type of business to be conducted
- The effective date of the agreement and the agreement's expiration date, if any
- An agreement as to the value of the assets to be contributed to the partnership by each partner
- The duties and rights of each partner, and the manner in which each partner shares profits, losses, and responsibilities
- The salary to be paid to each partner and the provisions for terminating the partnership

Additional factors pertinent to a partnership include:

- **The fiduciary relationship between each partner.** Each partner must maintain the highest standards of trust, good faith and integrity when dealing with his or her partners or acting on behalf of the partnership.

- **Agency relationship.** According to law, each partner is an agent for all other partners. This means that in transactions with others, the partnership is liable for the actions of a partner.

- **Terminating the partnership.** Ending a partnership is composed of two steps: dissolution and winding up. Dissolution sets the procedure into motion by announcing the partnership's intentions to close out business. Winding up is the actual settling, dividing, and terminating the partnership.

Articles of Partnership

THIS CONTRACT, made and entered into on the fifth day of December, 1989, by and between Paul E. Blake and Richard T. Nelson, both of Billings, Montana.

WITNESSETH: That the said parties have this day formed a partnership for the purpose of engaging in and conducting a wholesale automotive supply business in the city of Billings under the following stipulations, which are a part of this contract:

FIRST: The said partnership is to continue for a term of ten years from January 1, 1990.

SECOND: The business is to be conducted under the firm name of Blake & Nelson at 159 West Gilbert Street, Billings, Montana 59101.

THIRD: The investments are as follows: Paul E. Blake, cash, $60,000; Richard T. Nelson, cash, $60,000. These invested assets are partnership property in which the equity of each partner is the same.

FOURTH: Each partner is to devote his entire time and attention to the business and to engage in no other business enterprise without the written consent of the other partner.

FIFTH: During the operation of this partnership, neither partner is to become surety or bondsman for anyone without the written consent of the other partner.

SIXTH: Each partner is to receive an annual salary as follows: Paul E. Blake, $27,200.00; Richard T. Nelson, $26,000.00. One twelfth of the annual salary is payable in cash on the last business day of each month. At the end of each annual fiscal period, the net income or the net loss shown by the income statement, after the salaries of the two partners have been allowed, is to be shared as follows: Paul E. Blake, 60 percent; Richard T. Nelson, 40 percent.

SEVENTH: Neither partner is to withdraw assets in excess of his salary, any part of the assets invested, or assets in anticipation of net income to be earned, without the written consent of the other partner.

EIGHT: In case of the death or the legal disability of either partner, the other partner is to continue the operations of the business until the close of the annual fiscal period on the following December 31. At that time, the continuing partner is to be given an option to buy the interest of the deceased or incapacitated partner at not more than 10 percent above the value of the deceased or incapacitated partner's proprietary interest as shown by the balance of his capital account after the books are closed on December 31. It is agreed that this purchase price is to be paid one half in cash and the balance in four equal installments payable quarterly.

NINTH: At the conclusion of this contract, unless it is mutually agreed to continue the operation of the business under a new contract, the assets of the partnership, after the liabilities are paid, are to be divided in proportion to the net credit to each partner's capital account on that date.

IN WITNESS WHEREOF, the parties aforesaid have hereunto set their hands and affixed their seals on the day and year above written.

Paul E. Blake (Seal)
Richard T. Nelson (Seal)

Corporation

Corporations are quite different from proprietorships and partnerships for a number of reasons. Among them are:

- **Legal entity.** A corporation is a legal entity and may come into existence only by the sanction of a state.

- **An entity distinct from its owners.** A corporation is a legal entity in and of itself, separate and distinct from its owners. It's owners are stockholders. Whereas partners and sole proprietors are personally responsible for their debts, stockholders are not personally responsible for a corporation's debts.

- **Continuous existence.** A corporation has a continuous existence independent of the existences of its members. Partnerships and proprietorships have limited lives.

Because a corporation is a separate legal entity, it must seek approval to operate. Permission is granted by either State or Federal authorities after review of the requesting organization's **Articles of Incorporation.**

A corporation's *Articles of Incorporation* (see page 131) contains several pieces of information of interest to the financial investigator. Items of interest include the following:

- The name and purpose of the corporation and the location of the corporation's main office
- The date of the incorporation, the name of the state where incorporated, and the names and addresses of the incorporators
- The amount and kinds of capital stock that are authorized for the corporation, and the number of shares into which the ownership may be divided
- The amount of capital with which the corporation will begin operations

The *Articles of Incorporation* are normally filed with the Secretary of State in the state where the corporation is being formed. After approval by the State or Federal authority, a certified copy of the document is sent to the corporate office. This cer-

Articles of Incorporation
of
SNOWMOBILE CORPORATION

FIRST: The name of the corporation is Snowmobile Corporation.

SECOND: The principal office of said corporation is located at 21014 Beckett Avenue, in the City of Wilmington, County of New Castle, Delaware 19805.

THIRD: The nature of the business, or objects or purposes to be transacted, promoted, or carried on, is to engage in the business of selling snowmobiles and all business incidental to such sale.

FOURTH: The total number of shares of stock that the corporation shall have authority to issue is Two Thousand (2,000) and the par value of each of such share is One Hundred Dollars ($100.00), amounting in the aggregate to Two Hundred Thousand Dollars ($200,000).

FIFTH: The amount of capital with which the corporation will begin business is One Hundred Thousand Dollars ($100,000).

SIXTH: The names and places of residence of the incorporators are as follows:

Melvin C. Dahl	1336 Vine Place, Dover, Delaware 19901
David E. Gates	2547 Trimble Avenue, Wilmington, Delaware 19808
Gordon W. Rotz	139 Beechcrest Road, Newport, Delaware 19804

SEVENTH: The corporation is to have perpetual existence.

WE, THE UNDERSIGNED, being each of the incorporators hereinbefore named for the purpose of forming a corporation to do business both within and without the State of Delaware, under Chapter 65 of the Revised Code of Delaware, and the acts amendatory thereof and supplemental thereto, do make this certificate, hereby declaring and certifying that the facts herein stated are true and accordingly have hereunto set our hands and seals this fifth day of June, 1990.

In the presence of: Melvin Dahl (Seal)
Carl Downs David Gates (Seal)
Kenneth Rubin Gordon Rotz (Seal)

State of Delaware) ss.:
County of New Castle)

BE IT REMEMBERED, that on this fifth day of June, A.D. 1990, personally came before me, Mary D. Manning, a Notary Public for the State of Delaware, all of the parties to the foregoing certificate of incorporation, known to me personally to be such, and severally acknowledged the said certificate to be the act and deed of the signers respectively and that the facts therein stated are truly set forth.

GIVEN under my hand and seal of office the day and year aforesaid.

Mary Manning Notary Public

tified copy is known as the **Corporate Charter.**

After incorporation, a corporation may hold an organizational meeting where a Board of Directors and/or corporate officers are elected. Also, a set of bylaws may be adopted. The corporate bylaws regulate the actions and affairs of the corporation.

In Chapter 5, the securities market was discussed. It is through issuing securities that corporations obtain financing for their operation. Investors can either purchase stock (equity securities) or bonds (debt securities). An investor who purchases stock becomes an owner of the corporation, with each share of stock representing a valued interest. Even though stockholders are the owners of a corporation, they normally have no direct dominion over the management of the business. Stockholders exercise their power indirectly through the election of the Board of Directors. The duty of the Board of Directors is to determine corporate policy and oversee the carrying out of the policy by the corporate employees. Bondholders do not purchase an ownership interest in the corporation, they lend money to the corporation. The corporation promises to repay the bondholders what they have lent, plus interest.

All corporate security sales are reviewed by government authorities to protect the investing public from fraudulent offerings. Accordingly, corporations often provide detailed financial information to the reviewing authorities. These authorities, which include state incorporation departments and Federal agencies such as Securities and Exchange Commission, have valuable information to provide the financial investigator.

A Comparison of Business Organizations

A table that lists the advantages and disadvantages of the three basic types of business organizations is found on the next page.

Business Organization Derivations

There are derivations of the three forms of business organizations. Descriptions of some follow:

- **Limited Partnership.** A limited partnership permits partners to limit their risk of loss on their investment to the amount of their

A comparison of three types of business organizations

Sole Proprietorship	General Partnership	Corporation
Advantages	**Advantages**	**Advantages**
Ownership of all profits	Larger capital resources than sole proprietorship	Limited liability of stockholders
Ease of organization	Better credit standing than single individual	Very large capital resources
Freedom of action	More managerial talent than single individual	Ease of transfer of ownership
Minimum of legal restrictions	Few legal restrictions	Long or perpetual life
Maximum personal incentive	High degree of personal incentive	Ease of expansion
No tax on the business entity	No tax on the business entity	Legal entity distinct from others
Ease of dissolution	Ease of dissolution	Some Federal tax incentives
Disadvantages	**Disadvantages**	**Disadvantages**
Unlimited liability for business debts	Unlimited liability for business debts	Tax on business income
Limited capital resources	Existence ends with death or withdrawal of any partner	Extensive legal restrictions and regulations
Business ends with the death of the proprietor	Restricted transfer of organization ownership	Expenses of incorporation
		Possibly limited personal incentive

investment. Their risk is similar to the limited liability of a stockholder. A limited partnership agreement must be in writing and there must be at least one general partner who assumes unlimited liability. Limited partners may not participate in the management of the firm, although they may meet from time to time to vote on general policies of operation. This form of organization is popular in oil well drilling, cattle feeding, and real estate businesses.

- **Cooperative.** A cooperative is a corporation in which profits are distributed to shareholders not in proportion to the number of shares each owns, but in proportion to the amount of business each shareholder does with the cooperative. Unlike normal corporations which generally allow one vote per share, each member of a cooperative has only one vote.

- **Mutual Company.** A mutual company is a type of corporation that has no stockholders. It is common in the fields of life insurance and savings, and is owned by its customers (policyholders or depositors) who, depending on the provisions of the charter, may or may not have the right to vote for the directors. If any profits are distributed, they are paid out according to the size of the policy or the size of the deposit.

- **Shell Corporation.** A shell corporation is one that has no assets or liabilities. It simply has a charter to do business. The attraction of a shell corporation is confidentiality. An application to do business may take weeks to approve and the names of persons on the charter are subject to review; however, the names of subsequent stockholders and directors are not identified on public records.

- **Joint Stock Company.** A joint stock company is an unincorporated association that closely resembles a corporation, but for most purposes, it is treated like a partnership.

- **Joint Venture.** A joint venture, which is sometimes called a **joint adventure** or **joint enterprise,** is a partnership created for a limited purpose or duration.

- **Syndicate.** A syndicate, also known as an **investment group,** is a group of investors usually involved in a specific enterprise (i.e. financing a real estate development).

After identifying the type of business organization, the next step for the investigator is to analyze financial transactions effecting the organization itself. Through such analysis the movement of money, from both legal and illegal activities, can be systematically detected.

What is Accounting?

ac′ count-ing \ e′ kaunt-ij \n. 1. The system of recording and summarizing business and financial transactions in books and analyzing, verifying, and reporting the results.[2]

Archaeologists have traced accounting's roots back more than 3,000 years. Clay and stone tablets which contain a recorded history of ancient financial transactions have been found in various locations around the world. During the reign of the Roman Empire, sophisticated accounting methods were developed to record military records and maintenance of other monetary data. Other cultures also used accounting methods and systems—Chinese dynasties preserved tax information, Middle Eastern cultures kept census records, and American Indians used an accounting system to identify the accumulation of possessions (by notches on sticks or the number of beads on a string).

Accounting evolved slowly until commerce achieved a degree of complexity which necessitated a more sophisticated system of recording financial transactions. Could IBM or Apple Computer keep a record of its customer warranties on clay and stone tablets? Could the Federal Government maintain its payroll records for its civil and military personnel by placing notches on sticks? Of course not! Ever since Europe's Industrial Revolution established the foundation for the current climate of business and finance, the need for recording, summarizing, and verifying financial information has become paramount. Today, accounting establishes, in monetary terms, the framework for a business— a framework for evaluating the efficiency of a business's operations, for recording a history of a business's failures and accomplishments, and for projecting a business's future.

The American Institute of Accountants defines accounting as "the art of recording, classifying, and summarizing, in a significant manner and in terms of money, transactions and events which are, in part at least, of a financial character and interpreting the results thereof."[3] Accordingly, the cornerstone of accounting is the classification of "pieces of paper" (invoices, sales receipts, payroll records, etc.) involving financial transactions. To the financial investigator, these "pieces of paper" represent valuable information about monetary events.

Since the function of accounting is to record and summarize the accumulation, spending, and/or transportation of money by an individual or organization, a financial investigator should be conversant in fundamental accounting principles and understand the role of an accountant in the business organization. Since financial information is the key to unlocking the hidden answers to the riddles encountered in an investigation, accounting becomes, for the financial investigator, the key to reading the map of unknown events which leads to resolving a crime.

Accounting Systems

Businesses produce goods and provide services to be bought and sold. It makes sense that the exchange of goods and services can be observed and measured. Accounting is the language of business because it objectively measures and records the business exchanges that occur throughout society.

For accounting purposes, a **transaction** is the exchange of goods and services and begins with recording, in dollars and cents, what is received and what is paid out. All businesses use some system of accounting, from the sole proprietor who runs his or her business out of a checkbook to General Motors which employs hundreds of accountants to keep its books. Everyone who is faced with earning a living needs to keep track of what they earn. That is what accounting is about.

The ultimate objective of accounting is to show, in a summary form, the results of a business's transactions. In order to achieve this goal, two systems of accounting have been developed.

Single-Entry Bookkeeping

The single-entry bookkeeping system has been used for most of accounting's 3,000-year history. It is the simplest form of noting and recording a financial transaction. In this system, financial transactions from all source documents are chronologically recorded in one place, usually in columnar form. A checking account register, an example of which is shown on the next page, is a type of single-entry bookkeeping system.

Double-Entry Bookkeeping

For most businesses, recording single transactions in chronological order in a checkbook register is not a sufficient way to track their business affairs. Let's say you are a business owner and you want to know how much you paid your employees in 1991. Your

Record all charges or credits that affect your account

Number	Date	Description of Transaction	Payment/Debit (-)	✓ T	Fee (If Any) (-)	Deposit/Credit (+)	Balance $
813	5/12	Jakes Cafe	19 43				793 12
							250 —
	5/12	Deposit - RM, Inc.				250—	1043 12
							83 29
814	5/13	Walker Ridge	83 29				959 83
							72 91
815	5/13	Kilroy's Deli	72 91				886 92
							84 26
	5/13	Deposit - Sam Jones				84 26	971 18
							293 80
816	5/13	Sally Torrence	293 80				677 38

Remember to record automatic payments/deposits on date authorized

accountant would have to pull out the checkbook register related to 1991, find each transaction related to paying each employee, and total them. Wouldn't it be easier to record all the payroll payments in one place rather than have them scattered throughout a checkbook register?

Since it is easier to look at the summary of a group of transactions, an accountant must have a means of compressing similar transactions. The device employed for this purpose is called an **account.** Typically, accounts are established to record the movement of cash into and out of the business, the payments of expenses, the purchase of assets, and the equity of the owner. A business may have many different types of accounts: payroll, sales, cash, office furniture, and insurance expenses to name just a few.

In a double-entry bookkeeping system, a single transaction always affects two or more accounts. Let's say your business purchases a new desk and pays $200 cash for it. Two accounts are affected, cash and office furniture. You have increased the amount of furniture your business has, but, at the same time, the amount of cash available has decreased. The double-entry bookkeeping system allows this financial transaction to be recorded in the two accounts it affects, thereby showing the full effect of the financial transaction on the business.

Comparison of Accounting Systems

Single-Entry	Double-Entry
Transactions are recorded by one entry into business records	Two or more entries are required to record transactions into business records
Relatively simple form of bookkeeping	Relatively complex form of bookkeeping
Transactions are not classified according to type	Transactions are classified according to type
May not show full effect of transaction on business	Shows full effect of transactions on the business

Methods of Accounting

Within the double-entry bookkeeping system there are two recognized methods or ways of recording transactions, cash and accrual.

Cash Basis

With this method, business receipts (revenue) are recorded when cash is *received* and business expenditures (expenses) are recorded when cash is *paid out.*

The pivotal words are "received" and "paid out". In other words, *only* when the business has physically received the cash (i.e. currency, check), as opposed to a promise to pay, or *has actually paid* the expense— does the business record the transaction. For example, a business orders $500 worth of computer paper for delivery in December, however, it does not pay for the paper until January. When using a cash basis method of recording transactions, the $500 would be recorded as an expense *when paid* in

January. Professionals such as doctors and lawyers usually maintain their accounting records on a cash basis.

Accrual Basis

With this method, business revenues are recorded when *earned* (regardless of when collected) and expenses are recorded when *incurred* (regardless of when cash was disbursed). Let's look at that same $500 purchase of computer paper described above. The $500 would be recorded as an expense when *incurred* (or committed for) in December if the accrual basis of accounting is used. Most businesses maintain their accounting records on an accrual basis.

Hybrid Method

A method of accounting that combines the features of both the cash and accrual methods is called the **hybrid method.** It is permissible to use the hybrid method when it is consistently applied and clearly reflects income. This method is most commonly used in small businesses where the "timing" between the incurring of expenses and the paying of expenses is usually of short duration and when "income" is reported on the cash basis. If there is no material distortion of the matching of business income and expenses, a hybrid method may be used.

A Comparison of the Accounting Methods

The table below provides a comparison of the three types of accounting.

Comparison of Accounting Methods

Cash	Accrual	Hybrid
Receipts are recorded when they are received	Receipts are recorded when they are earned	Receipts are reported via the cash method
Expenses are recorded when they are paid	Expenses are recorded when they are incurred	Expenses are reported via the accrual method
Transactions are recorded when they are entered into the business's books	Transactions are recorded when they are entered into the business's books	No material distortion of income and expenses
Matches income and expenses	Matches income and expenses	

The Fundamental Accounting Equation

Matching a business's income and expenses is the important function of accounting. This matching concept is based on the principle that every item of value in a business is owned or claimed by someone. This concept may be expressed by the following equation:

Items of Value = Claims

- **Items of Value.** The various things owned by a business are called **assets.** Examples of assets include cash, supplies, machinery, furniture, fixtures, land, and other tangible objects. Additionally, there are assets which are not tangible items. These types of assets include the right to collect money from others, patents, investments, and goodwill (the dollar value assigned to a business's managerial skills and reputation). To be considered an asset, an item must meet the following two requirements:

  – It must be owned by the business

  – It must have monetary value

- **Claims.** There are two types of claims against assets:

  – Claims of the owner

  – Claims of the creditors

The claims of the owner are called **Capital Account Equity** or **Owner's Net Worth.** In a proprietorship, all owner equity belongs to the sole proprietor. In a partnership, the share of owner equity belonging to each partner is designated in the *Articles of Partnership.* In a corporation, the claims of the owner are called **corporate net worth.** Corporate net worth is divided into two separate accounts. One account is called the "Retained Earnings" or "Surplus Account," and it records profits or losses. The second account is called "The Capital Stock Account," and it represents shareholder investment.

The claims of the creditors are called **liabilities.** These claims may be made by suppliers, banks, mortgage holders, and bondholders.

The equation "Items of Value = Claims" can now be converted to the fundamental accounting equation shown below:

Assets = Liabilities + Owner's Equity

A = L + OE

You may also see the equation as:

A = L + C (Capital)

Although business transactions effect different components of the equation, **the total assets must always equal the total claims (liabilities and owner's equity).** Therefore, if the equation is to be maintained, it is impossible to change a single item without changing another. For example, when an asset is increased, a corresponding adjustment must be made in the equation or it will not balance; either another asset must be decreased, or a liability or owner's equity account must be increased.

Business Financial Statements

Business owners, potential investors, and creditors need some type of summary or report that describes the financial condition of a business during a specific period of operation. Also, they need to know whether or not the business is making or losing money. Accounting records provide the information that creates these types of financial reports. One of the important functions of an accountant is to summarize transaction entries and prepare the financial reports for a business. These reports are called **Balance Sheets** and **Income Statements** and they represent the summary of financial activity entered into by a business during an identified period of time.

Balance Sheet

The Balance Sheet, often called the Statement of Financial Condition or Statement of Financial Position, depicts the assets, liabilities, and owner's equity of a business organization at a specific point in time. It is called a balance sheet because, upon its completion, it must be in balance. In other words, the total value of the business's assets must equal the total value of the liabilities plus owner's equity— a reference back to the fundamental accounting equation, A = L + OE.

A balance sheet is prepared at the close of business of the last day of the accounting period. It identifies the business by name, sets out the fact that it is a balance sheet, and gives the date of the statement. The date assigned to a balance sheet does not cover a period of time, but rather represents a moment in time. One prepared on Tuesday the 12th will differ from one prepared on Monday the 11th and Wednesday the 13th. A balance sheet presents a picture of the business's financial position, as if frozen for a split second, on the statement date.

Balance sheets are usually formatted in one of two ways. The account form lists liabilities and owner's equity to the right of assets. The report form lists liabilities and owner's equity below the assets. A balance sheet in account form is shown below; one in a report format is shown on the next page.

Account Form

123 Company
Balance Sheet
December 31, 1991

Current Assets		**Current Liabilities**	
Cash	$130,000	Accounts payable	$270,000
Accounts receivable	486,000	Accrued expenses	117,000
Inventory	602,000	Income tax payble	30,000
Pre-paid expenses	90,000	Notes payable	320,000
Total current assets	$1,308,000	Total current liabilities	$737,000
Fixed Assets		**Long-Term Liabilities**	
Machinery	364,000	Payables	500,000
Equipment	116,000	Total liabilities	$1,237,000
Furniture	300,000		
Total fixed assets	$780,000	**Owner's Equity**	
		Paid-in capital	$701,000
		Retained earnings	150,000
		Total equity	$851,000
Total Assets	$2,088,000	**Total Liabilites and Equity**	$2,088,000

Report Form

123 Company
Balance Sheet
December 31, 1991

Assets

Current Assets		
Cash	$130,000	
Accounts receivable	486,000	
Inventory	602,000	
Pre-paid expenses	90,000	
Total current assets		$1,308,000
Fixed Assets		
Machinery	$364,000	
Equipment	116,000	
Furniture	300,000	
Total fixed assets		$780,000
Total assets		$2,088,00

Liabilities

Current Liabilities		
Accounts payable	$270,000	
Accrued expenses	117,000	
Income tax payable	30,000	
Notes payable	320,000	
Total current liabilities		$737,000
Long-Term Liabilities		
Payables	$500,000	
Total long-term liabilities		$500,000
Total liabilities		$1,237,000

Owner's Equity

Paid-in capital	$701,000	
Retained earnings	150,000	
Total equity		$851,000
Total liabilities and equity		$2,088,000

Each separate asset, liability, and owner's equity entry shown on the balance sheet represents an **account.** The balance sheet does not report the flow of funds into and out of the accounts during the accounting period. Only each account's ending balance as of the statement date is shown.

Look back at the two balance sheets shown above. Note that both classify and organize the individual accounts listed. Under the category "Current Assets," you find the following accounts: cash, accounts receivable, inventory, and pre-paid expenses. The categories shown on the preceding balance sheets often appear on a balance sheet and do so in the order presented. Keep in mind that not all balance sheets require all of the categories listed, and some may require others not shown. A discussion of the different categories follows.

Current Assets

This class of assets includes cash and any other asset that could be converted to cash within one accounting cycle or balance sheet period (normally one year). Current assets should be listed according to their degree of liquidity (likelihood of being converted to cash). Examples of current assets include:

- Cash— The bills and coins in the business as well as the money on deposit in savings and checking accounts.

- Notes Receivable— A formal written promise by a debtor to pay a specified amount of money, usually with interest, at a definite time.

- Accounts Receivable— Claims against customers arising from the sale of merchandise or services on credit.

- Allowance for Bad Debt— An estimated amount of accounts receivable which will probably be uncollectible due to nonpayment by a customer. This account is normally shown as a reduction to current assets. The balance in this account is deducted from the original receivable balance in the asset account.

- Merchandise Inventory— Goods purchased or produced for the purpose of sale to customers.

• Pre-Paid Expenses— Expenses paid in advance, such as rent and insurance.

Fixed Assets

This class of assets, sometimes called **Property, Plant, and Equipment,** includes assets that are not intended for sale but are to be used by the business over several years. Examples of fixed assets include:

• Furniture and Fixtures— The furniture and fixtures owned by the business.

• Allowance for Depreciation— The total amount set aside for the decline in the useful value of the fixed assets due to wear and tear from usage and the passage of time. This account is normally shown as a reduction to fixed assets. The balance in this account is deducted from the original cost balance in the asset account.

• Delivery Equipment— The vehicles used to get the goods from the business to the customer.

• Building— The physical structure which houses the company.

Current Liabilities

This class of liabilities includes all debts of the business that will come due within one year of the balance sheet date. Examples of current liabilities include:

• Notes Payable— A promissory note given by the business to a bank, individual, or other business entity as evidence of a debt owed for the purchase of merchandise or some other asset.

• Accounts Payable— A short-term liability usually arising from the purchase of merchandise for credit. Unlike the note payable, no formal written promise to pay is issued.

• Accrued Expenses Payable— Expenses which are owed but not yet paid. A common example is salaries owed to the employees but not paid until the end of the pay period.

Long-Term Liabilities

This class of liabilities involves all debts with maturity dates more than one year after the balance sheet date. One account that you might find under this category is **mortgage payable.** This liability deals with debts secured by mortgages on specific assets of the business. Failure by the business to pay this obligation would give the creditor a legal right to force the sale of the pledged asset as a means of obtaining payment.

Owner's Equity

Owner's equity shows how much of a business has been "furnished" by its owner(s). There are two basic accounts for owner's equity. These accounts are:

- Paid-in Capital— When the owners invest their assets (i.e. cash, property, etc.) into the business, they are contributing capital which increases the worth of the business.
- Retained Earnings— The accumulated profits and losses of a corporation.

Income Statement

The second accounting report that is important to a financial investigator or anyone else interested in the financial condition of a business organization is the Income Statement. The income statement, also called the Profit and Loss Statement, reports revenue and expenses incurred by a business for a designated period of time.

While the balance sheet reports the financial condition of a business at a given date, the income statement reports the business's operating activities for the whole accounting period. The income statement matches the amounts received from selling the goods and/or services produced by the business (income) against all the costs and/or services (expenses) needed to operate the business. The result of this matching process is a financial statement of the business's profit or loss for the period.

Like the balance sheet, there are two general formats for an income statement, single-step and multi-step.

Single-Step Format

In its simplest format, the single-step income statement presents the following three items:

- Revenue for the period
- Applicable expenses
- Net income or loss (revenue minus expenses)

The following shows a single-step income statement.

ABC Company
Income Statement
For the year ended December 31, 1991

Revenue:		
Sales		$4,212,000
Expenses:		
Cost of goods sold	$2,808,000	
Selling expenses	936,000	
Administrative expenses	116,000	
Interest expense	52,000	
Income tax expense	120,000	
Total expenses		$4,032,000
Net Income		$ 180,000

Note the heading of the income statement. Like the balance sheet, it consists of the name of the company, the name of the financial statement, and the date. However, unlike the balance sheet, the income statement date is preceded by the term "for the year, period, or month ending." The income statement reflects a business's net income or loss for the entire period stated in the heading.

Multi-Step Format

Many income statement users maintain that there are a number of significant relationships between total revenue and net income which are not brought out in a single-step income statement. They contend, for example, that some intermediate subtotals such as gross profit, operating earnings, and earnings before tax are as important as total revenue, total expenses, and net income.[4] They prefer an income statement format which presents intermediate steps, the multi-step format.

The multi-step format is designed to be read in a stairstep manner. Each step down is a deduction of one or more expenses. Look at the sample income statement in multi-step format shown on the next page. The first step down deducts the cost of goods sold from the business's sales revenue. This deduction results in the line entitled *gross profit.* This measurement is captioned "gross" because other expenses are yet to be deducted.

In the next step down, operating expenses (selling expenses and administrative expenses) are deducted from the gross profit figure. Then other expenses (i.e. taxes, interest, etc.) are also subtracted from the calculation to arrive at the final step down— **net income.** Net income is the bottom line in the matching process between business income and business expenses. If income remains after the deduction of expenses a net income (profit) is reported. Correspondingly, if the business expenses for the period exceed the business income, a net loss is reported.

ABC Company
Income Statement
For the year ended December 31, 1991

Sales revenue		$4,212,000
Less: cost of goods sold		2,808,000
Gross profit		$1,404,000
Less: selling expenses	936,000	
Administrative expenses	116,000	
Total operating expenses		1,052,000
Operating earnings		$352,000
Less: interest expense		52,000
Earnings before tax		$300,000
Less: Income Tax expense		120,000
Net Income		$180,000

Recording Financial Transactions

The effect of each individual financial transaction entered into by a business during the accounting period is eventually reflected on a business's balance sheet and income statement. Since a business may engage in hundreds or even thousands of transactions daily, an accounting procedure is needed to record and classify financial transactions in order to organize this type of financial information inside the business's bookkeeping system. Every check written, invoice paid, and sales receipt issued by a business represents a **source document** of accounting information. The financial information from the source documents is entered into the business's bookkeeping system through the establishment of **accounts.** As was stated earlier, accounts are established to record the movement of cash into and out of the business, the payments of expenses, the purchase of assets, and the equity of the owner.

Chart of Accounts

The number of accounts needed by a business will depend on its size, nature of operations, and the extent to which management wants detailed classification of information. To assist in tracking its accounts, a business will create a **chart of accounts.** A chart of accounts is a listing, in sequentially numbered order, of a business's established accounts. The chart of accounts for Ogle Insurance Company is found on the next page.

Bookkeeping Systems and Accounts

Single-entry bookkeeping only accounts for the cash coming into or cash going out of a business. It does not separate financial transactions into individual accounts or attempt to balance the effects of each transaction in the business's books and records.

In a double-entry system of accounting, financial transactions are recorded in a manner that balances the effect of each individual transaction in the business's books and records. Under the double-entry system, recording a financial transaction in the business's books affects two or more accounts.

Ogle Insurance Company
Chart of Accounts

Assets

101	Cash on Hand
101.5	Cash in Bank
102	Accounts Receivable
105	Merchandise Inventory
106	Pre-paid Insurance
117.0	Delivery Equipment
117.5	Accumulated Depreciation – Delivery Equipment
118.0	Office Furniture
118.5	Accumulated Depreciation – Office Furniture
119.0	Office Equipment
119.5	Accumulated Depreciation – Office Equipment
120	Goodwill
130	Land
140	Building
150	Petty Cash

Liabilities

201	Accounts Payable Expense
202	Salaries Payable
204	Employees' Income Tax
205	FICA Tax Payable
206	State Unemployment Tax Payable
207	Sales Tax Payable
208	Notes Payable
209	Mortgage Payable
210	Loans Payable

Net Worth

251	Capital, Robert Ogle
252	Drawing, Robert Ogle
253	Profit and Loss

Revenue

301	Sales
302	Sales Returns and Allowances
303	Sales Discount
311	Purchases

Operating Expenses

401	Delivery Expenses
402	Depreciation Expenses – Delivery Equipment
403	Salaries Expenses
404	Payroll Expenses
405	Miscellaneous Selling Expense
407	Depreciation Expense – Office Furniture
408	Depreciation Expense – Office Equipment
409	Insurance Expense
410	Office Supplies
412	Bad Debt Expense
413	Miscellaneous General Expense

Other Income

501	Gain on Disposal of Plant Assets
502	Interest Income

Other Expenses

601	Rent Expense
602	Telephone Expense

Journals

Financial information is taken from source documents and entered into the accounting system through a business's **journals.** Journals are called the Books of Original Entry and they maintain, in chronological order, the details of each financial transaction entered into by a business. In the double-entry system of bookkeeping, each transaction affects two or more accounts and, accordingly, two or more journal entries must be made to record the transaction, never just one.

The example below shows how a single transaction is recorded in a journal within a double-entry bookkeeping system. Three entries are needed to record the following transaction:

Company X sold $2,000 worth of merchandise to MLB Limited. The invoice shows that MLB Limited paid $500 cash and put the remaining $1,500 on account.

General Journal

page J-16

Date 1992	Accounts and Explanations	Ledger Folio*	Debit	Credit
8/13	Cash	101	500	
	Accounts Receivable	102	1,500	
	Sales	301		2,000
	Sold merchandise to MLB Limited.			

* **Account number - refer to chart of accounts**

Note that a description of the transaction, and the actual increase and decrease in terms of money are recorded in the journal. The dollar value of the transaction is recorded in one of two columns in the journal. The column on the left is called the **debit column** and the column on the right is called the **credit column.**

The terms debit (Dr.) and credit (Cr.) represent accounting nomenclature for "making an entry on the left side or right side of an account," and hold no other meanings or connotations. To "debit an account" means to make an entry on the left side or in the left column of an account. To "credit an account" means to make an entry on the right side or in the right column of an account. The accounting rules for recording the increases and decreases resulting from financial transactions are found on the next page.

Rules for Recording Increases and Decreases

Assets	
Increases on the left (debit)	Decreases on the right (credit)
Liabilities and Owner's Equity (Capital)	
Decreases on the left (debit)	Increases on the right (credit)
Revenue	
Decreases on the left (debit)	Increases on the right (credit)
Expenses	
Increases on the left (debit)	Decreases on the right (credit)

Let's look back at the sample journal entries on page 151 to see if the rules above were properly applied. The $500 cash (an asset that increased) was debited to the "Cash" account and the $1,500 balance, also an asset that increased, was debited to the Accounts Receivable account. Sales, a revenue account, was increased by the credit of $2,000.

Why is it important that a financial investigator understand how information from source documents eventually finds its way into a business's journals? Journals provide the financial link between the outside world's source documents and the business world's accounting records. Through analysis of journal entries, often a determination can be made as to whether or not the business has properly recorded the financial event as shown on the source document. This analysis can be completed by:

- Determining the accounts affected by the transaction
- Determining the affect in dollar terms of the transaction on each account
- Reviewing the recorded journal entry for the correct debit/credit entries relating to the financial transaction

Types of Journals

Special types of journals are devoted to particular kinds of business transactions. Examples of these different types of journals are the following:

- **Cash Receipts Journal.** Records the dates, sources, and amounts of money received into a business.
- **Cash Disbursements Journal.** Records the dates, amounts, and recipients of payments made by a business.
- **Sales Journal (Accounts Receivable Journal).** Lists sales invoices in date or numerical order for sales made on credit.
- **Purchases Journal (Accounts Payable Journal).** Records all acquisitions of merchandise or services purchased on credit by the business.
- **General Journal**. Reflects transactions not covered by specific purpose journals. It is also used to record adjustments to the books and records.

The following pages illustrate various types of journals and journal formats. Read each of the examples to see how various transactions are recorded. Refer to the chart of accounts on page 150 and the rules for recording increases and decreases to journals on page 152 as necessary.

Cash Receipts Journal Entries

1992	Financial Transactions
7-14	Received $250 from Redbay and Co. on account.
7-18	Sold $175 merchandise for cash to Reed Manufacturing.
7-22	Received a $300 payment from Bur, Inc. for cash sale.

Cash Receipts Journal

Date	Received From	Folio #	Debit	Credit
1992				
7/14	Cash	101	250.00	
	Accounts Receivable	102		250.00
	Redbay & Co. - paid acct.			
7/18	Cash	101	175.00	
	Sales	301		175.00
	Sold merchandise to Reed Mfg.			
7/22	Cash	101	300.00	
	Sales	301		300.00
	Sold merchandise to Bur, Inc.			

Cash Receipts Journal Entries

1992	Financial Transactions
7-6	Received $7,800 from Pike Mfg. on account.
7-8	Sold $7,000 of merchandise for cash to Iron Works.
7-10	Received a $9,000 payment from Bates Motel for a cash sale.
7-14	Sold $2,500 of merchandise for cash to Wilcox Motors.
7-18	Received $1,500 from Cloud Mfg. on account.
7-19	Cash sale to Hickory Co. for $2,500.

Cash Receipts Pg. CR-3

Date	Payee	Cash Debit (101)	A/R Credit (102)	Sales Credit (301)
1992				
July				
6	Pike Mfg.	$7,800.00	$7,800.00	
8	Iron Works	$7,000.00		$7,000.00
10	Bates Motel	$9,000.00		$9,000.00
14	Wilcox Motors	$2,500.00		$2,500.00
18	Cloud Mfg.	$1,500.00	$1,500.00	
19	Hickory Co.	$2,500.00		$2,500.00

Cash Disbursements Journal Entries

1992	Financial Transactions
1-25	$500 is paid to Sylvester Sage on account.
1-25	$75 is paid to the Telephone Company for the monthly bill.
1-27	$250 is paid to John Woods on account.
1-29	$300 is paid to Realty Management.

Cash Disbursements Journal

Date 1992	Paid to	L.F.	Debit	Credit
1/25	Accounts Payable	201	$500	
	Cash (CK #275)	101		$500
	Paid to Sylvester Sage on account			
1/25	Telephone Expense	602	$75	
	Cash (CK #276)	101		$75
	Paid telephone bill for month			
1/27	Accounts Payable	201	$250	
	Cash (CK #277)	101		$250
	Paid to John Woods on account			
1/29	Rent Expense	601	$300	
	Cash (CK #278)	101		$300
	Paid to Realty Management			

Sales Journal Entries

1992	Financial Transactions
1-3	Sales to XYZ Company on account = $1,000
1-4	Sales to 123 Company on account = $500
1-5	Sales to Bob Company on account = $250
1-6	Sales to XYZ Company on account = $1,000
1-7	Sales to 123 Company on account = $500

Sales Journal Pg. SJ-1

Date 1992	Customer Name	(103) Accounts Receivable (DR)	(301) Sales (CR)
1/3	XYZ Co.	$1,000	$1,000
1/4	123 Co.	500	500
1/5	Bob Co.	250	250
1/6	XYZ Co.	1,000	1,000
1/7	123 Co.	500	500
		$3,250	$3,250

Purchase Journal Entries

1992	Financial Transactions
1-1	Bought merchandise on account from wholesaler X for $250
1-2	Bought merchandise on account from vendor Y for $500
1-3	Bought merchandise on account from wholesaler Z for $750
1-4	Purchased merchandise on account from vendor Y for $500
1-4	Purchased merchandise on account from wholesaler Z for $750

Purchase Journal Pg. PJ-1

Date 1992	Vendor Name	Purchases (DR)	Accounts Payable (CR)
1/1	X Wholesaler	$250	$250
1/2	Y Vendor	500	500
1/3	Z Wholesaler	750	750
1/4	Y Vendor	500	500
1/4	Z Wholesaler	750	750

The Ledger

Journalizing entries, recording each business transaction from a source document into the journals, continues throughout the accounting period. Because of this, financial information contained within the journals grows during the accounting period, particularly in businesses that engage in a high volume of transactions. It would be difficult for a business owner, accountant, or financial investigator to analyze a journal full of financial transactions entered in chronological order, particularly when he or she is searching for specific account information (i.e., "all the rent expense payments" or " all sales to a particular customer"). An accounting device called a **ledger** is used to summarize journal entries by specific accounts. The summary of account information contained in ledgers is used to prepare a business's balance sheet and income statement.

A ledger is established to accumulate all the transactions affecting a specific account during the accounting period. For example, all transactions affecting the "cash account," a business's receipt of cash (debit) and pay outs of cash (credit) recorded in the journals, would be summarized in the ledger account entitled "cash". At the end of the accounting period, the balance of the ledger account (the mathematical difference between the total debit entries and total credit entries) is used as the basis for balance sheet and income statement reports.

A popular format for a ledger is the "T-account." A ledger account in the T-format looks like the following:

Cash (101)			
1/4/92	900.00	1/3/92	394.00
1/7/92	1,435.00	1/8/92	13.95
		1/13/92	52.43

In the T-account format, ledger entries to show increases and decreases in different types of accounts are made as follows:

Assets	
+	−
(Dr.)	(Cr.)

Liabilities	
−	+
(Dr.)	(Cr.)

Owner's Equity	
−	+
(Dr.)	(Cr.)

Expenses	
+	−
(Dr.)	(Cr.)

Revenue	
−	+
(Dr.)	(Cr.)

The T-account format is very convenient for illustrative purposes; however, in formal accounting records, more information is needed and the T-account is replaced by something similar to the following:

Date		Explanation	Ref	Debit	Credit	Balance

The Date column shows the date of the transaction, which is not necessarily the same date that the entry is made into the account. The Explanation column is needed only for unusual items— often it is not used. The Ref (Reference) column is used to list the page number of the journal in which the transaction is recorded. This makes it possible to trace ledger transactions back to their source.

When financial information that has been entered into journals is transferred to and entered in the appropriate ledger account, it has gone through the process known as **posting.** Thus, transactions are journalized and then posted to a ledger. Note how the journal entries on the following page are posted to ledger accounts.

General Journal Page J-16

Date 1992	Accounts and Explanations	Ledger Folio	Debit	Credit
9/1	Cash	101	60,000	
	Owner's Equity	251		60,000
	Owner invests $60,000 cash in business.			
9/3	Cash	101		21,000
	Land	130	21,000	
	Company purchases land for $21,000 cash.			
9/5	Building	140	36,000	
	Cash	101		15,000
	Accounts Payable	201		21,000
	Company purchases $36,000 building, pays $15,000 cash and $21,000 on account			

Cash (101)

9/1	60,000	9/3	21,000
		9/5	15,000

Owner's Equity (251)

		9/1	60,000

Land (130)

9/3	21,000		

Building (140)

9/5	36,000		

Accounts Payable (201)

		9/5	21,000

Trial Balance

If the computation of account balances has been accurate, it follows that the total of the accounts with debit balances must be equal to the total of the accounts with credit balances. This proof is called a **trial balance.** A trial balance is a two-column listing of the names and balances of all accounts in the order in which they appear in the ledger. The debit balances are listed in the left col-

Frank's Turkey Farm
Trial Balance
August 31, 1992

Cash	15,278	
Accounts Receivable	3,925	
Land	9,998	
Building	4,276	
Office Equipment	1,934	
Accounts Payable		11,254
Frank Lyn, Capital		24,157
	35,411	35,411

umn, the credit balances in the right. The trial balance is prepared prior to the creation of the balance sheet and income statement.

Keep in mind that the trial balance proves only one aspect of the ledgers, the equality of debits and credits. It does not prove that ledger entries are correct or accurate.

Analyzing Business Books and Records

Financial investigators rarely are asked to construct, or have a need to reconstruct, a full set of financial books and records. However, searching through or analyzing information in financial records is a common investigative technique. Analysis of these types of business records tie financial transactions to criminal activity. There exists a ruthless logic in accounting which overcomes deceit and deception.

Analyzing accounting records is known as **auditing.** Audit techniques are based on three action words— analyze, scrutinize, and compare. They are key terms in dissecting and tracing financial transactions. Investigators need to look beyond the written figures in books and records. They need to:

- **Analyze.** During analysis, the accounting books and records are broken into their component parts. For example, journals are analyzed by reviewing individual entries and seeing if they are compatible with the account to which they are charged.

- **Scrutinize.** Look for leads in unusual notations on documents, absence of a business purpose for a transaction, or lack of documentation for a transaction.

- **Compare.** Evaluate and compare the accounting source document to independent indicators available from sources outside the business. Analyze for inconsistencies and out-of-the-ordinary transactions.

Money Laundering Example

Let's look at two situations to see how a financial investigator might approach them. The first situation, which is described below, depicts an investigation into alleged money laundering.

> *Information indicates that Robert Ogle has started an insurance business to conceal his true business— that of a money launderer. Prior findings show that Ogle appears to have limited financial resources and little experience in the insurance industry. Also, investigative research reveals that Ogle has never before owned or operated a business, nor has he received any training in bookkeeping or accounting. When contacted, Ogle declined the opportunity to discuss the matter but provided his business's journals and ledger accounts to the investigator stating, "It is all there in black and white."*

For the investigator's purposes, financial analysis of a money laundering allegation could be completed through the examination of every source document associated with each transaction entered into by Ogle and his insurance company. However, attempting to identify "suspect transactions" from this perspective is often a time consuming and labor intensive process. The process is made even more complex when the analysis includes a high volume of transactions over an extended period of time. What the investigator needs to facilitate his or her analysis is a "transactional road map," a written record of financial events entered into by a business— **the journal.**

The following page contains entries into the Ogle Insurance Company's General Journal during January 1992. Upon *scrutiny* of the entries, several seem to merit further inquiry within the investigative context. These entries are:

- Entry (a)— The $10,000 investment by Ogle to start up the business.
- Entry (b)— The ability of R. Ogle Insurance Company, a new business, to secure a $95,000 mortgage with only a 5 percent ($5,000) down payment.
- Entry (e)— The sale of a $15,000 insurance policy.

- Entries (f) and (h)— The sale of a $13,000 insurance policy on credit.
- Entries (g) and (k)— The particular details of the $30,000 loan and subsequent repayment.

The journal entries provide information which narrows the scope of inquiry from eleven transactions to seven "suspect transactions." However, the journal entries leave certain questions unanswered: Who are L. Able, T. Albert, and E. Drew?, who provided the $30,000 loan? and what is meant by the 1/31 journal description "equally divided?"

The answers to the questions can be found in the business's ledger accounts. By analyzing ledger accounts, the investigator can determine the details, in terms of dollars, for every transaction during the accounting period for each specific account.

Ogle Insurance Company
General Journal

J-1

Date 1992	Account titles	Ref.	Debit	Credit
(a) 1/1	Cash	101	10,000	
	R. Ogle, Capital	251		10,000
	Investment by R. Ogle to start business			
(b) 1/6	Land	130	10,000	
	Building	140	90,000	
	Cash	101		5,000
	Mortgage Payable	209		95,000
	Purchase of office building			
(c) 1/7	Office Furniture	118	2,000	
	Cash	101		2,000
	To record purchasing office furniture			
(d) 1/9	Office Equipment	119	1,000	
	Accounts Payable	201		1,000
	Purchasing office equipment			
(e) 1/15	Cash	101	15,000	
	Sales	301		15,000
	Record cash sales to L. Able			
(f) 1/20	Accounts Receivable	102	13,000	
	Sales	301		13,000
	Record sales on account to T. Albert			
(g) 1/20	Cash	101	30,000	
	Notes Payable	208		30,000
	To record loans to the business notes issues in exchange			
(h) 1/24	Accounts Receivable	102	14,000	
	Sales	301		14,000
	Record sales on account to E. Drew			
(i) 1/29	Accounts Payable	201	500	
	Cash	101		500
	Paid on account			
(j) 1/30	Cash	101	10,000	
	Accounts Receivable	102		10,000
	Receipt of cash on account of T. Albert			
(k) 1/31	Notes Payable	208	5,000	
	Cash	101		5,000
	Paid on note/equally divided			

The following illustrates, in T-account format, Ogle Insurance Company's ledger accounts as of 1/31/92.

Cash (101)

(a)1-1-92	10,000	1-6-92	5,000(b)
(e)1-15	15,000	1-7	2,000(c)
(g)1-20	30,000	1-29	500(i)
(j)1-30	10,000	1-31	5,000(k)
	65,000		12,500
1-31 Bal.	52,500		

Accounts Receivable (102)

(f)1-20-92	13,000	1-30-92	10,000(j)
(h)1-24	14,000		
	27,000		10,000
1-31 Bal.	17,000		

Office Furniture (118)

(c)1-7-92	2,000		

Office Equipment (119)

(d)1-7-92	1,000		

Land (130)

(b)1-6-92	10,000		

Building (140)

(b)1-6-92	90,000		

Accounts Receivable Subsidiary Ledger

Thomas Albert
P.O. Box 123
N.Y., N.Y. 001

(f)1-20-92	13,000	1-30-92	10,000(j)
1-31 Bal.	3,000		

Accounts Receivable Subsidiary Ledger

Edward Drew
P.O. Box 123
N.Y., N.Y. 002

(h)1-24-92	14,000		

Accounts Payable (201)

(i)1-29-92	500	1-9-92	1,000(d)
		1-31-92 Bal.	500

Notes Payable (208)

(k)1-31-92	5,000	1-20-92	30,000(g)
		1-31 Bal.	25,000

Mortgage Payable (209)

		1-6-92	95,000(b)

Notes Payable Subsidiary Ledger

Henry Brown
P.O. Box 123
N.Y., N.Y.

001

(k)1-31-92	2,500	1-20-92	15,000(g)
		1-31 Bal.	12,500

R. Ogle, Capital (251)

		1-1-92	10,000(a)

Sales (301)

		1-15-92	15,000(e)
		1-20-92	13,000(f)
		1-24-92	14,000(h)
		1-31 Bal.	42,000

Notes Payable Subsidiary Ledger

Dell Clark
P.O. Box 123
N.Y., N.Y.

002

(k)1-31-92	2,500	1-20-92	15,000(g)
		1-31 Bal.	12,500

Ledger accounts offer additional investigative information relating to the movement of money. The posted journal transactions for the Ogle Insurance Company reveal:

- The business generated sales in the amount of $42,000 for the month. However, the business incurred zero expenses for the month. (Sales ledger)

- The identities of Thomas Albert and Edward Drew, two individuals who purchased insurance on credit, have been determined. (Accounts Receivable subsidiary ledgers 001 and 002, respectively)

- The providers of the $30,000 loan, Henry Brown and Dell Clark, have been identified (Notes Payable subsidiary ledgers 001 and 002, respectively)

• The mailing address for Albert, Drew, Brown and Clark has been identified— P.O. Box 123, New York, New York.

Some specialized ledgers, called **subsidiary ledgers,** are mentioned in the discussion above. These ledgers are used by accountants to provide details about certain accounts. Business owners need to know not only the total amount of outstanding accounts receivables owed to the business, but also what each individual customer owes. The same holds true for the business's accounts payable, loans payable, and certain expense accounts. This internal control is maintained through the use of subsidiary ledgers where the particulars (name, address, credit limits, etc.) of the accounts are shown.

Based upon the financial analysis of Ogle Insurance Company's accounting books and records, various transactions appear to be suspect. Analysis of the source documents relating to these particular transactions will be the next investigative step. The following illustrates, in narrative form, the source documents pertaining to the Ogle Insurance Company financial transactions. The letters (a, b, etc.) that precede the descriptions can be traced back to ledger and journal entries.

a. On 1/1/92, a $10,000 certified check, made payable to "Cash" was deposited into the Ogle Insurance Company checking account.

b. On 1/6/92, Ogle Insurance Company completes a real estate purchase by buying an office building. The closing statement, loan application, mortgage note, and repayment agreement are maintained by the insurance company. The loan is extended to Ogle Insurance Company and a Mr. Thomas Albert, as an individual. The total cost of the transaction is $100,000 with 90% of this cost allocated to the building and 10% to the land.

c. On 1/7/92, Ogle purchases office furniture in the amount of $2,000. Ogle Insurance pays for the furniture via a check (#101). The store issues a receipt for the purchase.

d. On 1/9/92, Ogle purchases office equipment in the amount of $1,000. The purchase is made on credit. The terms of the repayment are $250 a month with the first month's payment due

30 days after purchase. The store issues a receipt and a credit terms agreement to Ogle Insurance Company.

e. On 1/15/92, Ogle Insurance sells an insurance policy to Lyle Able in the amount of $15,000. Able pays for the policy in cash. Able is issued a receipt for his payment.

f. On 1/20/92, Ogle Insurance sells an insurance policy to Thomas Albert in the amount of $13,000. Albert promises to pay for the policy by making a $10,000 payment by 1/30/92 and $1,000 payments every 30 days after that. A credit agreement is issued to Thomas Albert.

g. On 1/20/92, two of Robert Ogle's friends each loan the insurance company $15,000. Both Henry Brown and Dell Clark provide $15,000 in currency. The insurance company prepares a repayment agreement stating the terms of the repayment to be $2,500 within 30 days and the balance repaid within one year. Robert Ogle, Henry Brown, and Dell Clark agree to and sign the loan note. The $30,000 in cash is deposited into the business's checking account.

h. On 1/24/92, Ogle Insurance sells an insurance policy to Edward Drew in the amount of $14,000. Edward Drew promises to pay for the policy within 30 days. A credit agreement is issued to Edward Drew by the insurance company.

i. On 1/29/92, Ogle Insurance check #102 is issued in the amount of $500 to the store where their office equipment was purchased in partial payment of the outstanding bill.

j. On 1/30/92, cash in the amount of $10,000 is received by the insurance company from Thomas Albert. This amount is applied to his outstanding account.

k. On 1/31/92, Ogle Insurance Company checks #103 and #104, both in the amount of $2,500, are mailed to Henry Brown and Dell Clark, respectively. These payments are made according to the agreed upon terms of repayment as outlined in (g) above.

As shown through the Ogle Insurance Company example, investigative analysis of the movement of money into and through a business is accomplished through an understanding of the accounting principles of journal and ledger entries. With the Ogle Insurance Company investigation, journal entries were scrutinized to determine if any appeared suspicious or required further inquiry. Once specific entries were selected, the ledger postings related to them were analyzed. Finally, the documentation related to a transaction was examined.

Political Corruption Example

Now let's see how auditing investigative techniques are used in a case of alleged political corruption.

> *The contractor, Woodruff Contracting Company, writes a check to a supplier, York Company, for "service", in the amount of $10,000. The check was endorsed and deposited by the York Company. In reviewing Woodruff Contracting Company's Cash Disbursements Journal, the investigator notices that other checks to York Company are* usually *in amounts less than $1,000.*

Woodruff Contracting Company

Cash Disbursements Journal

Date	**Vendor**	**Amount**
March		
1	Tye Co.	$6,000.00
2	York Co.	500.00
3	Mill Co.	3,500.00
6	York Co.	450.00
9	Smith Co.	3,250.00
10	York Co.	750.00
14	Tye Co.	5,000.00
16	Mill Co.	3,500.00
17	York Co.	10,000.00
19	York Co.	950.00
20	Miller Co.	750.00
21	See Co.	7,000.00

The investigator **scrutinized** the check and then went one step further and **compared** that check to other payments made to York Company. *Something was out of the ordinary.*

> *Inspection of York Company's Cash Receipts Journal shows* **NO** *entry for the Woodruff Contracting Company payment during the month of March.*

York Company

Cash Receipts Journal

Date	Customer	Amount
March		
10	Russell Co.	$800.00
10	Moore Manufacturing	$500.00
12	Falls Inn	$400.00
13	Grand Co.	$910.00
14	Franklin Co.	$450.00
17	Sussex Contracting	$780.00
19	Campbell Co.	$950.00
20	Branch, Inc.	$700.00
22	Calhoun, Inc.	$1,000.00
23	Adams Co.	$600.00
25	Roberts Contracting	$500.00

The investigator **scrutinized** York Company's Cash Receipts Journal and **compared** it to what should have happened. (When York Company receives money, normally it is recorded in the Cash Receipts Journal).

> *Review of York Company's General Ledger reveals a large debit entry to the Miscellaneous Expenses Account and a credit to the Cash Account, both in the amount of $10,000 on 3/17.*

General Ledger

Cash 101

Date	Folio	Debit	Credit	Balance
				$82,500
3/2			$ 400	82,100
3/3			1,000	81,000
3/4			4,000	77,100
3/9			300	76,800
3/11			825	75,975
3/15			1,250	74,725
3/17			10,000	64,725
3/22			650	64,075
3/23			1,250	62,825
3/26			750	62,075

Misc. Expenses 800

Date	Folio	Debit	Credit	Balance
				$1,000
3/2		$ 200		1,200
3/4		75		1,275
3/7		500		1,775
3/9		200		1,975
3/10		400		2,375
3/12		925		3,300
3/17		10,000		13,300
3/26		350		13,650
3/27		1,300		14,950
3/29		450		15,400

A canceled check, made payable to cash and noted "Misc. Exp.," was located. The check was dated March 17 and was prepared by the president of the York Company. The check was endorsed with a stamp and the notation "CC-1-59199" was written below the endorsement.

York Company
1115 Lancaster Street
Alexandria, Virginia 22308

1308

68-999
561

March 17 19 92

Pay to the Order of: CASH 10,000.00

Ten thousand dollars and 00/100 Dollars

Pinkerton Bank

Misc. Exp.

Gregory A. York

⑆056109991⑆ 084931121⑈ 1308 ⑈ 0001000000 ⑈

YORK COMPANY
CC-1-59199

The investigator **analyzed** the general ledger and then **scrutinized** canceled checks for possible leads. A $10,000 check, made payable to "Cash," drawn on March 17, was located. It was signed by the president of York Company, endorsed with the company stamp, and the notation "CC-1-59199" appeared below the endorsement.

The notation "CC-1-59199" was placed on the York Company check by a financial institution. It indicates that the check was used to buy Cashier's Check #1-59199. A copy of the Cashier's Check was obtained from the financial institution. It was to be paid to Bache & Co.

American Security and Trust
Washington, DC 20001

1-59199

15-999
560

March 19 19 92

Remitter G. York

Bache & Co. 10,000.00

Ten thousand dollars and 00/100

Cashier's Check

Lois E. Smith

⑆056009991⑆ 084931121⑈ ⑈ 0001000000 ⑈

The investigator **scrutinized** the check, saw the Cashier's Check notation, and *again* **scrutinized** the endorsement of that check.

An interview with a representative of Bache & Co. revealed how they recorded the receipt of the Cashier's Check. The check was credited to a customer's account. Bache & Co. records disclose that the customer is Thomas Foster, a city building inspector. Foster used the money to buy stock and he is having it held in a "street" name (Recall from Lesson 5 that stock held in "street" name is held in the name of the broker or brokerage firm, not in the name of the owner).

Through financial investigative techniques, the investigator traced the movement of money from a business's books and records through two financial institutions to the resolution of a financial crime.

The investigator now has the documentary evidence to confront the president of York Company. Confronted by such evidence, the president admits his involvement as the "go-between" and confirms the political corruption scheme.

Indicators of Fraud

Fraud investigations usually are initiated when several small events, taken together, point to a possible pattern of deception. Within a business's accounting system, there are often physical indicators that point to a pattern of deception. The following indicators may signify that financial fraud is taking place:

- Maintaining two sets of books and records
- Concealment of assets
- Destruction of books and records
- Large or frequent currency transactions
- Payments to fictitious companies or persons
- False or altered entries and documents

- False invoices or billings
- Purchase or sale of under or over-valued assets
- Use of nominees
- Large company loans to employees or other persons
- Frequent cashing of checks received
- Frequent use of cashier's checks
- Using photocopies of invoices or receipts instead of original documents
- Personal expenses paid with corporate funds
- Payee names on checks left blank and inserted at a later date
- Excessive billing discounts
- Excessive spoilage or defects
- Double payments on billings
- Unnecessary use of collection accounts
- An individual negotiating checks made payable to a corporation
- Second or third-party endorsements on corporate checks
- Excessive use of exchange checks or clearing accounts

Summary

For the financial investigator, analysis of a business's journals and ledgers and an understanding of accounting procedures can assist in:

- Identifying the movement of money during a financial crime
- Identifying the sources and/or applications of funds made by an individual or business for a given period of time
- Determining participants in specific financial transactions
- Uncovering additional leads for further investigative analysis

The accounting principles and audit techniques described in this chapter should not be considered tools to be rigidly memorized and applied, but rather an inventory of perspectives which will broaden the base of knowledge for the investigator.

Questions and Exercises

Answer the following questions then check your responses with those provided at the back of the book.

1. How do the three major forms of business organizations compare when it comes to being responsible for debts? In other words, who is responsible for the debts of a proprietorship, a partnership, and a corporation?

2. Why are a corporation's *Articles of Incorporation* and a partnership's *Articles of Partnership* important to the financial investigator?

3. Describe the terms "liability," "asset," and "owner's equity."

4. The balance sheet you are reviewing has coffee stains on it. You can barely make out that the total amount of assets is $675,325 and the owner's equity is $276,580. What is the total amount of liabilities reported?.

5. The objective of accounting is to show in summary form the results of financial transactions on a business. How is this objective accomplished?

6. What does the phrase "the balance sheet represents a snapshot of a business's condition" mean?

7. What does the following journal entry indicate?

Cash	10,000	
Accounts Receivable		10,000

8. Make the appropriate ledger account entries (in T-account format) that would result from the journal transaction in question 7.

9. Based on the following information, prepare a balance sheet for Collier Company (statement date is 12/18/92).

- On 12/12/92, the company sold 25,000 shares of stock. Each share sold for $1 with the proceeds of the sale placed into the company checking account.

- On 12/14/92, the company purchased a machine for $12,000. It paid $6,000 and financed the balance with a bank note.

- On 12/15/92, the company bought production materials (inventory) for $40,000. It paid $15,000 and promised to pay the balance in 30 days.

- On 12/16/92, the company bought a second machine for $3,000 cash.

10. Journalize the entries (as they would appear in the general journal) for the transactions listed in question 9.

11. Make the appropriate ledger account entries (in T-account format) that would result from the journal transaction in question 9.

12. Based on the following information, prepare an income statement (in multi-step format) for Pratt, Inc. (period ending 12/31/92):

- Cost of goods sold $30,000
- Selling expenses $5,000
- Interest expense $10,000
- Administrative expenses $100,000
- Sales revenue $155,000
- Sales returns and allowances $5,000

13. Why is a knowledge of accounting important to the financial investigator?

Endnotes

1 *Uniform Partnership Act,* Section 6

2 *Webster's New Collegiate Dictionary,* (Websters New World, 1977).

3 James Edwards, Roger Hermanson, and R.F. Salamonson, *Accounting: A Programmed Text* (rev ed.), (Homewood, IL: Richard D. Irwin, Inc. 1972), p. 47

4 Kenneth W. Perry, *Accounting: An Introduction,* (New York: McGraw-Hill Book Company, 1971), p. 510

CHAPTER 7

Tracing Funds Using the Direct Method of Proof

For the financial investigator, the proof of a financial crime is accomplished by documenting a suspect's receipt and/or disposition of the proceeds from an illegal activity. Proof, like evidence, can be either direct or circumstantial. In this chapter and the next, you will learn about methods of proof. Chapter 8 focuses on three methods of indirect (circumstantial) proof. This chapter deals with the specific item method, a direct method of proof. This method of proof is the simplest method of proving that a suspect has paid for something using illicit funds or received funds through an illegal means. The investigator looks for specific illegal transactions. Nothing is implied or inferred. A direct link is established between the suspect and a financial transaction.

The specific item method can be used to document the movement of money from either the point of payment or the point of receipt. An example of each is contained in this chapter. This chapter also describes several schemes a business or individual may use to cover illegal activities. Once a specific financial transaction is discovered, the investigator needs to review the information surrounding the transaction. This chapter contains a discussion on reviewing "suspect payments." The chapter concludes with some thoughts on using the specific item method. After studying Chapter 7, you should be able to:

- Explain the concept of "direct proof."
- Describe various point-of-payment schemes.

- Describe information surrounding "suspect payments" that cause an investigator to become suspicious.

The goal of a financial investigator is to trace the movement of money. In doing so, the investigator tries to prove that a suspect received or tendered illegal funds. The proof can be either direct or circumstantial. This chapter focuses on the specific item method of tracing funds, a direct method of proof.

What is the Specific Item Method?

The specific item method is the technique most commonly used by the financial investigator. It enables an investigator to offer proof of a suspect's receipt and/or disposition of funds from an illegal activity. This proof, like evidence, can be categorized as either direct or circumstantial. The proof obtained via the specific item method is direct proof— proof precise to the point at issue. This direct proof is achieved when investigative findings identify specific financial transactions involving the suspect. Such findings show a direct link between financial transactions and the suspect. Direct proof reveals the suspect's personal involvement and knowledge of the illegality of the financial activity under investigation. With the specific item method, the investigator tries to uncover a specific illegal or unusual financial transaction and then analyze the information obtained from the transaction to identify the parties involved. The specific item method is the preferred technique of proving financial criminal activity because it is the easiest to present at trial and the proof that results from its application is the most difficult for the suspect to refute.

There are two sides to every financial transaction: payment and receipt. The specific item method can be used to document the movement of money from either side of a transaction. **Point-of-payment analysis** begins at the transaction's origin— the payor of the funds. Alternatively, **point-of-receipt analysis** begins with the receiver— the recipient of the funds. Usually, the choice of which type of analysis to use is contingent upon the circumstances of the investigation. Normally, the investigator chooses the method which appears to be the easiest.

Example of Point-of-Payment Analysis

William Drawer, president of Leo, Inc., is suspected of purchasing illegal drugs. During an interview with him, he denies the allegation and contends that he is not financially able to purchase narcotics. The investigator reviews the books and records of Mr. Drawer's business and compares the Cash Receipts Journal (the journal used to record the dates, sources, and amounts of money received into the business) to the bank statements. Everything balances. The investigator then interviews the company bookkeeper who states that all payments to Leo, Inc. are received in the mail. The bookkeeper further states that before Mr. Drawer sees the mail, the payments are extracted and deposited into the bank. Next, the investigator reviews Mr. Drawer's personal finances. That review tends to support Mr. Drawer's statement relating to his financial inability to purchase illegal drugs.

The investigator contacts Leo, Inc.'s customers and finds that their records balance to the receipts recorded in the Leo, Inc.'s Cash Receipts Journal. Next, the investigator reviews the expenses recorded in Leo, Inc.'s Cash Disbursements Journal (the journal used to record the dates, amounts, and recipients of payments made by the business). The investigator locates an entry for a $1,500 check made payable to Gemini Corporation. A review of Gemini Corporation's books reveals that they have no record of receiving the $1,500 check.

The bookkeeper at Leo, Inc. locates the canceled check and provides it to the investigator. Analysis of the check shows that it was cashed at the bank where Mr. Drawer has his personal account and, through analysis of handwriting exemplars, a handwriting expert determines that Mr. Drawer, not the appropriate person from Gemini Corporation, endorsed the check. These specific items, the transaction recorded in Gemini Corporation's Cash Disbursements Journal and the canceled check, provide the proof the investigator needs. The investigator now has a source of funds that Mr. Drawer could have used for the purchase of illegal drugs.

Example of Point-of-Receipt Analysis

Harold O'Brien is a witness in the case against AKP Paints. A review of his bank records reveals a $2,000 check made payable to AKP Paints. The check is notated "supplies" and the encoding on the bottom right corner confirms the amount paid as $2,000. Upon review of AKP Paints's Cash Receipts Journal, the investigator discovers that the business recorded a $750 payment for supplies from Harold O'Brien. The bank statement balances to the entry made in the journal. However, there is a discrepancy of $1,250 between the amount of the check and the entry in the Cash Receipts Journal. It is this discrepancy, this specific item, that the financial investigator will want to trace.

The investigator reviews the back of the canceled check and sees a "For Deposit Only" stamp on it, indicating that the check was deposited into AKP Paint's corporate account. Next, the investigator reviews the deposit slip used to deposit the check. It reveals a split deposit transaction. Only $750 was deposited into the account while the remaining $1,250 was returned in currency. Now, the investigator can question the suspect (the person who deposited the check) as to the disposition of the $1,250 in currency. When confronted with the proof, the suspect confesses to cashing the check and taking the currency for her own use.

Point-of-Payment Schemes

The specific item method often becomes difficult to use as an investigative technique when tracing the flow of funds from the point of receipt. For example, in instances where payments are received in cash or the movement of money is not reflected in a business's books and records, tracing from the point of receipt is difficult. Luckily, the financial investigator has other options to use in these instances— methods of indirect proof. Those methods are discussed in Chapter 8. For now, we will concentrate on applying the method of direct proof, the specific item method, to resolving criminal financial activity from the point-of-payment approach.

Financial fraud, whether in the form of kickbacks, embezzlement, insider trading, or money laundering, is often discernible through investigative analysis using a point-of-payment approach. There are various "point-of-payment" schemes a business may use to cover its illegal activities. These schemes, and the investigative steps used to detect them, are discussed below.

Fictitious Payable Schemes[1]

Within a business setting, fraudulent activity is often perfected through the establishment of fictitious accounts payable or fraudulent entries in the Accounts Payable journal. Through the creation of fictitious vendors and false billings, fraudulent financial transactions can occur. Detection of these transactions can best be accomplished by analyzing the following types of records:

Accounting Books and Records

- Cash Disbursement Journals
- Cash Receipts Journals
- Ledgers

Sales Documentation

- Purchase Orders
- Invoices
- Documentation showing receipt of goods ordered, etc.

Bank Account Information

- All records of payments: canceled checks, wire transfer receipts, receipts for purchases of cashier's checks and money orders, and withdrawal slips
- Check Registers
- Account Statements

The most important of the above information, and often sufficient in and of itself, is the bank account information. When reviewing bank account information, the investigator should look for the following:

- **Payments by check and other types of account withdrawals made payable or charged to the account on which the illicit payments are suspected.** For example, if the investigator suspects that kickbacks were paid on sales to the Teaparty Corporation, the search would begin with checks made payable to "Teaparty Corporation" and continue with the analysis of those checks as they move through the bookkeeping system.

- **Payments by check for services rendered.** Be sure to look into transactions involving sales commissions and consulting fees. These types of services do not require the delivery of goods, and relatively little documentation, other than the check itself, is required as a record of payment.

- **Atypical charges for the business.** Look for out-of-the-ordinary charges relating to unusual/unnatural services that the business is not normally involved in. For example, a video production company would not normally be involved in business transactions with a plumbing supply company.

Ghost Employee and Payroll Kickback Schemes

Illicit funds may be generated and disguised as salary payments to fictitious or former employees. For example, payments to current employees, in the form of bonuses or expense reimbursements, can be returned to the payor or passed on to another individual. In instances where ghost employee or payroll schemes are suspected, the following records should be obtained by the investigator from the suspect company in order to trace the flow of funds:

- Payroll and employee lists (e.g., time and attendance records)
- Personnel files, employment applications, tax withholding forms, and social security numbers
- Payroll checks

Investigative attempts to identify the ghost employee or payroll kickback scheme can be completed through the following steps:

- **Compare personnel office employee records with the payroll records.** Discrepancies should be analyzed. Any employee who does not have taxes withheld from his or her paycheck or does not participate in the company's health insurance program should be scrutinized.

- **Verify the employee's claimed social security number.** A fictitious employee may be given a social security number which does not exist.

- **Look for inflated salaries and travel expenses.** An employee's normal salary may also be inflated or, more commonly, his or her travel and expense reimbursements may be padded to generate illicit payments. Look for unusual disbursements from the accounts where such checks are deposited.

Once a suspicious paycheck has been identified, the flow of the check through the bank system can be traced by using the applicable bank statement and the bank's proofing system.

Overbilling Schemes

Illicit funds may be added to legitimate payments for goods or services provided by actual suppliers, with the additional amounts being passed on by the supplier, or returned, usually via currency to the payor for distribution. The records required for tracing phony payables from both the original payor and any intermediaries (shell companies and/or straw/nominee individuals) are available to the investigator. Important indicators of overpayment schemes are:

- Notations on invoices or other billing documents that break out "extra" or special charges, particularly those which require no delivery of goods

- Discrepancies between the purchase order or invoice amount and the amount of payment

• Unusually large amounts appearing on particular bills, or bills which break a consistent pattern as shown on the books and records

Offbook and Currency Schemes

Using the specific item method of tracing funds from the point of payment becomes more complex when those payments do not go through a business's books and records or when they are made in currency. For example, customers of the suspect's business may demand that their illegal payments be diverted to off-book accounts; therefore, they will not be reflected in the suspect business's books and records. These types of transactions may be discovered through contact with the suspect business's competitors or by analyzing unusual costs and expenses shown on the company books which are not associated with known sales or business activity.

In most industries, there is a fixed relationship between the cost of producing and selling a particular item and the revenues that the item generates. In other words, the amount of raw materials and labor used to produce a product or perform a service usually is fairly consistent. The same is normally true with respect to utility usage, transportation cost, etc. Therefore, a significant imbalance in these ratios indicates possible unrecorded transactions. For example, an investigator should be suspicious if a company's records show that it ordered twice the amount of raw materials that it usually does but did not produce twice the amount of product.

Currency payments can be traced from the point of payment by matching the payor's currency withdrawals to the recipient's corresponding currency deposits, expenditures, or visits to a safe deposit box. Another strong indicator of currency payments is the purchase of a cashier's check or a wire transfer made payable to the recipient at or shortly after cash withdrawals or disbursements by the payor. Unexplained or unusual currency disbursements or withdrawals, particularly from a business which does not normally deal in currency, may itself indicate illicit transactions.

Reviewing Suspect Payments

Tracing the flow of funds from the point of payment often involves reviewing the "suspect payments" themselves. In a transaction involving a canceled check, this would include:

- **Reviewing the endorsement on the check.** This endorsement may be a signature, but more commonly it is an endorsement stamp in the name of the business payee. The identity of the endorser frequently is the corrupt recipient.

- **Noting the location where the check was negotiated.** When the endorsement is not obvious, the identity of the bank at which the deposit was made becomes important. The depository bank's stamp will appear on the back of the check as a part of the proofing system. Through the check's routing symbols (ABA transit number and check routing symbol), the geographical location of the depository bank can be identified and the locale of the suspected recipient can be determined. This type of information can be used to determine the location of the recipient's bank account if it becomes necessary to analyze his or her bank records.

- **Checks with a second endorsement.** A check payable to a business which is endorsed by that business and then endorsed a second time by a specific person, thereby allowing the check to be cashed or deposited into that person's personal account, is typical of a fictitious payable scheme. Another example would be a check payable to a third party which is endorsed by that third party and then endorsed over to the issuer of the check.

- **Checks payable to a business which are cashed-out.** Normal business practice calls for checks to be deposited. Usually, a "For Deposit Only" stamp appears on the back of deposited checks. When checks are cashed-out at a bank instead of deposited into an account, suspicions should arise.

- **Checks which fall into unexplained patterns.** Unusual or unexplained patterns of check transactions can be an indicator of illegal activity. For example, the discovery of a pattern of checks, one per month, written to a particular customer, with each check's amount equaling 10% of the monthly sales made to that customer, can indicate a potential kickback situation.

If the examination of the checks themselves do not yield any clear and convincing patterns relating to the illegal movement of money from the point of payment, the next step would be to compare the record of payment to "backup documentation" in the business's accounting system. Particular attention should be given to the following circumstances:

- **The absence of documentation to support a particular payment.** It is suspicious when no invoice is on file for payments to suppliers or no receipt exists to indicate that materials paid for were actually delivered and received.

- **Discrepancies between the payment information and the backup documentation.** For example, the amount of a check payable to a supplier is different from the invoice amount, or a check payable to a person or business is different from the person or business identified on the invoice itself.

- **Coincidences in the backup documentation**. Look for invoices from several suppliers which have different names but share the same business address. Also look for invoices from different companies that are signed by the same person.

- **Unnumbered or sequentially unusual invoices.** Unnumbered invoices are suspicious and a situation where invoices #101, #102, and #103 are dated 30 days apart is also suspicious.

- **Alterations or photocopies of backup documentation.** Photocopies of backup documentation may be made to conceal alterations to the originals.

Thoughts on Using the Specific Item Method

When using a specific item method to trace the flow of funds from the point of payment, it is important to remember that financial statements and accounting records are only representations of something that should exist in the real world. A financial statement for a business that reports cash of $5,000, means that somewhere that business should have $5,000 in cash. And, if a company claims an inventory of $10,000, that inventory should be observable. There always is an analytical relationship between representations in financial documents and the physical goods and assets.[2]

When searching for fraud, the investigator should be inquisitive and challenge things that appear to be out of the ordinary or out of sequence. If sales are rising, the cost of outbound freight should be rising. If purchases are increasing, the cost of inbound freight should be increasing. Every business has analytical relationships that should exist. Therefore, examining financial statement data, including bank financial statement data, to see if it makes sense with respect to non-financial statement data is one of the best ways to detect fraud. Investigators who ask themselves if reported amounts are too small, too large, too early, too late, too often, and too rare or who look for things that are reported at odd times, by odd people, and using odd procedures are much more likely to detect fraud than those who view the financial statements without any hint of skepticism.[3]

The embodiment of such skepticism is the specific item method of tracing the flow of funds. It provides financial proof of the receipt or disposition of illicit funds by the suspect under investigation.

Summary

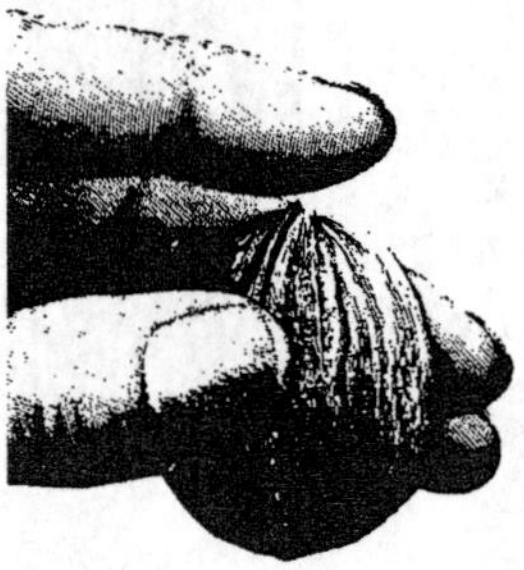

In this chapter, you were introduced to the technique most commonly used by the financial investigator, the specific item method of tracing funds. The proof obtained by the application of this method is direct proof, proof precise to the point at issue. When investigative findings reveal specific financial transactions being paid by or received by the suspect, direct proof of a financial crime is achieved. Such findings reveal a specific link between the suspect and the transactions at issue.

The specific item method can be used to trace the movement of money from either its point of payment or its point of receipt. In instances when specific financial events can be identified with particular financial crimes (i.e., insider trading, kickback payments, embezzlement, etc.) the specific item method can be successfully employed as an analysis technique. This method also can be applied when financial transactions leave an audit trail, either in a business's accounting records or a financial institution's recordkeeping system.

Questions and Exercises

Answer the following questions and then check your responses with those provided at the back of the book.

1. The specific item method is known as a "direct method of tracing funds." What does this mean?

2. What type of information is most useful when dealing with a fictitious payable scheme?

3. When investigating a possible payroll kickback scheme, why would an investigator want to look into an employee's travel expenses?

4. Describe, by example, an overbilling scheme.

5. Tracing currency payments via the specific item method is not an easy task. Identify two situations that may indicate currency payments in an illicit transaction.

6. What is unusual about the following information compiled from a suspect's Cash Disbursements Journal and bank statements?

1/18/91	Paid Lopez Electronics	$250
1/31/91	Paid Lopez Electronics	$25
2/16/91	Paid Lopez Electronics	$265
2/28/91	Paid Lopez Electronics	$26.50
3/17/91	Paid Lopez Electronics	$230
3/31/91	Paid Lopez Electronics	$23

7. Larry's Weight Club wrote a $3,500 check to Silver Ironworks, Inc. Silver Ironworks cashed the check. Why might an investigator become suspicious of this situation?

8. List three situations involving "backup documentation" that would cause an investigator to become suspicious.

Endnotes

1 Jack T. Wells, W. Steve Albrecht, Jack Bologna, and Gilbert Geis, *Fraud Examiner's Manual*, (National Association of Certified Fraud Examiners, 1989), Section 111, pp. 38 - 44.

2 *Fraud Examiner's Manual*, Section 111, pp. 17 and 18

3 *Fraud Examiner's Manual*, Section 111, pp. 13 - 19

CHAPTER 8

Tracing Funds Using Indirect Methods of Proof

In Chapter 7, the specific item method, a direct method of proof, was discussed. This chapter focuses on three indirect methods of proof: net worth analysis, the expenditures method, and the bank deposit method. Each of these methods can be used to show that a suspect's expenses exceed his or her known sources of income. However, none of them can prove where the extra income comes from. That is why the three methods are called "indirect methods of proof," for, like circumstantial evidence, inference is needed to establish the fact at issue. And just what is that fact? It's that somehow, the individual under investigation is receiving more income than he or she legitimately "earns."

With the specific item method, an investigator searches for a specific financial transaction to investigate. With the indirect methods of proof, an investigator gathers all sorts of financial information and then plugs the information into mathematical formulas. This chapter contains an example of a calculation for each indirect method of proof.

After studying Chapter 8, you should be able to:

- Differentiate between direct proof and indirect proof.
- Describe what types of information are gathered through the completion of a financial profile.
- State when it is appropriate to use an indirect method of proof.

- State the requirements of proof for each indirect method of proof.
- Write the formula for each indirect method of proof.
- Perform net worth analysis.
- Perform expenditures analysis.
- Perform bank deposit analysis.

It is not always possible to use the specific item method when tracing the flow of funds. For example, it is difficult to use the specific item method when cash payments are made or the movement of money is not reflected in a business's books and records. It's hard to find a specific item to investigate when transactions are not recorded in financial records. So, while it is not always possible to use the specific item method, the investigator need not worry— other methods are available, indirect methods of proof. Through indirect or circumstantial methods, the investigator can trace the proceeds from almost any type of illegal activity— from fraud and corruption to tax evasion or drug dealing— all from the point of receipt.[1]

The indirect methods of tracing funds are based on a simple, and almost invariably true, principle—

> *Money, in any significant amount, will eventually show up, directly or indirectly, in the accounts, assets, or expenditures of the recipient.*

The indirect methods of proof are most useful when the suspect is taking currency or other payments that cannot be directly traced. As an investigative tool, the indirect methods can corroborate testimony alleging hidden illicit payments. They not only provide the investigator with the evidence of a financial crime, but provide "leads" pointing to further investigative inquiry as well.

The Financial Profile[2]

The specific item method relies on a microscopic view of financial transactions through the review of books, records, or bank accounts of the recipient and payor of illegal funds. In contrast, the indirect methods of proof require a macroscopic view of the financial situation under investigation. Since the indirect methods of proof do not allow the investigator to directly trace transactions, he or she must prepare an overview of the suspect's financial condition— a financial profile. This is accomplished by uncovering what the suspect owes, owns, earns, and spends at a given point in time or over a given period of time. Also, it entails finding out the sources and applications of funds used to make purchases or pay expenses. The financial profile may uncover direct proof of illegal income or hidden assets, or circumstantially show that the suspect's expenditures exceed his or her known sources of funds.

A financial profile is completed via techniques used by the investigator during the investigative process. Of major importance to the completion of the financial profile is a thorough interview with the suspect. Other information can be gathered through third-party contacts and from public information sources. Financial transactions maintained within the records of financial institutions that the suspect deals with are important sources of information in the completion of the financial profile. Historically, illicit funds in any significant amount eventually pass through a suspect's account in his or her financial institution. Such movement creates a record that can lead to other accounts, assets, and information.

When developing a financial profile for use with any indirect method of proof, the analysis should mirror the suspect's method of accounting (cash or accrual). For example, if the suspect business's accounting system is on the accrual basis, the indirect proof analysis should be completed utilizing the accrual basis of accounting.

The table on the next page contains information concerning the development of a financial profile. The left side of the table lists typical assets, liabilities, sources of funds, and expenditures a suspect may own or have. The right side lists questions the financial investigator will want to pursue to complete a detailed financial profile.

The financial Profile

Typical assets		For each significant asset, determine —
Residence	Jewelry	• When was it acquired and from whom?
Real estate	Clothing	• How much did it cost?
Bank accounts	Collectibles	• How was it paid for (currency, check, cashier's check, etc.)?
Stocks and bonds	Pensions	• What source of funds was used to acquire it?
Automobiles	Home furnishings	• What documentation exists for the purchase and where is it?
Insurance	Boats	
Cash on hand		
Typical liabilities		**For each significant liability, determine —**
Mortgage(s)		• What was the original amount of the liability?
Other loans		• What is the present balance due?
Lines of credit		• When was the liability incurred?
Credit cards Installment purchases		• What was the purpose for the loan or debt?
Accounts payable		• How were the proceeds used and where were they deposited?
Taxes and other bills		• What security (collateral), if any, was given for the debt?
Alimony and child support		• What documentation exists for the transaction and where is it?
		• Was the debt written off as a bad loan for tax purposes?
		• Who was the creditor or lender?
Typical sources of funds		**For each source of funds, determine —**
Salary	Insurance proceeds	• What was the total amount during a given period?
Gifts	Commissions and fees	• What was the source?
Rental income	Awards	• How was it paid for (currency, check, by other means)?
Dividends	Inheritances	• When were the funds received?
Interest	Disability payments	• Where was it deposited?
Sale of assets		• How was it spent?
		• What documentation exists (i.e., W-2 or 1099 form) and where is it?
Typical expenditures		**For each major expenditure item, determine —**
Rent and mortgage	Clothing	• What was the total amount spent?
Health costs	Utilities	• How was it paid for (currency, check, credit card, etc.)?
Interest on loans	Food	• Where were the funds obtained to pay the expense?
Credit cards	Insurance	• What documentation (i.e., receipts, bills, etc.) exists and where is it?
Car payments	Travel	
Travel		• When was the payment made?

Net Worth Analysis

Any recipient of funds, honest citizen or suspect, has only four possible ways of disposing of that income:

- **Saving it.** An individual may place income in a financial institution or keep it in his or her possession.
- **Buying assets.** Individuals may expend their income on assets.
- **Paying off debts.** Individuals may use income to reduce their liabilities.
- **Spending it.** An individual may use his or her income to make personal or business expenditures.

Indirect methods of proof show the relationship between a suspect's receipt and subsequent disposition of funds. The results of the indirect methods of proof do not identify specific financial transactions entered into by the suspect (i.e. they cannot prove that illicit funds were used to pay the mortgage), however, they do reveal that the suspect was able to partake in financial transactions above and beyond his or her known sources of funds. Indirect methods of proof result in inferences— inferences that an unknown source of funds must be present and available to the suspect.

Net worth analysis begins with the completion of a suspect's financial profile. Through identification of the suspect's assets, liabilities, income, and expenses, a net worth statement (the difference between a person's assets and liabilities at a given point in time) can be determined. Once completed, changes in the suspect's net worth can be compared to his or her known income, and differences, if any, may be inferred as coming from unknown sources. *(Note: For the purposes of this textbook, payments received from legal sources will be labeled as* **known sources** *and payments determined to be received from illegal sources will be labeled as* **unknown sources.***)*

The Net Worth Formula

The basic component in computing net worth is the establishment of a starting point— the base year. For investigative purposes, the base year is the year prior to the year that the alleged illegal activity began. For example, if the investigator believes that the suspect began embezzling money in 1991, 1990 becomes the base year, the point of reference for comparison to subsequent years' net worth changes. Why does the investigator need to establish the suspect's financial profile for 1990? Because in 1990, the suspect was living as he or she "normally" would— without income from the alleged embezzlement.

Once the investigator has developed financial profiles for the base year and each of the years of alleged illegal activity, the net worth analysis formula can be applied. The formula for computing funds from unknown sources using the net worth method is:

Net Worth Analysis Formula

	Assets
Minus:	Liabilities
Equals	**Net worth**
Minus:	Prior's year's net worth
Equals	**Increase in net worth from previous year**
Plus:	Known expenses*
Equals	**Total net worth increase**
Minus:	Funds from known sources
Equals	Funds from unknown sources

* For net worth purposes, the payment of an expense represents the reduction of an asset. Therefore, these reductions must be accounted for and added back into the calculation.

Performing Net Worth Analysis

The suspect, Jim Dealer, is being investigated for some alleged illegal activity which occurred in 1991 and 1992. This means that the investigator must develop financial profiles for the years 1990, 1991, and 1992. The results of the profiles are described below and are calculated into the net worth computation on the next page.

(a) Mr. Dealer stated that as of 12/31/90 he had $1,000 cash-on-hand. He had no cash-on-hand at the end of 1991 and 1992. (Cash-on-hand is currency in possession of the suspect.)

(b) On 12/31/90, Dealer's bank account reflected a balance of $1,500. On 12/31/91, it contained $4,750 and on 12/31/92, it contained $5,225. The account earned $250 in interest in 1991, $475 in 1992. Total deposits in 1991 were $22,160, with redeposits of $660. Total deposits in 1992 were $19,585, with redeposits of $100.

(c) As of 12/31/90, Dealer owned $1,000 worth of jewelry. In 1991, he purchased jewelry worth $5,000, and in 1992, he bought $6,000 more.

(d) Sometime in 1990, Dealer purchased a boat costing $17,500. He still owned the boat as of 12/31/92.

(e) During 1992, Dealer purchased an $18,250 car. He paid cash.

(f) Dealer purchased a $150,000 residence on 1/1/91. He made a cash downpayment of $50,000 and financed the balance, interest free.

(g) As of 12/31/90, Dealer owed $275, interest free, to a finance company. He made no payments on this note during 1991 or 1992.

(h) Dealer borrowed $3,000, interest free, from a loan company on 6/30/91. Beginning 7/1/91, he made monthly payments of $100.

(i) Beginning 1/1/91, Dealer made monthly payments of $500 per month on his new residence. He made eleven similar payments in 1991 and twelve similar payments in 1992.

(j) Dealer paid $1,460 on his credit cards in 1991 and $3,000 on them in 1992.

(k) Dealer was able to document personal living expenses in addition to those listed in (a) through (j). In 1991, the expenses totaled $11,000, and in 1992, they were $10,000.

(l) Dealer earned $25,200 from his job in 1991 and $22,200 in 1992.

Net Worth Analysis

Suspect– Jim Dealer

Assets	**Base Year (1990)**	**Year One (1991)**	**Year Two (1992)**
Cash on hand (a)	$ 1,000	$ 0	$ 0
Bank account balance (b)	1,500	4,750	5,225
Jewelry (c)	1,000	6,000	12,000
Boat (d)	17,500	17,500	17,500
Car (e)	0	0	18,250
Real estate (f)	0	150,000	150,000
Total Assets	$21,000	$178,250	$202,975
Liabilities			
Note payable - finance company (g)	$ 275	$ 275	$ 275
Loan (h)	0	2,400	1,200
Mortgage on real estate (f, i)	0	94,000	88,000
Total Liabilities	$ 275	$96,675	$89,475
Net Worth (assets - liabilities)	$20,725	$81,575	$113,500
Minus: Prior year's net worth		20,725	81,575
Equals: Increase in net worth		$60,850	$ 31,925
Plus: Known expenses			
Credit card payments (j)		$ 1,460	$ 3,000
Other personal living expenses (k)		11,000	10,000
Equals: Total net worth increase		$73,310	$44,925
Minus: Funds from known sources			
Interest on bank account (b)		$ 250	$ 475
Wages (l)		25,200	22,200
Equals: Funds from unknown sources		$47,860	$22,250

A review of the previous table shows that between 1990 and 1992, Jim Dealer's assets increased significantly. In 1991, he was able to purchase a $150,000 house (with a $50,000 downpayment) and $5,000 worth of jewelry. Also, his bank account increased by $3,750. All this from a man with an income of $25,450. Mr. Dealer's assets increased again in 1992 and, in that same year, he was able to decrease his liabilities.

Keys to Net Worth Analysis

From the net worth analysis done on Jim Dealer, it seems pretty obvious that he has some other source(s) of funds that he is keeping quiet about. That is, if the information the investigator obtained while doing the financial profiles is complete and accurate. The key to a successful net worth analysis is reliable base year, or "opening net worth," information. The starting point must include all assets and liabilities of the suspect as of that time. If assets or liabilities are uncovered at a later date, it will cast doubt on the entire analysis and require a complete recalculation.

An inverse relationship exists between one year and the next in a net worth analysis. For example, an understatement of the net worth in one year will result in an overstatement of the increase in the net worth for the subsequent year. Conversely, an overstatement of the net worth in a year results in an understatement of the increase in net worth for the subsequent year. Accordingly, the investigator should pay special attention to the following elements when completing a net worth analysis:

Keys to Net Worth Analysis

- *Cash-on-hand*
- *Cash in banks*
- *Asset Valuation*
- *Known Expenses*

- **Determining Cash-on-Hand.** When developing a financial profile to use with net worth analysis, possibly the most important asset to establish is "cash-on-hand." For net worth purposes, cash-on- hand represents currency in the possession of the suspect. This does not include currency in financial institutions or currency that is tied up in investments or other assets. Cash-on-hand is all the suspect's currency— whether on the person, under a mattress, or buried in the backyard. The inability of the investigator to establish a firm and accurate amount of cash-on-hand can be fatal to the investigation. Suspects may try to inflate their cash-on-hand figure by saying that they have more cash-on-hand than they really do. "I was able to buy that boat because I had $20,000 stuffed away in a cookie jar." This alleging a "cash hoard" is a common defense in a net worth case.

Cash-on-hand is almost always shown by circumstantial evidence. The best source for determining this figure is during the interview process with the suspect. Questions such as: "Did you ever have more than $100 in cash-on-hand?" or, "more than $500?" or, "more than $1,000?" may result in admissions that can be used to establish cash-on- hand at a particular time. The location and denomination of cash-on-hand may also be useful information to support or refute a suspect's claims. Even without an interview or answers to the questions, an investigator can determine a suspect's cash-on-hand. It can be determined through analysis of previously filed financial statements, loan and credit card applications, and other records relating to the suspect's financial activity.

- **Cash in Banks.** Most likely, the suspect will have funds deposited in financial institutions. Since many account statements have cut-off dates other than the end of the net worth analysis period, they must be reconciled to determine the balances as of the end of the period. Unusual transactions (large deposits and/or withdrawals) that occur near the end of the analysis period must be traced to their ultimate source or disposition. Unusual financial transactions can affect the net worth analysis. For example, a large withdrawal of funds that was not used to purchase an asset, reduce a liability, make a personal expenditure, or pay a business expense, must be treated as an increase in cash on hand. Similarly, large deposits made early in the analysis year must be scrutinized and then allocated to the appropriate net worth year. A consistent treatment of transactions is vital to the validity of the net worth analysis.

- **Asset Valuation.** All assets should be valued at cost as opposed to fair market value. Subsequent appreciation or depreciation of assets is ignored for purposes of net worth analysis.

- **Known Expenses.** The amount of a suspect's expenditures, his or her actual "cost of living," can be difficult to document. The amount a person spends on items such as food, entertainment, cleaning, clothing, health and beauty aids, and sundry items is difficult to obtain. Therefore, estimates, if used, should be low or eliminated entirely. Any doubts should be resolved in favor of the suspect. Assuming that the net worth will still show substantial unexplained funds, the result will be an even more convincing demonstration of the dependence on illegal sources.

A Court-Approved Method

Because net worth analysis provides circumstantial evidence, its validity as a method of proving criminal activity had to be approved by the courts. The landmark case, decided by the Supreme Court in 1954, that established net worth analysis as prima facia evidence of a crime was Holland v. United States, 348 U.S. 121, 75 S.St. 127. An overall description of a net worth method is also set forth in United States v. Sorrentino, 726 F.2d 876, 879, 880 (1st Cir. 1984) and is stated in part as follows (note that these cases relate to Federal income tax evasion, thus the references to terms relating to taxability):

> *"The government makes out a prima facia case under the net worth method of proof if it establishes the defendant's opening net worth (computed as assets at cost basis less liabilities) with reasonable certainty and then shows increases in his net worth for each year in question which, added to his non-deductible expenditures and excluding his known non-taxable receipts for the year, exceeded his reported taxable income by a substantial amount. The jury may infer that the defendant's excess increases represent unreported taxable income if the government either shows a likely source or negates all possible non-taxable sources; the jury may further infer wilfulness from the fact of underreporting coupled with the evidence of conduct by the defendant tending to mislead or conceal."*

The Court established the following three requirements that the investigator must meet in order to establish a prima facia net worth case:

- Establish a reliable opening net worth
- Investigate all relevant leads that might show the suspect's innocence
- Establish a likely taxable source of income together with evidence indicating an increase in net worth

How do investigators establish a prima facia net worth case? Well, through the development of a financial profile, they can establish a reliable opening net worth. During this same process, investigators can develop relevant leads indicating potential non-taxable sources of net worth increase (gifts, inheritances, insurance settlements, etc.). Investigators also must either prove a likely source of taxable income for the suspect or negate all non-taxable sources of income. A "likely source of income" does not have to be from the suspect's principal business activity. Sources of net worth increases could be from interest or dividend income, gambling winnings, or from transactions involving illegal activities (narcotics, embezzlement, kickbacks, or other fraudulent activity).

Expenditures Method

With the expenditures method, a comparison is made between the suspect's known expenditures and known sources of funds during a given period of time. Any excess expenditures must be the result of income from unknown sources. The expenditures method also can be used to compute "cash-on-hand" for the base year of a net worth computation.

In theory, the expenditures method is closely related to net worth analysis. They are merely accounting variations of the same principle. Both of these indirect methods of proof look at a suspect's source of funds, expenditures, assets, and liabilities. However, each method examines the items in a different way. Let's take another look at our suspect, Jim Dealer. Through the completion of financial profiles for the years 1990, 1991, and 1992, an investigator was able to determine that Mr. Dealer's bank account held $1,500 in 1990, $4,750 in 1991, and $5,225 in 1992. Each of these figures is used in the net worth computation in the table on page 90. However, in the expenditures method, the investigator will look at only the net effect (the difference between the ending balance and beginning balance) of a transaction (increase of an asset or decrease in a liability). In Jim Dealer's case, the investigator will note a $3,250 increase in Dealer's bank account between 1990 and 1991, and a $475 increase between 1991 and 1992. With the expenditures method, only the year-to-year increases or decreases in the suspect's assets and liabilities are considered for analysis purposes. When the suspect's assets and liabilities remain unchanged during the period, they are not listed in the analysis.

The Expenditures Method Formula

The formula for computing funds from unknown sources using the expenditures method is as follows:

Expenditures Method Formula

	Total expenditures
Minus:	Known sources of funds
Equals	Funds from unknown sources

The two main factors in the above formula are expenditures and sources of funds. But the investigator also gathers information concerning assets and liabilities. So, how does this information fit into the formula?

As was stated previously, the expenditures method focuses on the net effect of a transaction. So, if an asset or liability is involved in a transaction, it will be classified as either an expenditure or a source of funds— depending on its net effect (increase or decease). The table on the next page classifies the net effect of different types of transactions.

Expenditures Method Transaction Treatment

If during the period under analysis, the net effect of a transaction results in an increase or decrease for the period, this net effect is recorded as a(n):

Expenditure (Application of Funds)	**Source** (Source of Funds)
• When cash-on-hand increases	• When cash-on-hand decreases
• When bank accounts increase	• When bank accounts decrease
• When assets increase	• When assets decrease
• When liabilities decrease	• When liabilities increase
• When personal living expenses are made	• When loans, gifts, or inheritances are received
• When cash expenditures are made	• When assets are sold
	• When salaries or business profits are earned
	• When other sources of income are known

A sample expenditures computation is found on the next page. Note that, unlike the net worth analysis computation, there are no figures listed for the base year. And, unlike the net worth analysis, the dollar amounts shown reflect the *differences* between one year and the next, not an absolute amount.

Expenditures Computation

	Year One	Year Two
Application of funds		
Increase in cash-on-hand	$ 0	$ 1,000
Increase in cash in banks	5,000	2,500
Increase in inventory	5,000	12,500
Increase in loans and accounts receivable	1,000	3,000
Increase in furniture and fixtures	0	1,500
Increase in real estate	0	25,000
Decrease in accounts payable	500	0
Decrease in notes payable	0	5,000
Decrease in mortgage payable	13,000	0
Personal living expenses	14,000	12,300
Federal income tax	1,100	1,000
Gifts made	1,500	0
Total application of funds	$41,000	$63,800
Minus:		
Known sources of funds		
Decrease in cash-on-hand	$ 500	$ 0
Decrease in securities	3,500	0
Increase in notes payable	10,000	0
Increase in mortgage payable	0	18,000
Increase in accumulated depreciation	500	1,000
Life insurance proceeds	0	8,100
Inheritance	0	5,000
Total sources of funds	$14,500	$32,100
Equals: funds from unknown sources	$26,600	$31,700

The difference between the amount of the suspect's expenditures and his or her known sources of funds is attributed to unknown sources.

The table on page 200 contains the net worth analysis of our suspect, Jim Dealer. The following example presents the same facts relating to the Jim Dealer financial investigation, only this time the expenditures method is used. The figures in the table reflect the financial profile information found on page 199.

Expenditure Analysis

Suspect– Jim Dealer

	Year One (1991)	Year Two (1992)
Expenditures		
Increase in bank balance (b)	$ 3,250	$ 475
Purchase of jewelry (c)	5,000	6,000
Downpayment on house (f)	50,000	0
Purchase of car (e)	0	18,250
Yearly mortgage payments (i)	6,000	6,000
Credit card payments (j)	1,460	3,000
Loan repayments (h)	600	1,200
Other personal living expenses (k)	11,000	10,000
Total expenditures	$77,310	$44,925
Minus: Known sources of funds		
Cash-on-hand (a)	$ 1,000	$ 0
Interest on bank account (b)	250	475
Loan (h)	3,000	0
Wages (l)	25,200	22,200
Total known sources of funds	29,450	22,675
Equals: Funds from unknown sources	$47,860	$22,250

In the Jim Dealer example, both the net worth and expenditures methods of tracing the flow of funds resulted in identical bottom line figures. In each case, $47,860 in funds from unknown sources was discovered in 1991 and $22,250 was discovered in 1992.

As with the net worth method, there is no statutory provision expressly authorizing the investigative use of the expenditures analysis for criminal purposes. Accordingly, court cases have established "case law" that sets forth the requirements of proof to establish a prima facia expenditures case.[3] The elements of proof requirement for the expenditures method is identical to that of the net worth method of proof:

- Establish a firm starting point
- Establish a likely source of income
- Investigate leads which tend to establish the subject's innocence

Bank Deposit Method

Through bank deposit analysis, unknown sources of funds are located through analysis of bank records and other financial transactions entered into by the suspect. The bank deposit method is applied in situations where assets and liabilities are constant from year to year and indications of extravagant expenditures are nonexistent, but investigative findings reveal that the suspect's known sources of income are being deposited into financial institutions.

Bank Deposit Analysis Formula

The formula for computing funds from unknown sources using the bank deposit method is:

Bank Deposit Analysis Formula

	Total deposits to all accounts
Minus:	Transfers and redeposits
Equals	**Net deposits to all accounts**
Plus:	Cash expenditures
Equals	**Total receipts from all sources**
Minus:	Funds from known sources
Equals	Funds from unknown sources

The details of each component of the bank deposit formula are described on the following pages.

Total Deposits to All Accounts

The bank deposit method considers all deposits made by a suspect, no matter what type of financial institution (banks, savings and loans, brokerage houses, credit unions, etc.) is involved. Also included in the "total deposits" element of the bank deposit formula is the amount of cash-on-hand the suspect accumulated during the period under investigation.

A key to establishing "total deposits" is to remember that only funds actually deposited into an account are included. If several checks are listed on a deposit slip and the suspect deducts an amount to be returned to him or her in cash (a split deposit), only the net amount of the deposit should be used in computing total deposits.

Transfers and Redeposits

The transfer of funds between a suspect's bank accounts (i.e., taking money from a checking account and depositing it into a savings account), and funds that are withdrawn and then redeposited (i.e., a "non-sufficient funds" check) must be considered in the bank deposit formula. These represent duplicate items for analysis purposes and must be subtracted from total deposits to arrive at the net deposits to all accounts.

Cash Expenditures

Cash expenditures consist of the total outlay of funds made by the suspect during the period in question minus net bank disbursements. Cash expenditures are calculated by the following formula:

Cash Expenditures Formula

	Total Outlay of Funds
Minus:	Net bank disbursements
Equals	**Cash expenditures**

The suspect's total outlay of funds for the period under analysis includes all payments in currency or by check. For analysis purposes, there is no need to determine which part was paid by currency and which part was paid by check. Total outlays could include purchases of capital assets or investments, loan repayments, known expenses, etc.

One of the elements in the formula shown above is "Net Bank Disbursements." To determine this element, a separate calculation is needed. This calculation is made as follows:

Net Bank Disbursements Formula

	Net deposits to all accounts
Plus:	Beginning balances
Equals	**Net bank funds available**
Minus:	Ending balances
Equals	**Net bank disbursements**

Net bank disbursements represent the maximum amount (in dollar terms) that could have been paid by the suspect through financial institution check withdrawals.

Funds from Known Sources

Funds from known sources include, but are not limited to: salaries, business profits, gifts received, loans received, and inheritances. Funds from known sources are subtracted from total receipts to derive the funds from unknown sources.

Sample Bank Deposit Analysis

The findings below pertain to the movement of money for a suspect named Dan Street.

The information is used in the bank deposit computation found on the next page.

Reference Number	Type of Transaction	Amount
(1)	Fees and commissions (known income)	$320,000
(2)	Total deposits into all accounts	400,000
(3)	Transfers between accounts	70,000
(4)	Known expenses	50,000
(5)	Cash placed into and maintained in a safe deposit box during the period under investigation	25,000
(6)	Deposit of proceeds from loan into checking account	25,000
(7)	Purchase of a car from the proceeds of a cash gift	20,000
(8)	Cash on hand at beginning of period under investigation	0
(9)	Net bank disbursements	40,000

Bank Deposit Analysis

Suspect– Dan Street

			Ref #
Total Deposits		$400,000	(2)
Minus: Transfers between accounts		70,000	(3)
Equals: Net deposits		$330,000	
Plus: Cash Expenditures			
Known expenses	$50,000		(4)
Increase in cash on hand	25,000		(5,8)
Purchase of car	20,000		(7)
Total Outlay of Funds	95,000		
Minus: Net bank disbursements	40,000		(9)
Equals: Cash Expenditures		$55,000	
Equals: Total receipts		$385,000	
Minus: Funds from known sources			
Fees and commissions	$320,000		(1)
Loan proceeds	25,000		(6)
Cash gift	20,000		(7)
Total from known sources		$365,000	
Equals: Funds from unknown sources		$ 20,000	

The example on the next page presents the information relating to the Jim Dealer financial investigation in the bank deposit method format. Again, the figures contained in the table reflect the financial profile information found on page 199.

Bank Deposit Analysis

Suspect– Jim Dealer

		1991		1992
Total deposits (b)		$22,160		$19,585
Minus: Redeposits (b)		600		100
Equals: Net deposits		$21,500		$19,485
Outlays				
Jewelry purchase (c)	$ 5,000		$ 6,000	
Downpayment on house (f)	50,000		0	
Car purchase (e)	0		18,250	
Monthly mortgage payments (i)	6,000		6,000	
Credit card payments (j)	1,460		3,000	
Loan repayments (h)	600		1,200	
Other personal living expenses (k)	11,000		10,000	
Total outlays	$74,060		$44,450	
Minus: Net bank disbursements*	$18,250		$19,010	
Equals: Cash disbursements	$55,810		$25,440	
Plus: Cash disbursements		55,810		25,440
Equals: Total receipts		$77,310		$44,925
Minus: Cash from known sources				
Cash-on-hand (a)	1,000		0	
Bank account interest (b)	250		475	
Loans (h)	3,000		0	
Wages (l)	25,200		22,675	
Total known sources	$29,450		$22,675	
Minus: Known sources		29,450		22,675
Equals: Funds from unknown sources		$47,860		$22,675

***Net Bank Disbursements Computation**

	1991	1992
Net bank deposits	$21,500	$19,485
Plus: Beginning balance	1,500	4,750
Equals: Net bank funds available	$23,000	24,235
Minus: Ending balance	4,750	5,225
Equals: Net bank disbursements	$18,250	$19,010

In the Jim Dealer example, all three indirect methods of proof resulted in identical bottom line figures. In each case, $47,860 in funds from unknown sources was discovered in 1991 and $22,250 was discovered in 1992.

Since there is no statutory authority for using the bank deposit method of proof, authority stems from case law.[4] The evidentiary facts most often used and accepted by the courts, to establish a prima facia bank deposit case are:

- The suspect was engaged in a lucrative income-producing business or profession
- The suspect made periodic deposits of funds into accounts in his/her own name, over which he/she had exercised control
- A thorough analysis of deposits was made by the investigating agent in order to negate the likelihood that the deposit came from non-taxable sources
- Unidentified deposits have the inherent appearance of income

The principle defense in a bank deposit case is that the deposits themselves represent non-taxable sources (i.e. other people's money, prior accumulated funds, redeposits of cash withdrawals, or transfers of funds between accounts). This type of a defense can be overcome by a thorough analysis of the deposit and withdrawal activity in the accounts under investigation.

Use of Each Indirect Method of Proof

Since there are three methods of indirect proof, an investigator must be able to determine which method to apply to a given situation. The following section explains when each indirect method of proof is applicable.

Net Worth Analysis

Net worth analysis is often used when several of the suspect's assets and/or liabilities have changed during the period under investigation and one of the following conditions exists:

- The suspect maintains no books and records
- The suspect's books and records are not available
- The suspect's books and records are inadequate
- The suspect withholds his or her books and records

In addition to being used as a primary method of proving income in civil and criminal financial cases, net worth analysis can also be used to:

- Corroborate other methods of proving income
- Verify the accuracy of known or reported income

Expenditures Method

The expenditures method is used as a primary method of establishing funds from unknown sources when a specific item case cannot be made. One of the following conditions must exist:

- The suspect maintains no books and records
- The suspect's books and records are not available
- The suspect's books and records are inadequate
- The suspect withholds his or her books and records

In cases where the suspect has several assets and liabilities whose cost basis remains the same throughout the period in which you are interested, the expenditures method may be preferred over net worth analysis because a more brief presentation can be made in the computation. Assets and liabilities which do not change during the period under investigation are omitted from the expenditures statement.

Bank Deposit Method

The bank deposit method is recommended as a primary method of proof when most of the subject's income is deposited and the subject's books and records are:

- Unavailable
- Withheld
- Incomplete

The use of the bank deposit method is not limited to the above circumstances. If the suspect's books and records appear to be complete and accurate, the methods can be used and there is no requirement to disprove the accuracy of the books and records in order to do so.

Indirect Methods of Proof an Investigative Tool

Besides being used to prove income, the indirect methods of proof can be used as an investigative tool. They can help evaluate information provided by informants and can be used to show that a suspect warrants investigation or prosecution. At trial, an indirect method of proof can be used to convince the jury that the suspect is guilty. The following scenario will be used to illustrate these usages.

An informant comes into an investigator's office and provides information concerning Billy Bob Smith. According to the informant, Billy Bob has embezzled money from the bank where he is employed. The informant does not know how much money has been taken, but alleges it is substantial.

An indirect method of proof can be used to evaluate the informant's allegation. A net worth, expenditures, or bank deposit computation could substantiate the informant's allegation and indicate Billy Bob Smith has funds in excess of his legitimate income. This analysis would show that an investigation is warranted.

While conducting the investigation, indirect methods of proof can be used as a measuring device. This investigative tool will indicate whether a substantial portion of the embezzled funds have been identified. For example, suppose the investigator uses the specific item method of proof and documents three acts of embezzlement by Billy Bob. In each case, Billy Bob took $5,000. However, the investigator's indirect method of proof computation shows $75,000 of unknown income. The investigator has documented only 20% of the embezzlement through the use of the specific item method. The investigation should be pursued further. Now, if the indirect method of proof computation reflected $20,000 of unknown income instead of $75,000, the investigator may decide to stop the investigation and present his or her findings to the prosecutor since it appears the major portion of the embezzlement has been documented.

The approach described above also can be used to convince a supervisor to allocate resources necessary to an investigation or prosecutors to take a case to trial. While the specific item method may document three acts of embezzlement, an indirect method of proof may indicate $100,000 was received from the embezzlement. This may convince a prosecutor to indict a suspect. It also may convince a jury that on three occasions Billy Bob Smith did embezzle money from his employer.

Indirect methods of proof also are useful in money laundering and forfeiture investigations. They can provide the information the investigator needs to prove that an asset was purchased with money obtained through illegal activity. Money laundering and forfeiture investigations are discussed in Chapter 11.

Summary

Since the key to proving a financial crime often rests on a showing of the suspect's disposition or receipt of illegal funds, the ability to follow the flow of funds and the movement of money is of utmost importance to a financial investigator.

The specific item method, the method of direct proof discussed in Chapter 7, relies on a microscopic view of the movement of money through a suspect's books and records or into and out of the suspect's bank accounts. In contrast, indirect methods require a macroscopic view of the financial situation. To prepare such an overview of the suspect's financial condition requires that the investigator complete a "financial profile" or detailed financial statement of what the suspect owns, owes, earns, and spends during the particular time period under examination. The financial profile identifies the assets, liabilities, expenses, and expenditures of the suspect. Additionally, it details the identified sources and applications of the funds used to make the purchases and payments. Through the use of the financial profile, financial events can be identified which trace the movement of money by indirect means.

Net worth analysis is one indirect method of proof. This analysis is based on the theory that increases or decreases in a person's or business's net worth, during a specific period, results in the identification of unknown/illegally received funds. The net worth formula is shown below.

Net Worth Analysis Formula

	Assets
Minus:	Liabilities
Equals	**Net worth**
Minus:	Prior's year's net worth
Equals	**Increase in net worth from previous year**
Plus:	Known expenses
Equals	**Total net worth increase**
Minus:	Funds from known sources
Equals	Funds from unknown sources

Expenditures analysis is a second indirect method of tracing the flow of funds. In the expenditures method, a comparison is made between known expenditures and known sources of funds during a given period of time. This analysis concludes that any excess expenditures must result from unknown funds received by the suspect. The expenditures formula is:

Expenditures Method Formula

	Total expenditures
Minus:	Known sources of funds
Equals	Funds from unknown sources

Bank deposit analysis is another method of tracing the receipt of unknown funds by indirect means. Through analysis of bank records and known sources of funds, a determination of funds received from unknown sources is derived. The bank deposit formula is shown below.

Bank Deposit Analysis Formula

	Total deposits to all accounts
Minus:	Transfers and redeposits
Equals	**Net deposits to all accounts**
Plus:	Cash expenditures
Equals	**Total receipts from all sources**
Minus:	Funds from known sources
Equals	Funds from unknown sources

Questions and Exercises

Answer the following questions and then check your responses with those provided at the back of the book.

1. When is it appropriate to use an indirect method of proof?

2. The base year is a key factor in the net worth computation. Explain why.

3. In an expenditures analysis, what effect does understating the "known sources of funds" have on the computation?

4. Compare and contrast the net worth and expenditures methods of tracing the flow of funds.

5. What is meant by the statement, "the specific item method represents a microscopic view of the movement of money, whereas indirect methods represent a macroscopic view of financial activity?"

6. When using the expenditures method, you must determine if a transaction is an expenditure or source of funds. Review the following list of transactions and for those that are expenditures, place an "E" in the blank space that precedes the transaction; for those that are sources of funds, place an "S" in the blank.

___ a. Suspect has a bank account balance of $1,300 on January 1, 1991, and $1,600 on December 31, 1991.

___ b. Suspect's mortgage decreased from $27,500 to $25,200 during the year.

___ c. Suspect's beginning inventory was $52,000 and ending inventory was $38,000.

___ d. Suspect sold stock costing $5,000 for $8,000.

___ e. Suspect paid $13,250 for a new car.

___ f. Suspect embezzled $40,000 from his employer.

___ g. Suspect took out a $50,000 loan to purchase a boat.

___ h. Suspect donated $10,000 to the University of Higher Education.

7. Given the following scenario and facts, compute the subject's funds from unknown sources using net worth analysis.

Scenario

Richard Ross operates a flower shop downtown. It is alleged that this business is a "front" for his bookmaking and loan sharking activities.

Facts

a. You find a financial statement signed by Ross and dated December 31, 1991. The statement indicates that Ross had $1,000 cash on hand.

b. Ross has a checking account which he opened on June 1, 1991. His balance as of December 31, 1991 was $4,000. During 1992, Ross made total cash deposits of $30,000 and withdrawals of $25,000. His balance as of December 31, 1992 was $9,000. During 1993, Ross made total cash deposits of $25,000 and withdrawals of $32,000. His balance as of December 31, 1993 was $2,000.

c. A search of your county real estate records shows that Ross purchased his present home in 1991 for $130,000 and that he obtained a $30,000 mortgage. Real estate taxes on the property amounted to $1,500 for each of the years 1992 and 1993. Contact with the lending institution shows that Ross made monthly payments of $1,000 to the lending institution during the subject years. The mortgage balances are as follows:

- December 31, 1991 $98,000
- December 31, 1992 $96,500
- December 31, 1993 $94,500

Interest payments are as follows:

- 1992 $10,500
- 1993 $10,000

d. Ross bought a new car in April, 1991. He paid $25,000 cash.

e. City records indicate that Ross applied for a building permit in 1992 for the construction of a swimming pool in his backyard. Contact with the pool construction company reveals that Ross paid $20,000 for the pool. He made a $10,000 cash downpayment and received an interest-free loan from the pool company for the remaining $10,000. The pool was completed in June, 1992. Ross made monthly payments of $500 to the pool company. The loan balance on December 31, 1992 was $7,000 and on December 31, 1993, the loan balance was $1,000.

f. An informant stated that since 1991, Ross had maintained a $1,500 a month apartment for his girlfriend, Becky Perry. The informant's information was verified as being accurate.

g. During your investigation, you find that on February 28, 1992, Ross purchased a diamond ring and necklace for $25,100 cash and on December 23,1993, he paid $15,900 cash for a mink coat.

h. During an interview with Ms. Perry, she told you that in addition to the apartment, Ross provided her with a new car which he leased on January 1,1992. Contact with the auto leasing company revealed that Ross made lease payments of $300 a month during 1992 and 1993.

i. Information obtained from a local boat company shows that Ross purchased a boat on June 4, 1993 for $24,000.

j. The county judgment index shows that Ross borrowed $5,000 from a local finance company in 1990. He has never made any repayments.

k. Records of the local travel agency disclosed that Ross took his girlfriend on a vacation to the Orient in 1993. It cost $12,000.

l. You interviewed Ross and he showed you the books and records for his flower shop which indicated that he had a net profit of $40,000 in 1992 and $45,000 in 1993.

Net Worth Analysis Computation

8. Given the scenario and facts listed for question 7, compute the subject's funds from unknown sources using the expenditures method.

Expenditures Method Computation

9. Given the scenario and facts listed for question 7, compute the subject's funds from unknown sources using the bank deposit method.

Bank Deposit Method Computation

Endnotes

1 Jack T. Wells, W. Steve Albrecht, Jack Bologna, and Gilbert Geis, *Fraud Examiner's Manual,* (National Association of Certified Fraud Examiners, 1989), Section 111, p. 46.

2 *Fraud Examiner's Manual,* Section 111, pp. 47 - 49.

3 U.S. v. William R. Johnson (319 U.S. 503, 63 S. Ct. 1233, 43-1 USTC 9470)

4 U.S. v. Gleckman (80 F 2d 394 (CA-8), 35-2 USTC 9645)

CHAPTER 9

Planning, Conducting, and Recording an Interview

"Talk is cheap because supply exceeds demand."

The above statement may be true in many situations, but when it comes to an investigator trying to get answers out of a witness, the opposite will probably happen. One of the most important skills investigators can develop is the ability to get people to open up and talk to them. In this chapter, you will learn about the "art" of interviewing. Yes, it is an art because those who do it well are more successful than those who shrug interviewing off as just "asking questions and writing down answers."

An interview is more than just going to someone's house, knocking on the door, and then asking questions. It takes planning. If you come across in a threatening manner or can't adequately explain why you need to interview a witness, you'll never get any voluntary cooperation. If you ask complex questions or don't allow witnesses to tell their story in their own words, you're not going to get what it is you are after. And finally, if you cannot adequately convey to others what you found out during the interview, it may as well not have taken place. The "art" of interviewing consists of three phases— planning, conducting, and recording— all of which are discussed in this chapter.

After studying Chapter 9, you should be able to:

- State the purpose of a financial interview.
- List the objectives of a financial interview.

- Describe the elements that must be considered when planning an interview.
- Describe techniques used when conducting an interview.
- Identify and describe methods used to record an interview.

"Just the facts." Remember Sergeant Joe Friday's famous phrase from the television show Dragnet? For years, every week like clockwork, Joe had the uncanny ability to detect, investigate, and resolve criminal matters in 30 minutes or less.

Television makes it look easy. Unfortunately it isn't. Detecting and investigating a financial crime can take weeks, months, and even years. So, while reality significantly differs from what happens on television, one thing remains the same— financial investigators, just like Joe Friday, search for facts by interviewing people.

Few skills are as important to the financial investigator as the ability to talk to people and successfully gather information from them. Yet, law enforcement officers are not empowered to force people to talk to them. These powers are granted only to courts, grand juries, and certain judicial and legislative bodies. Consequently, investigators face the double duty of convincing the interviewee (hereafter called the **witness**) to agree to be interviewed and then getting the witness to talk after getting inside the door.

What is an Interview?

An Interview

- *Face-to-face*
- *Task related purpose*

Phone interviews. Employment interviews. Counseling interviews. Investigatory interviews. As you can see, there are many types of interviews. And though they all serve different purposes, they are founded on the same definition: an **interview** is a specialized form of oral, face-to-face communication between people that is entered into for a specific task-related purpose associated with a particular subject matter.[1]

For the financial investigator, two aspects of this definition should be noted. The first one is that an interview is a face-to-face communication. Not only will investigators listen to what witnesses say, they will be able to see what the witnesses do. The visual and non-verbal aspects of an interview are very important and should not be overlooked. Secondly, the interview has a specific task-related purpose. This task-related purpose is what makes an interview different from mere conversation. A conversation can take off in many directions; an interview must be focused on relevant content.

Introduction to the Financial Interview

Before we get into a general discussion of the interview process, we should look at some specifics of the financial interview. The purpose of a financial interview, its objectives, and the type of question to be asked during a financial interview are discussed below.

Purpose and Objectives

For the financial investigator, the interview is a tool used to determine what knowledge a witness has concerning an investigation. Knowledge in this context includes information about the allegation or crime in question, and any relevant records in a witness's possession. The information and documents provided to the investigator form the basis of the **witness's testimony.**

A financial interview is different from a financial interrogation. Financial interviews are conducted to obtain information and documentation from witnesses. Financial interrogations are conducted with suspects and hostile witnesses to elicit confessions or admissions of culpability. An investigator may plan on conducting an interview and have it turn into an interrogation. Conversely, interrogation can commence only to discover that the witness appears to be innocent, and with that, an interrogation turns into an interview.

The financial interview is not something that investigators undertake haphazardly. Prior to each interview, they must decide what they hope to accomplish by interviewing a particular witness. In other words, they must determine the interview's objective(s).

The objectives of a financial interview are:[2]

- To obtain information that establishes or refutes the allegation or crime under investigation
- To obtain leads for further development of the case
- To obtain all information and documents in the witness's possession relative to the financial investigation
- To obtain the cooperation of the witness for any subsequent legal proceeding
- To obtain background and personal information about the witness and motivation for involvement in the crime

Type of Question Asked

A financial interview is a special type of investigatory interview. During most investigations, people are interviewed to obtain their recollections of events. For example:

"Can you describe the person who came into the bank?"

"Do you remember if anyone was with him?"

"What color was the car she purchased?"

Ask questions *related to specifics, not just general recollections*

Financial interviews go beyond recollection questions. Like the financial investigation itself, they are concerned with specific details of financial transactions and the movement of money. For example:

"Why did you have this check cashed?"

"You notarized two signatures on this document. One is the suspect's. Who is the other individual?"

"How did she pay for the car?"

The Three Phases of an Interview

For any investigator, an interview is more than just asking a witness some questions. Who should be interviewed? What questions should be asked? In what order should the questions be asked? Where should the interview take place? How can the witness be put at ease so that he or she cooperates? What happens to the information collected? These are just some of the questions an investigator must ask before, during, and after the interview.

A good interview requires a lot of forethought, skillful execution, and an ability to convey what happened during the interview to others. The interview process is comprised of the following three phases:

- Planning
- Conducting
- Recording

Planning an Interview

Prior to planning any interview, the investigator is usually faced with one or more of the following conditions:[3]

- A crime has been alleged or committed, but the facts relating to the situation have not yet been established
- A complainant or victim has been identified. This could be an individual, business, or governmental entity
- Records or documents reflecting financial transactions relating to the suspected criminal activity have surfaced
- Rumors, innuendo, or factual information pointing to a specific suspect have emerged

The investigator uses the interview to develop information about these existing conditions. The information collected will be used to support or dispel the allegations.

Selecting Witnesses

When an investigation begins, investigators must determine who they want to interview and in what order. Traditional criminal cases are generally investigated by first contacting the outer circle of honest, disinterested witnesses and then working inward to the co-conspirators and ultimately to the target. Law enforcement normally starts the interview process with the complaining witness and after exhausting his or her knowledge of the facts and reasons for suspicion, proceeds in a similar manner around the outer circle of witnesses.[4]

In a financial investigation this traditional sequence is often altered. Following the movement of money dictates talking to witnesses that have knowledge of financial transactions. Accordingly, the hierarchy of interviews is determined by the degree of knowledge or participation in financial activities created by the alleged criminal event or crime at issue. For example, in a political corruption investigation, documents showing the movement of money from the payer of the bribe to the taker of the bribe would be of paramount importance to the investigator. People with documents (bankers, money couriers, business associates) would be priority contacts. In an embezzlement or tax evasion investigation, the key interviews would be with custodians of accounting records and internal audit files, and tax return preparers. Even in a drug case, financial transactions decide the order of contacts for the investigator. The priority witnesses will have records reflecting the suspect's use of proceeds from the drug trade. While each investigation offers a different set of interview options and priorities, the bottom line in a financial investigation is that every person who has documents pertaining to financial transactions, or knowledge about them, should be interviewed.

Types of Witnesses

One of the things an investigator must consider prior to contacting an individual for an interview is what type of witness will that person be. Will he or she be cooperative, hostile, or have no feelings one way or the other? Prospective witnesses can be categorized into three general types:[5]

Types of Witnesses

Neutral
This is an uninterested third party such as a custodian of public or financial records. This person has no interest in the outcome of the investigation and provides documents and/or unbiased information.
Friendly
A friendly witness is one who cooperates. Witnesses are friendly for a variety of reasons. Certain people naturally tell anybody everything. Others realize that they stand to benefit from providing information about the suspect to authorities. Also, many people seem to enjoy "playing detective" and get caught up in the excitement of being a part of an important investigation.
Reluctant or hostile
This is an uncooperative party who is typically a friend or associate of the suspect. This witness may also be hostile due to his or her own culpability in the criminal activity under investigation.

Neutral and friendly witnesses usually agree to interviews upon request. No more than proper identification and introduction by the investigator opens the door. Interviewing hostile witnesses often presents greater challenges. Most likely, these witnesses will not voluntarily submit to an interview. They refuse to provide information and documents.

Since law enforcement cannot, on its own, compel any witness to say or do anything, investigators need assistance from the legal system. With approval from a government attorney (i.e. city or district attorney, or U.S. Attorney) the investigator can be issued a document (i.e., summons, subpoena) which commands a witness to appear and submit to an interview. The investigator serves this document on the witness and, if the witness disregards the document, contempt charges and incarceration possibly could result. But even an investigative tool that can command appearance before the investigator does not override a witness's constitutional guarantees. So, while a hostile witness can be ordered to open the door and submit to an interview, he or she cannot be compelled to say anything incriminating.

Contacting the Suspect

In Chapter 4, we stated that the suspect was a valuable source of information. It follows then that deciding when to interview the suspect is an important decision. Should he or she be contacted at the start of the investigation or confronted upon its completion? Should the investigator contact the suspect at all? The decision is determined by the investigator and is different for each investigation. Interviewing the suspect during the early stages of the investigation makes good sense if it is feared that records in his or her possession may be destroyed or an alibi may be concocted. Often, catching the suspect off guard results in a more responsive interview filled with more answers and more documents. Also, early interviews have resulted in quick confessions and/or early indications of innocence.

On the other hand, delaying contact with the suspect may be advantageous if information and documents gathered from other witnesses can be used to refute the suspect's alibis and lies. Additionally, confessions sometimes occur when the suspect is confronted face to face with the evidence of guilt.

In certain situations, the suspect may not be interviewed at all. He or she may be beyond the reach of law enforcement (i.e. out of the country) or may be represented by an attorney who refuses to allow his or her client to be interviewed on constitutional grounds.

Method of Questioning

While planning an interview, the investigator must determine the method of questioning to use. Questioning can be organized in a number of ways:

- **Chronological method.** The witness is questioned about the events in the order that they occurred from beginning to end. This is the usual organization of questioning.

- **Questioning according to documents.** In this type of interview format a particular document (financial statement, canceled check, tax return) is the focus. The witness may be the legal custodian of the record and have no other involvement in the investigation.

- **Questioning according to transactions or events.** The witness may have sold the subject a house or delivered a package for him or her. The questions in this situation would center on the event and radiate from there.

During the planning phase, the investigator should prepare a written outline that lists main topics to be covered in the interview. An outline allows the investigator to concentrate on important ideas and areas to be covered. However, writing down every specific question to be asked and in a specified order should be avoided as this has the tendency to make the investigator inflexible and tied to the next question. The investigator unwittingly becomes guided by what is written on the sheet of paper instead of what is being said by the witness. Also, the witness may catch a glimpse of the upcoming questions and prepare responses in advance. The following page contains a simplified example of an interview outline. The outline used for an actual interview would be more extensive.

Sample Interview Outline

Ray Austin Interview

Introduction:	Identify Self State Purpose
Background:	DOB SSN Address Married Wife (Maiden Name) Children Source of income Parents Education Military Prior Arrest, Convictions

Assets	Liabilities	Cash-on-Hand

Associates:	Adkins HTB Inc. Allen Cleveland Massey TB Trust Massey Cemetery Rosemary Westbury Tony Idaho Toni Boise Marc Fresno

Conducting an Interview

Once an investigator is finished with the planning phase, he or she is ready to conduct the interview. The interview itself is composed of three distinct parts:

- Introduction
- Body
- Close

Introduction

The introduction is critical as it sets the tone for the whole interview. It serves the following two purposes:

- Allows the investigator to identify himself or herself to the witness
- Allows the investigator to state the purpose of the contact

The following shows right and wrong ways for an investigator to introduce himself or herself.[6]

Wrong

"Mr. Smith, my name is John Jones and this is Mary Adams. We're with the government. We're investigating Jim Dealer and we need to talk to you."

Right

"Mr. Smith, my name is John Jones. I am a Special Agent with the Internal Revenue Service's Criminal Investigation Division. This is Special Agent Mary Adams from the Drug Enforcement Administration. We are currently conducting an investigation involving alleged violations of money laundering laws by Jim Dealer. May we speak to you for a few moments?"

The objective of the introduction is to put witnesses at ease and to get them to agree to answer questions. However, once the investigator identifies himself or herself, the next question normally is asked by the witness.

Witness:	"Why are you contacting me?"
Investigator:	"We would like to ask some questions about your financial dealings with Jim Dealer and his associates."

Since the investigator's goal is to put the witness in a frame-of-mind to answer questions, he or she must supply a reason which leads the witness to perceive that he or she will benefit from cooperating with the investigator. If the witness believes that the investigator represents a threat, voluntary cooperation is generally lost. The next page shows some right and wrong ways to gain the cooperation of a hesitant witness.

During the introduction, the investigator should ask general, almost generic, questions such as name, address, telephone number, and date of birth. Since many witnesses are apprehensive, the investigator needs to be patient and avoid rushing into important questions. Through reassuring the witness that his or her cooperation will not cause any undue hardships, inconveniences, or embarrassment, a rapport can be established that will assist both the witness and the investigator during the interview process. When the introduction has been completed and the witness is ready to talk, the investigator moves on to the second part of the actual interview— the body.

Right and Wrong Ways to Gain the Cooperation of a Witness

Wrong

Witness: "Why should I talk to you? I don't want to get involved."

Investigator: "You should have thought of that sooner— it's too late now. We can talk here or we can talk downtown. It's your choice."

Right

Witness: "Why should I talk to you? I don't want to get involved."

Investigator: "You certainly are not required to talk to me. I am just seeking some information on a serious matter which may or may not result in legal action. By speaking informally with me now, it may save you the trouble of having to testify later, depending on the information you have. Is that o.k.?"

or

Witness: "I don't want to answer any questions at this time without first talking to my lawyer."

Investigator: "You certainly don't have to talk to me, with or without your lawyer. Let's do it this way. Let me ask you a few questions and if you don't want to answer them, just say so. I'm not trying to get you into trouble, I'm just trying to do my job and get some answers. Is that o.k.?"

The Body

The body of the interview is the fact finding part of the interview process. Questions are asked and answers are provided. The structure of the interview is determined by the method of questioning (chronological, by document, or by transaction or event) which should have been pre-determined and outlined by the investigator.

In this stage of the interview, witnesses should be allowed to tell their story in their own words. Recognizing that a witness's story will usually be disjointed and rambling, the investigator must be prepared to put order to the material— find the details, focus for clarity, and ensure the accuracy. For the investigator, conducting an interview is much more than just asking questions and writing down answers. This process requires concentration and active participation by the investigator if his or her objectives are going to be achieved.

The time-honored questioning devices of *who, what, where, when, why*, and *how* allow investigators to push witnesses for details. Investigators should continue the questions until they are convinced that a witness's knowledge of a topic is exhausted. Details, details, details! Whether recollections or records, it is the detail provided by the witness that lays the foundation for a successful financial investigation. The following exchange between an investigator and a witness illustrates how to pursue the detail in a line of questioning.

Investigator: "How was the kickback payment made?"

Witness "At a meeting."

Investigator: "Where did this meeting take place?"

Witness: "In Mr. X's office."

Investigator: "How many people were there?"

Witness: "There were three of us."

Investigator: "Who were they?"

Witness: "Mr. X, Bill Baker, and me."

Investigator: "How was the kickback divided?"

Witness: "Mr X split it into three piles."

Investigator: "How much did each of you get?"

Witness: "I don't know. Mr. X didn't count the money. He just estimated the size of each pile."

Investigator: "Did you all get the same size piles?"

Witness: "Yes. I counted it at my office. I had just a little over $100,000."

Investigator: "Would you say that Mr. X received about $100,000 also?"

Witness: "That would seem about right."

A witness's opinion of events often clouds the facts. Although there is nothing wrong with requesting an opinion from a witness, the investigator, through proper questioning, needs to separate the facts (what was said) from the opinions (what was talked about). The goal is a verbatim recollection from the witness. For example:

Wrong

"What did you and Jim Dealer talk about?"

Right

"What did Jim Dealer say to you?
What did you say to him?"

As was stated earlier, an investigator must actively participate in the interview process. It's not as simple as ask a question, write down a response. The investigator must constantly analyze responses, and continually check for inconsistencies, inaccuracies, and incompleteness. For example:

Investigator: "How long did your meeting with Mr. Grey last?"

Witness: "It lasted all day."

Investigator: "What did Mr. Grey say?"

Witness: "Not much."

An all day meeting with not much said should raise a red flag in the investigator's mind. This line of questioning needs to be pursued.

During an interview, investigators have a multitude of tasks to handle simultaneously. From listening to a response and recording it, to formulating the next question, they have a lot to do. There are some general "do's and don'ts" that investigators should consider when performing an interview. They are found on the next page.

Interview Do's and Don'ts

- *Do* interviews as a team. One investigator listens and controls the questioning while the second records the responses.

- *Do* interview witnesses individually. Attempting to interview two witnesses in the same room at the same time results in one of two things—one witness influences the other's responses or one witness becomes mute thereby allowing the second witness to answer all the questions. Always separate witnesses and conduct their interviews simultaneously.

- *Do* control the interview. Don't let, for example, an attorney who is present disrupt the interview. Before beginning the interview, advise each participant of their role in the process. This should help eliminate any control problems.

- *Do* provide the witness with an out. If a witness has previously denied knowledge, or has supplied false information, there is often reluctance to admit it. The investigator should provide this witness an "out". It normally will be taken. For example:

  "Mr. Smith, I know when we talked before you denied knowing Mr. Dealer. You probably forgot about meeting him. Can we start over?"

- *Don't* ask compound/complex or negatively phrased questions, (i.e. "you didn't see the money, did you?"). Questions should be simple, to the point, and positively phrased.

- *Don't* make threats and avoid threatening remarks. Threats rarely work, so overbearing tactics should be avoided. The "good cop/bad cop" interview technique looks good on television but is usually inappropriate in financial investigations.

As was discussed in Chapter 3, in our legal system, documents cannot speak for themselves, either figuratively or literally. A witness must identify, explain, and introduce every financial document to give it meaning in any legal proceeding or court action. So what does interviewing have to do with the introduction of documents into a legal proceeding. Plenty! Successful interviewing creates cooperative witnesses who breathe life into financial records involving the movement of money.

Technical areas such as accounting procedures or business specialties should be covered in detail during the body of an interview. The investigator should ask questions concerning the document's entries, meanings, and purposes. The investigator should also determine the identity of the document's custodian and solicit the authenticity of the document. Investigators should not be afraid to ask questions and should keep that old saying, "There is no such thing as a stupid question" in mind. Any question can lead to a surprising answer.

The investigator's job during the interview process is not complete until he or she has exhausted the witness's knowledge on the important topics relative to the ongoing investigation. Successful interviews obtain information and financial leads, as opposed to solving the case. If enough interviews are conducted and enough information is uncovered, the case will solve itself.[7]

The Close

After the witness has provided information, the investigator should review the key points gathered during the body of the interview. This process of summing up the important facts serves the following two purposes:

- It allows the investigator to clarify the facts
- It provides an opportunity for the investigator and witness to agree with the investigator's summation

Once the summation has been agreed on, the investigator should ask the following three questions:[8]

- **"Is there anything that I have forgotten to ask?"** Probably the number one reason investigators fail to get the answers they seek is that they simply fail to ask the question. Using this "catch-all" question allows the witness the opportunity to play detective.

- **"Is there anyone else you think I should speak with?"** This question is designed to find more leads. If the witness is hesitant, it's ok to say that his or her name will not be revealed to the person(s) suggested.
- **"Is there anything else that you would like to say?"** This should be the investigator's last question. It gives the witness one final chance to say anything that he or she wishes.

Exit gracefully, even after encounters with hostile witnesses. Soothe the apprehensive witness by mentioning that all the information that he or she provided will be held in confidence and/or for official purposes only. If the witness was cooperative, thank him or her for the cooperation; if nothing was said, express regrets and leave the door open for future contacts.

Recording an Interview

Investigators conduct interviews to obtain information and documents in an attempt to resolve financial crimes. It is also necessary to prepare a permanent record of each interview for future reference and use. Often in a financial investigation, persons interviewed become trial witnesses. The record of the financial interview as prepared by the investigator can be used to refresh the witness's memory and assist the witness in the identification process relative to a financial document.

The complexity and investigative importance of an interview determines the best method to record it. In situations where no information is secured, a limited report or record of interview is acceptable. However, in situations where "case critical questions" are answered, or denials are made by an important witness, a more formal record becomes necessary. The only constraint in the recordation process is the requirement for **accuracy** and **completeness** by the investigator preparing the written summary.

When an investigator plays the role of an interviewer, he or she must be accurate, fair and just. The prosecuting attorney relies on the investigator's written notes taken during an interview. The investigator's portrayal of the interview process should accurately and completely reflect the witness's testimony.

Informal Notes

The **"informal notes"** taken by investigators during the course of the interview, in conjunction with their recollections, provide the basis for the written record. Informal notes should contain sufficient detail to permit investigators to refresh their memories as to what transpired during the interview. Any method of recording the details is sufficient if it shows the date, time, place, persons present, and what occurred. The following is an example of the informal notes taken by Special Agent John Jones during an interview with Richard Smith. Special Agents Jones and Adams interviewed Smith concerning a financial transaction (the purchase of a car) he had with the suspect, Jim Dealer.

Example of Informal Notes

John Jones, IRS
Re: Jim Dealer
Mary Adams, DEA
Talked w/Richard Smith
July 25, 1991
123 A. Street
10am - 10:47am

Dealer called Smith about truck Smith advertised. Dealer came to see truck about ½ hour after call. Test drove truck around block then paid $25,000 in cash, in $100 bills, for truck.

1990 truck, serial # 1173945

Memorandum

A second way to record interviews is to "formalize" the investigator's informal notes into a **"memorandum of interview".** A memorandum should be prepared when details of an interview are too numerous to be fully and properly related through informal notes. It should state what occurred during the interview and show the date, time, place, and persons present. If the person interviewed was advised of his or her constitutional rights during the interview, this fact should also be noted in the memorandum. The final typed memorandum should be prepared as soon as possible, and promptly signed and dated by the investigators present during the interview. The actual date of preparation should be shown at the bottom of the memorandum. If it becomes necessary to correct or supplement a memorandum after it has been finalized, the supplemental memorandum should clearly state the date and reason for such action, and the previous memorandum should be attached.

Handwritten notes made during an interview and used as the basis for a more detailed memorandum may be subject to inspection by a court and should be retained in the case file. Investigators should confine memorandums to the facts developed in the interviews and should avoid opinions, conclusions, and other extraneous matters.

When deciding whether or not to use a memorandum as a means of recording interview notes, an investigator should consider the following advantages and disadvantages:

Advantages and Disadvantages of the Memorandum

Advantages	Disadvantages
Informal	Does not contain the exact words of the interviewee
Contains all pertinent testimony obtained in the interview	Since information was not mechanically recorded, there is a chance for some information to be forgotten
Memorandums can be prepared by topic and therefore are easy to follow	
Does not require an oath or affirmation	

An example of a memorandum appears on the following page.

Example of Memorandum of Interview

In re: James Dealer
115 South Street
Miami, Florida

Present: Richard Smith, Witness
Special Agent, Mary Adams
Special Agent, John Jones

Place: Office of Richard Smith
117 Elm Street
North Miami, Florida

Date: July 25, 1991

Time: 10:00 a.m. to 10:47 a.m.

1. S/A Adams and I made a field call to a travel agency located at 117 Elm Street, the known employer of Richard Smith. Records obtained from State vehicle registration files reveal that Smith transferred the title of a truck (serial number 1173945) to Dealer in May, 1990.

2. After proper introduction and identification (by displaying our credentials and badges), I asked Mr. Smith if he would answer a few questions about the sale of his truck. Mr. Smith agreed and when asked, stated the following:

   a. He advertised his truck for sale in a newspaper at $25,000.

   b. Dealer responded to the ad and bought the truck by paying $25,000 in currency, composed of one hundred dollar bills.

   c. The sale was completed on May 29, 1990, when the currency was exchanged for the truck and registration paperwork.

3. Mr. Smith further stated that he would agree to reducing the information to a written affidavit and swear to it's accuracy.

4. I suggested that we meet again tomorrow at his home to prepare the affidavit. Mr. Smith agreed.

5. This interview concluded at 10:47 a.m. when we left Mr. Smith's office.

I (prepared/dictated) this memorandum on July 26, 1991, after refreshing my memory from notes made during and immediately after the interview with Richard Smith.

John Jones
Special Agent

I certify that this memorandum has recorded in it a summary of all pertinent matters discussed with Richard Smith on July 25, 1991.

Mary Adams
Witness

Question and Answer Statement

A question and answer statement is a complete transcript of the questions, answers, and statements made by each participant during an interview. It may be prepared from a stenographer's notes or from a mechanical recording device. The source used to prepare the transcript should be preserved and associated with the case file as it may be needed in court to establish what was said.

A question and answer statement should contain:

- When and where the testimony was obtained
- The name and address of the person giving the testimony
- The matter the testimony relates to, including the purpose of the interview
- The name and title of the investigator asking questions and the name and title of the person giving answers
- The names and titles of all persons present during the testimony and the reason for each person being present, if not obvious
- The consent of the person being interviewed to use a tape recorder if a mechanical recording is being made
- Information given to the person being interviewed concerning his or her rights to counsel and against self-incrimination, if appropriate
- Administration of an oath if given
- Questions and answers establishing that the statement was made freely and voluntarily, without duress, and that no promises or commitments were made by the investigators
- Signatures of the investigators who conducted the interview and the person being interviewed
- Signature and the certification of the person transcribing the statement, showing the source of the original information used
- Information that the person being interviewed was given the opportunity to examine the statement, correct any errors, and sign it

The following is a format that can be used for question and answer statements.

Question and Answer Statement Format

Testimony of (name, address) given at (location including address) at (time) on (date) about (subject of investigation and their address).

Present at this interview are (names and titles of all persons present).

Questions were asked by (name and title of person asking the questions) and answers given by (person being interviewed).

This interview is being recorded, as agreed upon, by means of (method of recording).

1. **Q.** You were requested to appear at (location) to answer questions concerning (subject matter). (If appropriate, advise the person being interviewed of his or her rights to counsel, etc..)

2. **Q.** Please stand and raise your right hand. Do you (person being interviewed) solemnly swear that the answers you are about to give to the questions asked will be the truth, so help you God?

3. **Q.** Did you sell a truck that you owned to Mr. Jim Dealer?

   A. (answer)

4. **Q.** How much did he pay you for the truck?

   A. (answer)

• Note: The interview is brought to a close with the following questions.

120. **Q.** Have I, or has any other investigator or officer, threatened or intimidated you in any manner?

   A. (answer)

121. **Q.** Have I, or any other investigator or officer, offered you any rewards, promises or immunity, in return for this statement?

   A. (answer)

122. **Q.** Have you given this statement freely and voluntarily?

   A. (answer)

123. **Q.** Is there anything further you care to add for the record?

   A. (answer)

After this statement has been transcribed, you will be given an opportunity to read it, correct any errors, and sign it.

• Note: When transcribing the statement include the following:

I have carefully read the foregoing statement consisting of page 1 to (last page number), inclusive, which is a correct transcript of my answers to questions asked me on (date of statement) at (location where statement was given), relative to (subject of investigation and their address). I hereby certify that the foregoing answers are true and correct, that I have made the corrections shown, have placed my initials opposite each correction, and that I have initialed each page of the statement.

(signature of person giving statement)
Subscribed and sworn to before me at (time), on (date) at (present location).
(signature and title of investigator)
(signature and title of witnessing investigator)
I (name of person transcribing statement), do hereby certify that I took the foregoing statement of (person giving statement) from (method of recording) and personally transcribed it and have initialed each page.
(signature and title of transcriber)

Normally people will review and sign a question and answer statement after it has been put in its final form. Sometimes, for various reasons, the person may change his or her position and refuse to sign the statement. When an investigator is faced with such a refusal, he or she should request that the statement be read and verified for correctness. In such situations, the following can be inserted at the end of the statement:

> *This statement was read by (name) on (date) who stated that it was true and correct, but refused to be placed under oath or to sign it.*

Just as there are advantages and disadvantages to using a memorandum as a recording device, so there are for the use of a question and answer statement.

Advantages and Disadvantages of the Question and Answer Statement

Advantages	Disadvantages
Reflects both questions and answers	Usually contains unnecessary material
Questions are generally asked in a logical sequence	Is often very long and involved
Is difficult to dispute with claims of misunderstanding	It is unedited; therefore, it picks up incorrect grammar, etc
Is preferred when the issues are complicated	Tape recorder will pick up outside noises which can disrupt recording
	Unable to make voice distinction
Is useful when the person testifying under oath is illiterate or below average intelligence	Mechanical failure (if tape recorder used)
Can be used to challenge or discredit a witness	Can be viewed as intimidating by deponent; therefore, witnesses are often not willing to participate

Affidavit

An **affidavit** is a written declaration of facts made voluntarily and confirmed by oath or affirmation. The text of an affidavit may be prepared extemporaneously or composed by agreement between the **affiant**, the person making the statement, and the investigator. An affidavit can be either typed or handwritten, and prepared either by the affiant or investigator. There are certain advantages to allowing the affiant to compose and write an affidavit. These advantages are :

- The affidavit will be in the affiant's own words
- The affidavit will be more credible because it is in the affiant's own handwriting. It would be difficult for the affiant to later deny the affidavit was his or hers

One advantage to having the investigator prepare the affidavit is that the investigator will ensure that only relevant information will be covered and that the information will appear in an orderly fashion. In cases where the affiant is unable to either read or write, a witness other than the affiant or the investigator must read the affidavit to the affiant before he or she signs it. The affidavit must also be signed by both the investigator and witness.

No particular form of affidavit is required by common law. It is customary that affidavits have a caption or title, the judicial district in which given, the signature of the affiant, and the jurat. A **jurat** is the certification on an affidavit declaring when, where, and before whom it was sworn.

The affidavit is one of the most commonly used forms of recording testimony. It can be used during trial to impeach a witness, refresh memory, or it can be introduced as evidence. An affidavit should not contain hearsay or information about which the witness has no direct knowledge. If the person being interviewed was advised of his or her constitutional rights, this should be included in the affidavit.

A sample affidavit is found on the next page.

Sample Affidavit

United States of America Southern)
Judicial , District of Florida)

I, Richard L. Smith , state that:
I reside at 123 A Street, Miami, Florida
I am currently employed as a travel agent at Miami Travel, located at 117 Elm Street, Miami, Florida. On May 28, 1990, I placed a newspaper advertisement in the Miami Herald classified ads offering my 1989 truck for sale. I listed the asking price as $25,000. On May 29, I received a phone call from a man who said that he read the ad and would like to see my truck. He stated that he would like to look at it that afternoon. I gave him my address and he came over about 30 minutes later. I gave him the keys and we took a ride around the block. He said that he would buy the truck for $25,000. He opened the trunk of the car he was driving and pulled out a briefcase. We went into my house where he took $25,000 in one hundred dollar bills from the briefcase to pay for the truck. I was surprised at being paid in currency, but the man stated that he wanted the truck today and knew that it would take time for a check to clear the bank, so he brought cash. I gave him the ownership papers for the truck. I said thanks for buying the truck and gave him my business card requesting that he give me a call if he needed any travel planning. He gave me his business card and said he was in the import-export business. Jim went to his car and made a telephone call and a couple of minutes later two guys arrived and one drove Jim's car while Jim drove the truck away. I have not seen or heard from Jim since that day. On today's date, I gave Special Agent John Jones a copy of the truck registration, serial number 1173945, that I sold to Jim Dealer on May 29, 1990, and the business card I received from Jim Dealer on that same date. I have received a receipt for both of these items from Special Agent Jones.

I have read the foregoing statement consisting of 1 page(s), and have signed it. I fully understand this statement and it is true, accurate, and complete to the best of my knowledge and belief.

I made this statement freely and voluntarily without any threats or rewards, or promises of reward having been made to me in return for it.

Richard L. Smith
(Signature of affiant)
Subscribed and sworn to me before this 29th
day of July , 1991,
at Miami, Florida

John Jones
(Signature)

Special Agent
(Title)

Mary Adams
(Signature of witness, if any)

The affidavit, like the memorandum and the question and answer statement, has advantages and disadvantages to its use. Prior to using an affidavit, the items listed below should be considered.

Advantages and Disadvantages of an Affidavit

Advantages	Disadvantages
Preserves probable testimony	Does not reflect questions asked
Frequently used in requiring testimony from: Hostile witnesses Witnesses who have changed allegiance	May contain non-related information if prepared by affiant May not contain all pertinent information when prepared by affiant
May be used as grounds to impeach witness	May not be well written or clear if prepared by affiant
Usually is easier to write than other types	
Valuable in developing an investigation	
May be written or typed and prepared on the spot	
May be concise and brief	

Sworn Statement

A sworn statement is, in a general sense, a declaration of matters of fact. It may be prepared in any form and should be signed and dated by the person preparing it. A sworn statement has the same judicial bearing as an affidavit. The investigator taking the statement administers an oath prior to the witness signing the statement. The following is an example of an oath that can be administered:

Do you (name of person giving statement) solemnly swear that everything contained in this statement is true and correct.

Mechanical Recordings

A mechanical recording device may be used to record statements when a stenographer is not readily available— if all parties to the conversation consent. A recording device also may be used in conjunction with a stenographer, when necessary, again provided that all parties consent. When mechanical recording devices are used, the following guidelines are suggested:

- Identify, on tape, the individuals engaged in the conversation, any other persons present, and the time, date, and location

- Immediately after the original has been made, make a copy of the tape for use in transcribing the conversation. If the recording was made during an undercover operation, seal and store the original after a transcribed copy has been made

- Keep a written record of the tape's custodians and storage arrangements from the time it was recorded to the time it is submitted as evidence

- When tape recordings are going to be used in taking a confession, advise the suspect of his or her rights and have the suspect state at the start of the tape recording that he or she is aware that a recording is being made

- Off the record discussions between the investigator and the suspect should not be permitted during a recorded interview and should be kept to a minimum during a recorded interview with anyone else

Form Letter

A form letter can be used to request information of a similar nature from several third parties. An example of a form letter is found on the next page.

Sample Form Letter

Prosecuting Attorney's Office
Glynn County
300 South Main Street, 4th Floor
Brunswick, GA 31523
Telephone: (912) 555-5982

June 4, 1992

Ms. Michelle Tallmadge
1111 B Street
Glynco, GA 31520

Dear Ms. Tallmadge,

This office is conducting an investigation concerning Rosemary Westbury for the years 1989, 1990, and 1991. Ms. Westbury is a corporate officer of Massey TB, Inc. She is also the trustee for Massey TB Trust. We have reviewed the bank records of Massey TB, Inc., and Massey TB Trust. We found several checks made payable to you. Please answer the questions below which relate to the checks we found. We have included copies of the checks for your review.

Should you have any questions, please call investigator Dennis S. Paul at the telephone number listed above.

1. Did you receive checks number 1521, 1571, 1681, 1952, 1991?

____

2. Did you endorse these checks?

____

3. Please explain why these checks were deposited into Massey TB Trust's bank account.

____
____
____
____
____

4. We would like to talk to you about these checks. Please call us, or provide your daytime telephone number so we can schedule an appointment.

____

Sincerely, Dennis S. Paul

Grand Jury Transcript

A complete grand jury transcript will contain the questions, answers, and statements made by each participant before the grand jury. This transcript can be used as basis for a charge of perjury if the witness gives false information before the grand jury.

The Art of Interviewing

Through practice, an investigator can improve his or her interview skills. But, equally important is practicing the art of critical self-analysis when dealing with others. This starts by stripping away the prejudices and other self-imposed barriers to impartiality that surface when communicating with people. It continues by learning to converse in different styles of language. Interviewing a college graduate and a fifth grade drop-out require different communication skills. How something is said is just as important as what is said. Everyone communicates through speech patterns and non-spoken behavior patterns. Witnesses sense the presence of the investigator's questions, not only with their ears, but by watching his or her gestures, making or avoiding eye contact, and feeling the stress in the room.

The interview process should flow naturally. The investigator should enter into the interview with general questions in mind. After the first question is asked, the investigator assumes a new role— the listener. Contingent upon what is heard the investigator leads the interview toward the next question and then listens. This asking and listening process, controlled by the investigator, continues until the objectives of the interview have been achieved.

A successful interviewer has empathy for others. No one likes the thought of appearing foolish. Many witnesses are actually victims of fraudulent actions committed against them by the subject of the investigation and are embarrassed about being victimized. For example, businesses victimized by insiders are often reluctant to let the public know that they were vulnerable to fraud. A business may have more than money at stake. It becomes a matter of confidence and prestige in the public or industry's eye. An investigator who can become sensitive to a witness's situation quickly improves his or her interviewing techniques.

Summary

The goal of an investigator is to conduct each interview in such a manner as to gather all available information and documents pertaining to the investigation and then make a permanent record of each witness's testimony for further reference.

The planning phase of the interview process is the foundation of an interview. Poor planning will have the same effect on an interview as a weak foundation has on a building. Proper planning enhances the probability of a successful interview. A successful interview can create a cooperative witness who can breathe life into financial records. It could also provide additional leads for the investigator to solve the case.

Once the investigator has decided on who, when, where, and how to interview the witness, the investigator should prepare a topical outline of the questions to be asked. Just as planning is the foundation of the interview process, the opening of an interview sets its tone. The body of the interview is the fact finding part of the process. The closing summarizes the key facts and provides an opportunity for the witness and the investigator to agree with the summation.

The medium used to record an interview should be reflective of the significance of the witness and the information and records provided by the witness.

Interviewing is a skill that can be developed and improved upon through practice. Few skills are as important to the financial investigator as the ability to talk to people and successfully gather information from them.

Questions and Exercises

Answer the following questions and then check your responses with those provided on pages at the back of the book.

1. How does an interview differ from an interrogation?

2. How do questions asked in a financial interview differ from those asked in other types of investigative interviews?

3. What are some things an investigator should consider when planning financial interviews during the course of an investigation?

4. Identify and describe the three methods of questioning that can be used in a financial interview.

5. Why is the introduction critical to a successful interview?

6. How can an investigator gain the cooperation of a hesitant witness?

7. Explain the following statement:

The interview process is more than just asking questions and writing down responses.

8. What is wrong with the following question?

He didn't have anyone with him when he came into the bank did he, but if he did, do you remember if the person was male or female and can you give a description of the person?

9. What is the last question an investigator should ask during an interview?

10. You are preparing to record an interview and you can't decide which method of recordation to use. You are torn between the memorandum and the question and answer statement. Describe the pros and cons of each.

11. What advantages are there to having a witness compose and write his or her own affidavit?

Endnotes

1 Cal W. Downs, G. Paul Smeyak, and Ernest Martin, *Professional Interviewing,* (New York: Harper and Row Publishers, 1980), p. 5

2 Joseph T. Wells, W. Steve Albrecht, Jack Bologna, Gilbert Geis, and Jack Robertson, *Fraud Examiner's Manual,* (National Association of Certified Fraud Examiner's, 1989), Section 1, p. 15

3 *Fraud Examiner's Manual,* Section 1, p. 14

4 *Fraud Examiner's Manual,* Section 1, p. 7

5 *Fraud Examiner's Manual,* Section 11, pp. 15, 16

6 Format for examples adopted from *Fraud Examiner's Manual,* Section 1, pp. 20 - 23

7 *Fraud Examiner's Manual,* Section 1, p. 31

8 *Fraud Examiner's Manual,* Section 1, p. 23, 24

CHAPTER 10

Investigative Techniques

In the previous chapter, we discussed how to plan and conduct a financial interview. The financial interview, if properly done, is a very valuable tool for the investigator. In this chapter, we will explore some other investigative techniques. We will begin with a discussion of the search warrant for financial records: what it is, how it differs from a "general" search warrant, and how one is issued to an investigator. We will then explore the undercover operation, surveillance, the use of informants, recovering information from trash, gathering information from a suspect's mail, and retrieving evidence from a computer. We will look at how document examiners apply forensic science techniques to aid in investigations. The chapter concludes with an examination of a tool called "link analysis."

After studying Chapter 10, you should be able to:

- State the importance of obtaining a valid search warrant.
- Describe the terms "probable cause" and "curtilage."
- State the purpose of an affidavit.
- List and describe the types of information required in an affidavit for a search warrant for financial information.
- List the objectives of undercover operations.
- List the objectives of surveillance.
- Describe the different types of surveillance.
- Describe how informants contribute to an investigation.

• State why recovering evidence from a suspect's trash, reading the covers of a suspect's mail, and retrieving evidence from a computer are valuable investigative techniques.

• List and describe the types of analyses a document examiner can perform.

• Use link analysis to show relationships in an investigation.

Persons involved in criminal activities do not flaunt their indiscretions in the faces of law enforcement officers. They try to hide what they are doing. And some of the webs criminals weave are very complex. Because of this, investigators rely on certain investigative techniques to help them gather information concerning criminal activities. These techniques are discussed in this chapter.

The Search Warrant

"Revenuers" executing a court authorized search warrant on bootleg alcohol during the 1930's.

Special Agent Wilson Taggart is working on a narcotics investigation where Tim Anthony is the prime suspect. Taggart receives an anonymous letter indicating that David Anthony, Tim's father, recently paid cash for a new $23,000 car. Wondering if Tim provided his father with the money, Taggart decides to visit David Anthony. Taggart goes to Mr. Anthony's house, identifies himself, and says he'd like to ask a few questions about Tim. Mr. Anthony lets him in. Taggart asks if it is alright for him to take a look around and, even though Mr. Anthony says no, Taggart acts as if he doesn't hear. Taggart opens a briefcase that is sitting on a desk and finds that it contains $100,000. He asks Mr. Anthony where he got the money but Mr. Anthony just shrugs his shoulders. Then Taggart spies a checking account statement that indicates Mr. Anthony had a balance of $1,494 less than a month ago. Taggart wants to know if Mr. Anthony has other accounts, but, again, Mr. Anthony just shrugs his shoulders. "How did you get $23,000 to pay for a new car?" Taggart asks. "None of your business," Mr. Anthony replies. "Now, get out of here." When he leaves, Taggart takes the briefcase full of money and the checking account statement with him.

The scenario presented above is fictitious, but suppose it really happened. Will Special Agent Taggart be able to use what he collected as evidence against Tim Anthony?

The answer is no. Taggart obtained the evidence without a valid search warrant. Mr. Anthony was under the assumption that Special Agent Taggart wanted to ask him a few questions about his son. When he invited Special Agent Taggart in, he had no reason to believe that the agent was going to search the house. The Fourth Amendment to the U.S. Constitution protects citizens against actions such as Special Agent Taggart's. The amendment provides that the people have the right to be "...secure in their persons, houses, papers, and effects, against unreasonable searches and seizures..." If evidence is obtained by an unreasonable search and seizure, or in violation of the privileges guaranteed by the Fourth Amendment, the evidence will be excluded from trial. Investigators need to be aware of the importance of obtaining a valid search warrant. Otherwise, critical evidence will be ruled inadmissible.

What is a Search Warrant?

A **search warrant** is a written order issued by a judge or magistrate. It describes the place to be searched as well as the things to be seized. Search warrants are usually issued for the search of a premise, person, or vehicle. Generally, search warrants are issued based on evidence gathered by the investigator during the conduct of the investigation. This evidence must establish that a crime has been or will be committed.

A specialized form of search warrant is a **search warrant for financial records.** This specialized warrant directs a law enforcement officer to search for financial documents or records. If Company XYZ is a suspect in a kickback investigation, the investigators probably will not be interested in searching and seizing office equipment and personnel files. However, they will be interested in obtaining the company's journals, ledgers, and other financial records. That's what a search warrant for financial records will allow them to do.

A search warrant is usually prepared by the prosecuting attorney before it is submitted to a judge or magistrate. Search warrants are usually required to be executed during daytime hours on a given day and are executable within a 72 hour period. At the completion of the search, a detailed inventory of the items seized is prepared. A copy of the search warrant and the inventory are to be left at the place searched or with the person searched. The investigator will then return the warrant and the inventory to the judge or magistrate who authorized the warrant.

Probable Cause

A judge or magistrate will issue a search warrant only after a finding of **probable cause.** Probable cause is all the facts and circumstances within the knowledge of the investigator about a criminal activity that can be considered reasonable and trustworthy.

When developing probable cause, an investigator must keep the following two principles in mind:

- Probable cause must be current

- Probable cause must be reasonable and trustworthy to a degree sufficient to ensure that a reasonable person will believe that a crime has been or will be committed and that the evidence sought exists in the place to be searched

Probable cause may vary from investigation to investigation but only in matters of degree. It must be present and it must be sufficient to enable an impartial judicial officer to issue the warrant.

The Affidavit

Judges or magistrates issue search warrants and do so only after a finding of probable cause. To convince a judge or magistrate that probable cause exists, an investigator prepares a sworn statement called an **affidavit.** In affidavits, investigators summarize their expertise and the information gathered during their investigations. The investigator who prepares an affidavit is called the **affiant.**

An affidavit for a search warrant should contain certain types of information. Affidavits for "general" search warrants and search warrants for financial records should contain the following types of information:

- Affiant's experience
- Detailed account of the criminal activity
- Description of place(s) to be searched
- Financial evidence
- Items to be seized

An affidavit for a search warrant for financial records requires an additional type of information: **conclusions based on the affiant's expertise.**

The following paragraphs describe the types of information to be included in a search warrant for financial records. An example of a statement reflecting the type of information is also provided.

Affiant's experience

The affidavit should contain a sufficient amount of detail concerning the affiant's experience, training, and investigative background.

> *I am a Special Agent with the IRS, Criminal Investigation Division, and have been so employed since March, 1977. I have conducted or assisted in over forty investigations of alleged criminal violations of IRS laws; of the distribution of drugs and controlled substances; and of money laundering. For the past 2½ years, I have held the position of Intelligence Analyst. I have been in charge of the Division's High Level Drug Leaders Project, Project Narcotics Currency, and Project White Collar Currency. All of these projects analyze information relative to the flow of drug proceeds throughout the State of Wisconsin.*

Account of criminal activity

The affiant must detail the illegal activity that has been uncovered during the investigation.

> *In January 1992, four FBI informants who have previously provided reliable information reported that Tom Trio was selling cocaine in the Milwaukee area. Two of the informants stated that Trio was selling cocaine out of his residence. One*

informant reported that a friend of his had seen several trash bags of currency in Trio's house.

Description of place(s) to be searched

The affiant must show that the defendant exercises dominion and control over the location(s) to be searched. To do this, the affiant can cite information contained in documentation such as telephone and utility records. The affiant can also point to surveillance findings as well as information secured through interviews from third parties.

The Milwaukee City Phone Directory lists Tom Trio's address as 102 North West Street, Milwaukee, Wisconsin.

Financial evidence

The affidavit should document major asset purchases and expenditures made by the defendant. It should describe any acts of deceit or fraudulent schemes uncovered, such as the use of aliases or the existence of any money laundering activities. Tax information, if available, should be presented as financial evidence. Generally, a court order is needed before tax returns can be released to non-IRS law enforcement personnel because of confidentiality laws. However, tax returns can be obtained from non-IRS sources such as an ex-spouse, bookkeeper, accountant or return preparer, or loan documents.

Federal income tax records reveal that Tom Trio has reported a total income of $54,000 during the past two years.

Items to be searched/seized

An itemized list of specific property (documents and evidence) to be searched for and seized must be attached to the affidavit.

Search the residence located at 102 North West Street, Milwaukee, Wisconsin and the 1990 Mercedes with VIN number G1AB2323 for:

U.S. currency

Cocaine

Books, records, receipts, notes, ledgers, and other papers relating to the transportation, ordering, sale, and distribution of cocaine

Conclusions based on the affiant's expertise

As previously indicated, what distinguishes the affidavit for a search warrant for financial records from the affidavit for a "general" search warrant is the reliance on the affiant's expertise to establish that records and other evidence will be at specific locations.

> *Based upon my training and experience, and my participation in other investigations involving the distribution of cocaine, I know that:*
>
> *a. drug traffickers must maintain, on hand, large amounts of U.S. currency to maintain and finance their ongoing narcotics business*
>
> *b. drug traffickers maintain books, records, receipts, notes, ledgers, and other papers relating to the transportation, ordering, sale, and distribution of controlled substances*

A sample affidavit for a search warrant for financial records is shown on pages 270 through 272. Page 273 contains the search warrant issued as a result of the affidavit.

AFFIDAVIT

STATE OF WISCONSIN)
) ss
MILWAUKEE COUNTY)

John Smith, being first duly sworn on oath, here deposes and says:

1. I am a Special Agent with the IRS, Criminal Investigation Division, and have been so employed since March, 1977. I have conducted or assisted in over forty investigations of alleged criminal violations of IRS laws; of the distribution of drugs and controlled substances; and of money laundering. For the past 2 1/2 years, I have held the position of Intelligence Analyst. I have been in charge of the Division's High Level Drug Leaders Project, Project Narcotics Currency, and Project White Collar Currency. All of these projects analyze information relative to the flow of drug proceeds throughout the State of Wisconsin.
2. I have attended and instructed in-service training seminars which concentrated on currency reporting statutes (Title 31, U.S.C.), money laundering statutes (Title 18, U.S.C. §§ 1956, 1957) and drug statutes (Title 21, U.S.C. §§ 848, 851, 881). I have conducted net worth and expenditure investigations and I have planned, drafted and executed both financial and traditional search warrants. I have been qualified in the U.S. District Court as an expert in financial and money laundering investigations.
3. As part of my duties, I am involved in the investigation of Tom Trio for cocaine trafficking in violation of Title 21 of the United States Code. Special agents from the Federal Bureau of Investigation and the Drug Enforcement Administration and officers from the City of Milwaukee Police Department have participated in this investigation. The information in this affidavit comes from my own personal investigation and observation, or from the information provided to me by personnel of these other agencies.
4. In January 1992, four FBI informants who have previously provided reliable information stated that Tom Trio was selling cocaine in the Milwaukee area. Two of the informants stated that Trio was selling cocaine out of his residence. One informant reported that a friend of his had seen several trash bags of currency in Trio's house.
5. The Milwaukee City Phone Directory lists Tom Trio's address as 102 North West Street, Milwaukee, Wisconsin.
6. Real Estate records at the County Courthouse in Milwaukee, Wisconsin show that on August 12, 1991, Tom Trio purchased the residence at 102 North West Street from John Jakes for $64,000. No mortgage documents have been located for the property.
7. In an interview with John Jakes, he stated that Trio attempted to pay cash at the time of settlement. Jakes refused to accept payment in cash and Trio subsequently provided him with eight $8,000 cashier's checks.
8. Tom Trio is employed by Penders and Associates, Inc. This is his only place of employment.

9. Local income tax records reveal that Tom Trio has reported a total income of $54,000 during the past two years.
10. On February 6, 1992, I collected and went through the trash left for garbage collection at 102 North West Street. The garbage included bills addressed to Tom Trio of that address, M & I Bank envelopes, 12 money wrappers marked for $2,000 each, and the title to a 1990 Mercedes with VIN number G1AB2323. The garbage also contained freezer paper cut into small squares. Special Agent Thomas Gore of the Drug Enforcement Administration told me that such paper is commonly used to wrap 1 ounce quantities of cocaine. The garbage also included three large plastic garbage bags that contained fiber glass cartons. Special Agent Gore told me that cartons of that size and type commonly contain kilograms of cocaine. The inside of the packages had a powdery residue which Special Agent Gore tested for the presence of cocaine. The test was positive.
11. Documentation from the dealership where Tom Trio bought the 1990 Mercedes shows that he paid $27,000 in cash for the car.
12. Between February 16 and February 24, 1992, one of the previously mentioned informants purchased cocaine from Tom Trio three times. Each buy was a controlled buy. All three buys took place at Trio's house. Each time, the substance purchased was tested for the presence of cocaine. Each time, the substance tested positive.
13. Based upon my training and experience, and my participation in other investigations involving the distribution of cocaine, I know that:
    a. drug traffickers must maintain, on hand, large amounts of U.S. currency to maintain and finance their ongoing narcotics business;
    b. drug traffickers maintain books, records, receipts, notes, ledgers, and other papers relating to the transportation, ordering, sale, and distribution of controlled substances;
    c. the aforementioned books, records, receipts, notes, ledgers, etc., are commonly maintained where drug traffickers have ready access to them, i.e., homes, offices, automobiles;
    d. it is common for drug traffickers to hide contraband, proceeds from drug sales, and records of drug transactions in secure locations for ready access;
    e. cocaine traffickers usually keep paraphernalia for packaging, cutting, weighing, and distributing cocaine;
    f. the courts have recognized that unexplained wealth is probative evidence of crimes motivated by greed, particularly trafficking in controlled substances.
14. Based on the information contained herein, and my experience and training, I have probable cause to believe that Tom Trio is involved in cocaine trafficking in violation of Title 21 U.S.C. § 881 (B). The locations to be searched and property to be seized are included on the attachment to this affidavit.

John Smith

John Smith
Special Agent

Attachment

Search the residence located at 102 North West Street, Milwaukee, Wisconsin and the 1990 Mercedes with VIN number G1AB2323 for:

U.S. currency

Cocaine

Drug paraphernalia for packaging, cutting, weighing, and distributing cocaine, including, but not limited to, scales, freezer paper, and spoons

Books, records, receipts, notes, ledgers, and other papers relating to the transportation, ordering, sale, and distribution of cocaine

Books, records, receipts, bank statements and records, money drafts, letters of credit, passbooks, bank checks, and other items evidencing the obtaining, secreting, transfer, and concealment of assets and the obtaining, secreting, transfer, concealment, and expenditure of money

Income tax returns

UNITED STATES DISTRICT COURT
EASTERN DISTRICT OF WISCONSIN
AT LAW AND IN ADMIRALTY

UNITED STATES OF AMERICA,

Plaintiff,

Warrant No. 1

vs.

SEARCH WARRANT
(21 U.S.C. § 881 (B))

Thomas Trio

TO: **ANY DEPUTY UNITED STATES MARSHAL OR OTHER FEDERAL OFFICER**
An affidavit has been made before me by Special Agent John Smith of the United States Internal Revenue Service that he has reason to believe that Tom Trio of 102 North West Street, Milwaukee Wisconsin is involved in cocaine trafficking in violation of Title 21 U.S.C. § 881 (B). Special Agent Smith's affidavit further states that he has reason to believe that evidence needed to support such a claim is located at the residence of 102 North West Street. I am satisfied that there are sufficient facts and circumstances to support the probable cause standard to believe that the items listed on the attachment to this warrant are currently located at 102 North West Street in Milwaukee, Wisconsin, and that grounds exist for the issuance of this seizure warrant as stated in the supporting Affidavit.

YOU ARE HEREBY COMMANDED to proceed to 102 North West Street to seize the items listed or described on the attachment to this warrant within a period of three days, serving this warrant and seizing this property during daytime hours 8:00 a.m. to 5:00 p.m., leaving a copy of this warrant, preparing a written inventory of all the property seized, and promptly returning this warrant and bringing the inventory before this court as required by law within ten days after seizure.

Dated at Milwaukee, Wisconsin, this 2 day of March, 1992.

Alice Miller
United States Magistrate

Undercover Operations

Operation ABSCAM was an investigation into corruption among U.S. government officials. Over the course of a year and a half, FBI undercover agents approached public officials thought to be involved in political corruption and told them that oil-rich Arab sheiks would offer money in exchange for political favors. The agents met with the public figures and paid out considerable sums in cash. Several public officials were indicted and convicted.

In August 1989, 46 traders from the Chicago Mercantile Exchange and the Chicago Board of Trade were indicted on charges ranging from defrauding customers to tax evasion to racketeering. The charges were the result of a two-year undercover operation that put wired FBI undercover agents in the trading pits at the two exchanges.

In March 1991, law enforcement agents raided three University of Virginia fraternity houses and arrested 12 students for selling drugs to undercover agents. The raids came after more than six months of investigation by federal and state officials. The investigation involved undercover purchases of designer drugs, LSD, cocaine, and marijuana.

What is an Undercover Operation?

The undercover operation is something we hear about all the time. In an **undercover operation,** law enforcement officers or private individuals assume an identity other than their own for the purpose of gathering information relating to criminal violations.

Undercover operations require the highest degree of skill and planning to be successful. Used in a timely manner and with great care, the undercover operation can bring results to investigations that cannot be achieved in any other way. Used in the wrong way or handled poorly, these operations can lead to death, injury, serious financial liability, and agency embarrassment.[1]

An undercover operation is frequently the only investigative technique that can be used effectively against well-organized criminal groups or sophisticated criminal activities. Through the use of disguise and deceit, information is gathered directly from those involved in the criminal offense. Take, for example, the undercover activities of Joe Pistone. Pistone was an undercover agent who infiltrated the Bonnano and Columbo crime families, posing for five years (1976-1981) as jewel thief Donnie Brasco. Pistone was instrumental in gaining more than 100 federal convictions against organized crime members.[2]

Undercover activities can last a long or short period of time. As was just indicated, Joe Pistone was undercover for five years. The length of the undercover operation is contingent on the amount of information necessary to develop a picture of the alleged criminal activity. Situations involving organized crime figures and sophisticated financial crime networks dictate lengthy undercover operations.

At the other extreme are short-term undercover operations called **stings.** The previously described drug raid at the University of Virginia is an example of a sting operation.

Objectives of Undercover Operations

Undercover operations are accepted by the courts as a legitimate function of public and private law enforcement personnel, provided that the undercover operation is conducted in those situations where sufficient probable cause exists to believe that a crime has been or is being committed. Entrapment issues make it essential to establish that the suspect has a pre-disposition or prior intent to commit the crime. The only factor the government provides is the opportunity for the suspect to commit the offense.

The courts will not allow covert operations to be conducted as law enforcement "fishing expeditions." Undercover operations should be based on a written plan that details time frames and specific objectives. Specific objectives of an undercover operation may include:[3]

- Observing and attending planning sessions for future violations
- Identifying unknown violators and developing information related to violations currently in process
- Purchasing contraband (i.e., drugs, firearms, counterfeit currency)
- Identifying the fruits of a crime (illegal proceeds and profits)

- Developing information related to past crimes or criminal activities
- Locating contraband or weapons
- Locating violation sites
- Identifying co-conspirators and/or key witnesses
- Obtaining probable cause for search and arrest warrants
- Checking the reliability of informants
- Corroborating a witness' statements and testimony
- Gathering information and documents relative to the criminal investigation
- Obtaining information and leads to purchases and expenditures

Surveillance

Jonathan J. Pollard was a civilian analyst for the U.S. Naval Intelligence Center in Suitland, Maryland. In November 1985, Pollard's supervisor, Jerry Agee, began suspecting that Pollard was taking classified documents from his workplace and providing them to a foreign government. Agee shared his suspicions with a senior naval intelligence officer. The Naval Investigative Service and the FBI agreed to investigate. As the investigation progressed, the agents determined that Pollard was providing classified information to a foreign government. They just did not know which one.

Eventually the investigators discovered that Pollard was providing the classified information to Israel. How did they determine this? They placed a round-the-clock surveillance on Pollard.

On November 21, 1985, Pollard and his wife decided to make a run for it even though they knew that were going to be followed. Pollard felt sure he could shake the surveillance as he and his wife drove in circles around Washington, DC. Several unmarked FBI cars were involved in the surveillance— one car would pick up the tail then drop it when another car became involved. Would the Pollards lead them to the foreign government involved in the espionage ring? Yes. The Pollards revealed the government they were providing classified information to when they pulled up to the Israeli embassy.[4]

Surveillance vans assist investigators while conducting moving, stationary and electronic surveillance. Some surveillance vehicles contain hidden cameras, microphones, instamatic cameras that zoom in on license plates and two-way radios to communicate with a command base.

What is Surveillance?

Surveillance is the secretive and continuous observation of persons, places and things to obtain information concerning the identity and activity of individuals suspected of violating criminal laws. Like undercover operations, surveillance provides a means to obtain information and evidence which probably would not be available by any other means. It is a technique that requires experience, teamwork, and knowledge of the "thing" to be surveilled.

Private citizens who form neighborhood watch groups use surveillance to gather information. So do private companies that employ security cameras. Countries use intelligence agencies to set up surveillance operations that are a matter of national security. Even criminals perform surveillance on their suspects before committing crimes.

Objectives of Surveillance

The objectives of a surveillance are to:

- Obtain evidence of a crime
- Obtain probable cause for search and arrest warrants
- Identify co-conspirators and associates of the suspects
- Apprehend violators during the commission of a crime
- Develop investigative leads
- Provide protection and corroboration for undercover officers
- Locate persons and things
- Gather intelligence

Types of Surveillance

Various types of surveillance activities are utilized by law enforcement. They can be classified as follows:

- Stationary
- Moving
- Electronic

Stationary

Stationary surveillance is where neither the suspect or the agent maintaining the surveillance are mobile. Sitting in an unmarked car and watching someone's home or office is an example of stationary surveillance. A common term for stationary surveillance is **stakeout.** The surveillance on Jonathan Pollard began as a stakeout. But when Pollard and his wife decided to make a run for it, the surveillance requirements changed. A moving surveillance was needed.

Moving

A moving surveillance is one where the suspect does not remain in one position. Following a suspect in an automobile is an example of a moving surveillance. Following a suspect on foot or in a boat, or watching a car from an airplane also would be considered moving surveillances.

The risk of detection is higher in a moving surveillance than it is in a stakeout. Also, a moving surveillance consumes significantly more manpower. In the instance of following an automobile, a minimum of three cars with radio contact would be necessary. In most investigative situations, surveillance techniques mandate that it is better to lose the suspect than compromise the surveillance.

Electronic

The FBI agents who went undercover as traders in the pits at the Chicago Mercantile Exchange and the Chicago Board of Trade secretly tape recorded hundreds of incriminating conversations.

To make sure they would not lose touch with the Pollards during a moving surveillance, the FBI planted an electronic tracking device inside the bumper of the Pollard's car.

In each of the incidents above, electronic devices were used to assist law enforcement officers in obtaining evidence against their suspects. Used in a secretive manner, electronic surveillance can be of tremendous assistance to an investigation, but it must be used with care. Some devices available for use may require court orders.

In the trading pit incident, at least one of the people involved in the taped conversations knew the conversations were being recorded. This is called **consensual monitoring.** At the federal level, such monitorings are Constitutional and statutorily permissible; however, this investigative technique is subject to careful regulation in order to avoid any abuse or any unwarranted invasion of privacy. At the state level, some states have made consensual monitoring illegal. Therefore, it is important for an investigator to know the legal precedents in the state where an investigation occurs.

Today's sophisticated electronic monitoring devices can be concealed in virtually anything. Briefcases, light fixtures, and jogging suits can be used to conceal microphones and tape recording devices. Pen registers (telephone number recording devices) can be activated by the change in voltage and used to record the numbers dialed on outgoing calls. Other electronic devices can make a record of the incoming telephone calls to a suspect's number.

Informants

Larry Bullock was an Illinois State Representative who dreamed of becoming Chicago's first black mayor. His district encompassed McCormick Place Exposition Hall, a place that would play an active role in the 1992 World's Fair if Chicago was selected as the host city.

By law, a certain percentage of all public construction projects had to be awarded to minority business enterprises (MBE). Eugene Blackmon was an MBE general contractor and he was experiencing difficulty in getting his money from another general contractor to pay his sub-contractors. Blackmon approached Bullock to enlist his aid in securing his money. Bullock said he could help - for a price! Bullock also promised Blackmon that he would play a prominent role in the awarding of the World's Fair contracts.

Blackmon did not have the money to pay Bullock. But he was desperate to get his money, so one Friday afternoon he went to the Office of the U.S. Attorney and told them about his encounter with Bullock. The government and Blackmon reached an agreement where Blackmon would become an informant and would meet with Bullock to discuss fixing contracts and other matters in political corruption. In return, the government would give Blackmon money to "pay" Bullock so that his contract money would be released.

Over the next few weeks, Blackmon had a series of meetings with Bullock and paid him thousands of dollars of FBI money. Blackmon wore a concealed recording device to the first meeting but something went wrong with the equipment and, instead of recorded conversations, all the FBI got was a mess of spaghetti tape because the tape had come off the spool. At all subsequent meetings, Blackmon wore a recording device *and* had a transmitting device concealed in his briefcase.

Toward the end of the investigation, Bullock and his attorney were invited to the U.S. Attorney's Office and were treated to selected portions of the recorded conversations. The government offered Bullock the opportunity to cooperate with them in investigating political corruption. Bullock refuses, choosing rather to go to trial. After a long trial, during which Blackmon spent a week on the stand testifying, Bullock was found guilty of a multitude of offenses. He was sentenced to six years in prison.

What is an Informant?

In the case described above, it is important to note that the role of the informant was key in carrying out the investigation. An **informant** is a person who has specific knowledge of a criminal event and provides that information to a law enforcement officer.

The development of an informant to provide confidential information is a legitimate function of investigators. If properly developed, informants can greatly enhance an investigation.

Many criminal cases have originated from informant information. Others have been successfully completed only because an informant supplied information that would have otherwise been unknown. Take, for example, the case against Al Capone. Capone was one of the United States' most notorious gangsters. You'd think that when he eventually went to prison he would have gone for murder or racketeering. No, Al Capone was brought down by a mild-mannered tax investigator from the IRS. This investigator was able to build a case against Capone when one of Capone's associates told IRS agents where they could seize books reflecting Capone's income.[5]

Perhaps the most common reason informants supply information is because they themselves are involved in the criminal offense and by furnishing information on the suspect they can diffuse suspicion from their own activities. Particularly when looking at jail time, individuals are willing to become informants in order to get a reduced sentence based on their cooperation.

Many informants are motivated by revenge. They sense that they've been wronged or taken advantage of by the suspect and want to get even. For example, in the case of drug dealing, an informant may furnish information on the suspect because the suspect is a "business" competitor. Other informants feel a social responsibility to provide law enforcement their knowledge of any criminal wrongdoing. It is critical that the investigator be able to determine why the informant is cooperating and to use that information to properly assess how the informant and information provided should be handled.

Informants can be used in surveillances, consensual monitorings, and as participants in undercover operations. Control is a key element in dealing with an informant. Informants should take directions from the investigator, not the other way around. Without control, not only is the investigation in jeopardy, but the investigator could be at risk. If informants are willing to violate a basic tenet of our culture and inform on someone close to them, consider how quickly they would be willing to blackmail agents if they can discover some wrongdoing.

Informants can be powerful tools in a financial investigation. However, all informant information should be corroborated through independent verification to ensure it's accuracy.

Evidence Recovered from Trash

An informant tells an investigator that Billy Greenwood is dealing drugs. The investigator watches

Greenwood's home and observes a number of cars making brief nighttime stops at the house. Based on the informant's information and the surveillance, the investigator asks the garbage collector for the plastic garbage bags in front of Greenwood's house. While sifting through the garbage, the police uncover drug-related paraphernalia, straws containing cocaine residue, and phone bills listing calls to people with drug records. Based on this evidence, the investigators obtain a warrant to search the house and find cocaine and hashish. They arrest Greenwood. Can the evidence the investigators collected from the trash be used against Greenwood at trial?

Yes. In May 1988, the Supreme Court ruled that police may freely rummage through ordinary household trash left at a curbside without obtaining a search warrant.[6] This decision evolved from the incident described above.

Investigators often find that picking up a suspect's garbage is a useful tool for identifying leads. People often dispose of important documents and information pertaining to their criminal activities when they throw out their trash. Once the trash leaves the suspect's possession, they no longer have a reasonable expectation of privacy in the contents of their trash. However, the investigator must be careful not to violate the suspect's **curtilage.** Curtilage usually, but not always, refers to the area inside the boundary of a person's residence or business location, which has been marked off by any number of man-made or naturally occurring devices. These boundary lines include fences, sidewalks, tree lines, and rows of shrubbery. Inside this area, a person has a reasonable expectation of privacy based on the Fourth Amendment to the Constitution.

Reading Mail Covers

Since letters, packages, and other documents travel through the U.S. and other mail delivery services, a person cannot attach a reasonable expectation of privacy to the outside of the mail itself. Therefore, an investigator, in conjunction with the U.S. Postal Service, can make a record of the outside of any mail. Return addresses and postmark information can provide an excellent source of financial leads (i.e. names of banks, credit card companies, etc).

Forensic Science

Timothy Wilson Spencer was suspected of murdering a number of women in Richmond and Arlington, Virginia. Police had reason to suspect Spencer but had no confession, no witnesses, and a limited amount of physical evidence. Then it was found that Spencer's DNA perfectly matched that from semen found at three of the murder scenes. The likelihood that someone else could have produced all three matching patterns was 1 in 135 million. Subsequently, Spencer was found guilty on four counts of murder and sentenced to death.[7]

Genetic fingerprinting played a crucial role in the case against Spencer. Genetic fingerprinting is a technique used in forensic science. Forensic science is the application of scientific techniques to legal matters, in particular to investigations of criminal activities. The **forensic sciences** have been utilized in the investigation of violent crimes for centuries. Traditional techniques such as fingerprint identification, ballistics classifications, and drug, blood, and urine analyses have served the purposes of law enforcement successfully in the past.

Not all criminal cases evolve around forensic evidence like fingerprint identification and ballistics classification. Sometimes evidence comes from the forensic analysis of documents involved in the crime. Take, for example, the Lindbergh kidnapping case. On March 1, 1932, 20-month old Charles A. Lindbergh, Jr. was kidnapped. A ransom note left at the scene of the crime read:

> *Have fifty thousand dollars ready, 25,000 in twenty-dollar bills 15,000 in ten-dollar bills, and 10,000 in five-dollar bills. In 4-5 days we will inform you where to deliver the money. We warn you for making anything public of for notify the police. The child is in gut care. Indication for all letter are signature and three holes.*

On May 12, 1932 the child's body was found in some woods a few miles from the Lindbergh mansion. It wasn't until September, 1935 that a person was charged with the kidnapping and murder of the Lindbergh baby. On January 2, 1935 Bruno Richard Hauptmann went to trial. Since the ransom note was a key piece of evidence, the prosecution needed to show that Hauptmann wrote the note. They obtained other samples of his handwriting and compared them to the ransom note. Handwriting experts took the stand and stated that Hauptmann's handwriting and that of the ransom note were one and the same. This crucial testimony helped convict Hauptmann.[8]

What is a Questioned Document?

Since the end product of financial investigation is documentary evidence, scientific examination of documents by a qualified expert can be an important aspect of the investigation. Besides verifying a person's handwriting, a **document examiner** can analyze checks, kidnapping and hold-up notes, hate letters, wills, contracts, birth/death/marriage certificates, passports or any other document to determine if they have been forged, erased, or changed in any way.

Document examiners are called into an investigation when a **questioned document** is involved. A questioned document is a document that has been questioned in whole or in part with respect to its authenticity, origin, or contents. For example, a suspect denies that she signed a check used to make a bribe payment. Or Cousin Jane accuses Cousin Larry of altering Uncle Charlie's will so that Larry receives the bulk of Charlie's estate.

Types of Forensic Analyses

Document examiners can perform many types of analyses on a document. The following types of forensic analyses are discussed in this section:

- Handwriting analysis
- Typewriter analysis
- Alteration analysis
- Ink analysis
- Paper analysis
- Document restoration

Handwriting Analysis

Over the years, an individual's brain, arms, and fingers create a pattern of handwriting. Everyone's handwriting possesses "normal" or "natural" variations. But the basic pattern does not change. When analyzing handwriting, the document examiner has the suspect submit an **exemplar,** a sample to be used in comparison to the questioned document. The document examiner determines the range of variation in a person's handwriting from the exemplar and compares that handwriting to the questioned document. The document examiner can determine if the writing on the questioned document falls within the individual's "normal" or "natural" range.

Typewriting Analysis

Every typewriter is unique. Each one types differently from every other one because typewriters develop individual characteristics during the manufacturing process and through use. Examiners attempt to determine a document's type style and escapement (pica, elite, or proportional) to establish the make and model of the typewriter that created it. Also, the examiner attempts to find horizontal and vertical misalignment of characters, which if significant, is considered to be an identifying characteristic. Examiners also search for any typeface defects or damaged letters.

Alteration Analysis

Document examiners can determine if a document has been altered. They look for additions (inserts between lines, addition of a word, sentence, or paragraph to a document) and deletions (erasures or obliterations). Utilizing infrared and ultraviolet viewing techniques and photography, alterations unseen by the naked eye become apparent. By looking through a microscope, a document examiner can determine if information was erased by determining if paper fibers were disturbed due to abrasive action.

Sophisticated chemical deletions such as white-out obliterations or ink over-writes can be examined through infrared reflectants.

Interlineation, the addition of a word, sentence or an entire paragraph to a document can be detected because it is nearly impossible to perfectly realign paper in a typewriter once a document has been removed. The examiner can detect the misalignment of the added information by the use of typewriting test plates.

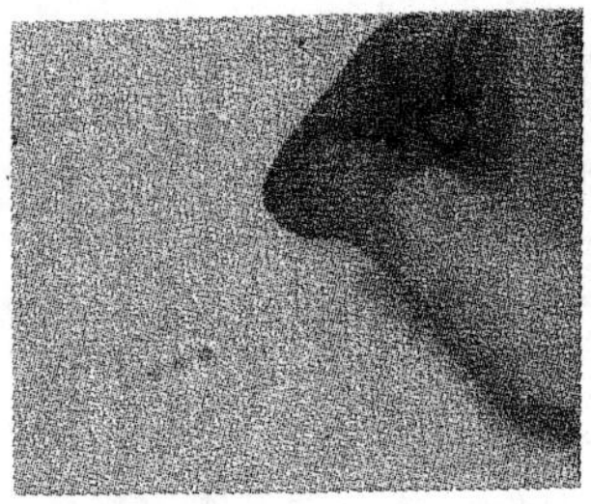

The ink components in various types of writing instruments can react differently to infrared lighting. Dissolved ink is tested by spotting it onto a thin layered chromatography plate which is placed into a solvent tank.

Ink Analysis

The ink on a questioned document can be examined through the use of scientific techniques. One ink can be differentiated from another by microscopy, infrared reflectants, transmission, florescence, and thin layer spectro-chromatography. Inks are identified and dated by their chemical properties. Even pencil writing can be dated within 50 years based on carbon methods.

Paper Analysis

Paper can be identified by characteristics such as dimensions, texture, thickness, color and opacity. Higher grades of paper have watermarks that identify both the brand of paper and its manufacturer. Some papers are coded by the manufacturer to show the year of make.

Document Restoration

It is possible to restore a document that has been torn, mutilated, or even burned. Through scientific processing, some documents that have been partially destroyed can be pieced together and used for investigative purposes.

In this age of desktop publishing, a new type of forgery has come about - desktop forgery. With a scanner, computer, and laser printer, desktop forgers can re-create almost anything: checks, invoices, etc. While some of the forensic analysis techniques described above can be applied to desktop forgery, new techniques will evolve.

Evidence Recovered from Computers

Recent law enforcement reports suggest that - just as legitimate business managers have found computers indispensable in conducting business - organized criminals, drug dealers, and even child pornographers increasingly depend on computer transactions.[9] The computer is a powerful tool in today's business society, providing access to many services and programs. Computers also can provide evidence of criminal activity. A computer could contain a drug dealer's database, the daily operations of a prostitution ring, or a pornographer's mailing list. Physical evidence including handwritten notes, printouts, manuals, sales invoices, photographs, and fingerprints may also be found in the area of the computer.

Link Analysis

Link analysis is a technique for evaluating, integrating, and presenting complex information by taking bits of information collected from various sources and putting them together to show patterns and meanings. It provides a graphic picture of associations and relationships among various of persons and organizations. Link analysis is ideally suited for showing the associations among identifiers such as:

- Telephone numbers
- Vehicle license plates
- Aircraft/boat/vehicle registration numbers

- Property ownership
- Financial transactions

For the investigator, link analysis converts written information into a graphic summary called an association matrix. The **association matrix** is converted into a link diagram which graphically depicts relationships among people, organizations, and activities. Look at how an association simplifies the following relationships:

> *Smith is the vice president of the ABC Corporation and President of DEF Corporation, a subsidiary of ABC. DEF is a general partner in two limited partnerships. Jones and Green are limited partners in the first partnership, Brown and Black are limited partners in the second partnership. Black is also a general partner in a third partnership. Smith may have an interest in the first partnership.*

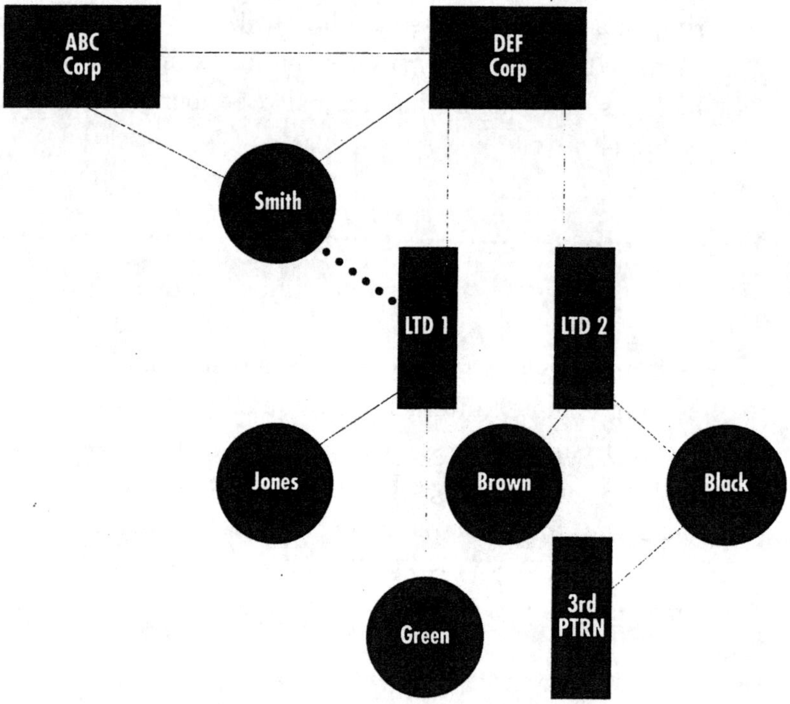

Link networking can also be used to identify the direction and frequency of telephone traffic between suspect parties. The numbers inside the small circles indicate the number of calls made to particular telephone numbers.

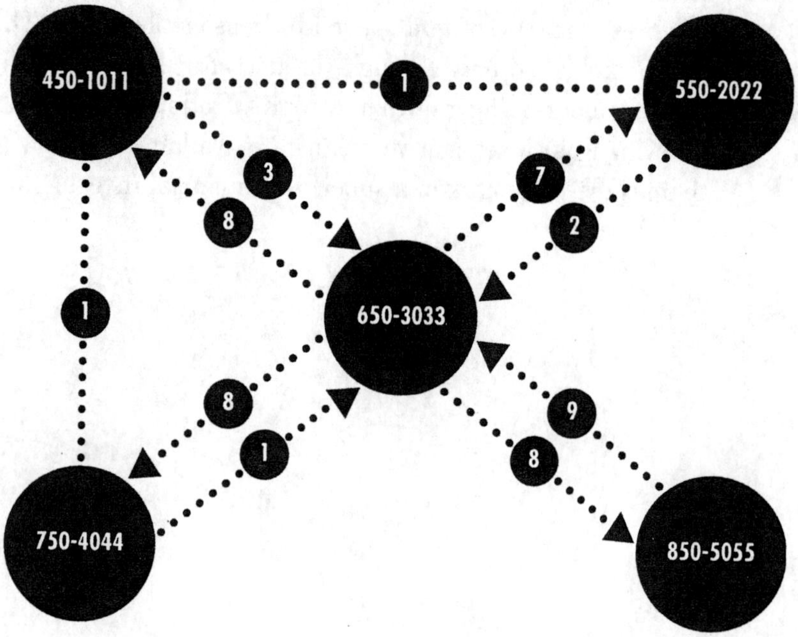

Link networking offers the investigator the ability to simplify and synthesize the relationships and suspected relationships of people in organizations involved in a criminal activity. This technique can be used to present material during the investigative process or at any legal proceedings that may occur subsequent to the investigation.

Summary

An investigator's success or failure is often determined by the investigative techniques used. "Proving a financial crime" requires evidence of guilt beyond a reasonable doubt. This often can be achieved only through the use of specialized techniques. With the continuing growth and sophistication of financial crimes, knowing what investigative means are available and how to apply them is the trademark of a successful financial investigator.

Questions and Exercises

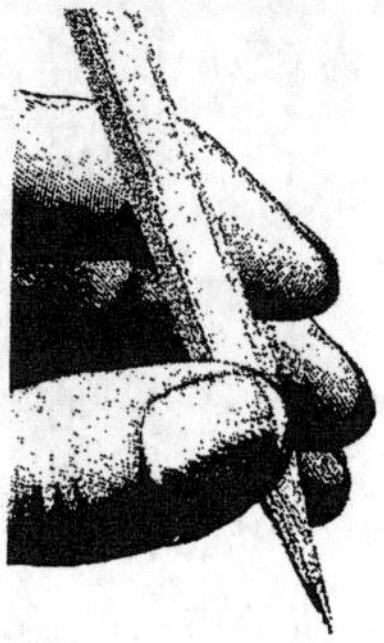

Answer the following questions then check your responses with those provided at the back of the book.

1. Why is it important that an investigator obtain a search warrant prior to searching a suspect's residence or place of business?

2. What is probable cause and how does an investigator show that probable cause exists?

3. What six types of information should be included in an affidavit for a search warrant for financial information? After you have listed the six, place an * beside the type of information that is not required in an affidavit for a "general" search warrant.

a.

b.

c.

d.

e.

f.

4. You are developing an affidavit for a search warrant for financial information. You are trying to obtain a warrant to search John Winkler's residence at 34 Tremont Avenue. Winkler is an accounting clerk suspected of embezzling money from the company he works for. In your affidavit, you include the following statement:

While going through the trash left for garbage collection at 34 Tremont Avenue, I found an electric and phone bill addressed to John Winkler of that address. I also found a bill from Haggler's Electronic Store indicating that Winkler recently bought $2,435 worth of stereo and video recording equipment.

How does the statement support your quest for a search warrant?

5. During the execution of a search warrant, a typewritten contract between the suspect, Toni Tuesday, and Frank Friday is seized. Mr. Friday claims that the contract is a fake, that it is not the contract his office created. What could a document examiner contribute to the investigation?

6. The University of Muckraker's basketball team is under investigation for its suspected involvement with professional gamblers in a point-shaving scandal. You have been tasked with going undercover as one of the team's tutors. What do you suppose are some of the objectives of this undercover operation?

7. During your undercover activities at the University of Muckraker, you discover the following:

- Sam Roundball and Terry Rebound are the starting forwards for the basketball team. They are also roommates and live in a fraternity house off campus.

- Roundball's uncle, Joe Bench, served time in prison. Bench shared a cell with Jack Dice. Dice was convicted of running an illegal gambling operation.

- Dice is a season ticket holder for University of Muckraker basketball games. Dice's son, Kurt, attends the university. Kurt Dice lives in the same fraternity house as Sam Roundball and Terry Rebound.

- Jack and Kurt Dice often attend University of Muckraker basketball games together.

Develop an association matrix that depicts the relationships described above.

8. How might an informant contribute to your investigation of the University of Muckraker's basketball team?

Endnotes

1 Jack T. Wells, W. Steve Albrecht, Jack Bologna, and Gilbert Geis, *Fraud Examiner's Manual,* (National Association of Certified Fraud Examiners, 1989), Section 11, p. 85

2 "Strife and Death in the Family," Time, January 18, 1988, p. 21

3 *Fraud Examiner's Manual,* Section 11, p. 85

4 Wolf Blitzer, *Territory of Lies,* (New York: Harper & Row Publishers, 1989), Chapters 7 and 8

5 Jay Robert Nash, *Encyclopedia of World Crime,* Volume 1, (Wilmette, IL: CrimeBooks, 1990), pp. 603-618

6 "Lifting the Lid on Garbage," Time, May 30, 1988, p.54

7 Gordon Hinkley, "The Search for the South Side Strangler," Reader's Digest, April 1991, pp. 73-78

8 Jay Robert Nash, *Encyclopedia of World Crime, Volume 2,* (Wilmette, IL: CrimeBooks, 1990), pp. 1479-1490

9 Catherine H. Conly, *Organizing for Computer Crime Investigation and Prosecution,* (U.S. Department of Justice, National Institute of Justice, 1989), p. 1

CHAPTER 11

Money Laundering and Forfeitures

Way back in Chapter 1, we described money laundering as "the investment or transfer of money from racketeering, drug transactions, and other illegal sources into legitimate channels so that its original source cannot be traced." This chapter identifies methods used to launder funds and techniques for detecting laundering schemes. Additionally, the specific laws used in prosecuting money laundering crimes are detailed. The evidentiary requirements for successfully imposing forfeitures are also discussed in this chapter. Forfeiture actions are a means to take the profit out of criminal activity. The knowledge and expertise of the financial investigator is particularly suited to dealing with the crime of money laundering.

After studying Chapter 11, you should be able to:

- Distinguish between the two types of transaction systems.
- Describe three methods of moving money from the cash transaction system to the business transaction system.
- Identify methods used to move money into and out of the United States.
- Identify characteristics of businesses used as money laundering fronts.
- Identify and interpret money laundering and forfeiture statutes.
- Distinguish between civil and criminal forfeitures.

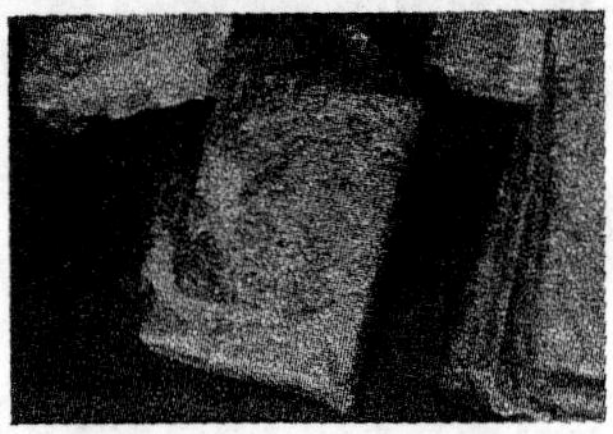

The illicit drug business is reportedly making $300 billion a year in the underground economy. This is more than the Gross National Product of the Netherlands. Traditional drug interdiction methods haven't been effective— the emphasis has now switched to hitting drug dealers where it really hurts: in the wallet.

- Describe the factors that assist an investigator in establishing probable cause for a forfeiture proceeding.

In 1989, it was reported that "the international trade in illicit drugs may now be worth $300 billion a year. Most of that cash must be laundered before it can be spent or invested. In the past, narco-cops have spent most of their time, resources, and energy trying to seize illicit drugs and arrest drug traffickers, many of whom were minor miscreants. Now the attention has switched to tracing flows of dirty money, arresting launderers, and confiscating the assets of traffickers."[1]

Even though the preceding quote focuses on drug trafficking and money laundering, it pretty much sums up what this textbook is all about. In Chapter 1, you read that an overwhelming majority of crimes committed in America today are motivated by money and that many of these crimes cannot be solved solely by the use of traditional investigative techniques. In fact, not only are new investigative techniques required, a whole new approach to investigation is needed - a financial approach. The quote above confirms all of this. Investigations are now being geared to the financial aspect of the crime.

This chapter deals with the crime of money laundering. The term "money laundering" typically invokes the thought of money being transported to a foreign country and, through some vague method, being "cleaned up." This clean cash is then somehow secretly transported back to the United States for use by narcotics traffickers. The truth is, money laundering can occur on any street corner or in any bank; may not involve currency; and does not exclusively relate to narcotics trafficking. The growth of this crime poses a major challenge to law enforcement because money laundering takes place in the majority of financial crimes committed in America.

In a report issued by the Presidential Commission on Organized Crime, money laundering was defined as "the process by which one conceals the existence, illegal source, or illegal application of income and then disguises that income to make it appear legitimate."[2] The financial criminal has a need to manipulate the proceeds generated from a crime so that he or she can use them for personal benefit. Both the embezzling bank teller and the top echelon narcotics trafficker need to be able to spend their illegal gains. And they want to achieve their goal without being detected by law enforcement. They must launder their money.

Transaction Systems

Everyone conducts financial transactions. Activities such as buying groceries, paying bills, carrying on a business, and conducting an illegal activity all involve financial transactions. These transactions are conducted either by a cash system or by what can be referred to as a business system. The **cash transaction system** is a method of conducting all financial transactions exclusively through the use of currency. The **business transaction system** is a method of conducting transactions that generates a trail of financial records (i.e., checks, receipts, invoices, deeds, etc.). The resultant records summarize the financial activity by reflecting specific sources, destinations, participants, and dates.

For the financial criminal there are advantages and disadvantages to both systems. The table on the next page lists the advantages and disadvantages of both transaction systems.

If it was feasible to remain entirely within one system, particularly the cash system, criminals would be afforded strong protection from law enforcement's detection and scrutiny. However, motivations exist for financial criminals to carry out some of their activities in both systems, and virtually all move from one system to the other. From an investigative viewpoint, the movement between systems is often where the criminal is most vulnerable.

Advantages and Disadvantages of Transaction Systems

Cash Transaction System	Business Transaction System
Advantages	**Advantages**
Everyone can come up with currency to pay for illegal goods and services	There is greater efficiency and security in the transfer of funds
Lack of records makes it difficult to connect a person with a criminal activity or with the purchase of illicit goods and services	Losses owing to employee theft are controllable
Unreported revenues are not taxed	Other business opportunities are available such as legitimate investments in real estate and securities
Currency is universally accepted	A legitimate business is a valuable base of operations and source of cash for criminal activities
	Ownership of a business permits acquisition of community standing and influence which provides additional camouflage for illegal operations
Disadvantages	**Disadvantages**
In large amounts, cash is suspicious and calls attention to those who hoard it	Taxes must be paid on reported revenues
Lack of records makes it difficult to prevent theft by employees	Business records are subject to examination by authorities
Large amounts of cash are difficult to handle and transport	Falsification of records is a criminal act and can lead to a prosecution even without proof of other criminal activities
Certain assets cannot be acquired for cash without an extensive inquiry into its source	Transactions have a source and destination which can lead to the criminal activity

Methods of Laundering Funds

There are three basic methods used by financial criminals to move their illegal funds from one transaction system to another. These methods are:

- Legitimate businesses
- Buy/sell transactions
- Offshore havens

Use Of A Legitimate Business

Legitimate businesses are often used to move money from the cash system into the business transaction system. The proceeds from an illegal activity can be laundered through a legitimate business by one or more of the following means:

- Overstatement of legitimate revenue
- Overstatement of legitimate expenses
- Deposits of currency

Let's look at how Stage One Records and Videos moves money between the cash and business transaction systems. We'll also introduce some investigative strategies that can be used to detect money laundering.

Stage One Records and Videos is located in a small metropolitan shopping mall. The bulk of its business activity is the sale of records, tapes, and compact discs. A smaller portion of business revenue is generated from the rental of video tapes. The owner, Greg November, a local narcotics dealer, works part-time in the store and has four full-time employees who are not aware of the his drug activity. November's wife, who is aware of the illegal activity, maintains the business's books and records. Customers are encouraged to pay cash for purchases, and when they do, they receive a 15% discount.

Overstatement of Legitimate Revenue

With this method of money laundering, illegal proceeds are added into the sales records of a legitimate business. Greg November employs this scheme at Stage One by doing the following three things:

- **Falsifying invoices.** November has his staff compute the 15% cash discount on purchases at the check-out line but has them show the full price on the sales invoice— "for bookkeeping purposes." For 1992, total legitimate cash sales as recorded on invoices amounted to $300,000. The 15% cash discount reduced actual cash receipts by $45,000, for net cash receipts of $255,000. Now November can deposit $45,000 of drug proceeds into the business's bank account to replace the discount reduction.

- **Generating phony invoices.** November generated phony sales invoices and video rental invoices totaling $65,000 and $32,000, respectively. The creation of fictitious sales involves a little more risk because it requires completely fabricating all elements of a sale rather than just modifying part of a normal sale. But apparently for November it's worth the risk. Now he can deposit an additional $97,000 in narcotics proceeds.

- **Inflating the cost of goods sold.** In 1992, the actual cost of goods sold was $260,000. November inflated this amount by $28,000 by copying, and then altering, purchase invoices.

The income statement on the next page shows the affect of November's money laundering activities on his business. The results of the activities described above can be seen in the Gross Income figure.

Stage One Records and Video
Income statement for year ending
December 31, 1992

	Without Money laundering	With Money laundering
Sales:		
Cash	$255,000	$365,000
Checks	120,000	120,000
Video rentals	52,000	84,000
Total sales	$427,000	569,000
Cost of goods sold	$260,000	$288,000
Gross income	$167,000	$281,000
Expenses:		
Salaries/wages	96,000	144,000
Supplies	6,000	10,000
Rent	36,000	36,000
Interest expense	12,000	12,000
Telephone	9,000	9,000
Consultants' fees	0	10,000
Total expenses	$159,000	$221,000
Net income	$8,000	$60,000

Overstatement of reported revenue does have one significant disadvantage; because the additional income is openly reported, the amount is taxable. Unless financial criminals want to pay a large portion of their laundered proceeds in taxes, they need to find some way to reduce their increased tax liability. They resolve this problem by overstating their legitimate business expenses.

Overstatement of Legitimate Expenses

Overstating business expenses compliments overstating revenues. Because inflated expenses, like real expenses, are tax deductible, the additional tax liability caused by inflated revenues can be reduced or eliminated. The possibilities of overstating expenses are limited only by one's imagination. Amounts can be "paid" for supplies or goods never received, fictitious consultants can be "paid" fees, nonexistent employees can be "paid" on a regular basis, and depreciation can be claimed on inflated or nonexistent assets.

By reviewing the income statement on page 301, you can see that Greg November inflated his legitimate business expenses in 1992 by $62,000. He added two of his narcotics distributors to his payroll ledger and increased his yearly salary expenses by $48,000. By withholding taxes and issuing year-end wage statements, he has provided his distributors with an apparent legitimate source of income. Throughout the year, he overpaid suppliers by $4,000 and then deposited their refund checks to the business's bank account as additional revenue from sales. The original amount paid the supplier is recorded as an expense and the canceled check is used as substantiation of the expense.

A consultant's fee of $10,000 is shown as an expense. This could be completely fictitious— maybe November paid the $10,000 to a narcotics confederate in his illegal activity or maybe he used the money to purchase a personal asset.

Greg November manipulated his business's financial activities by overstating both revenues and expenses. Not all money launderers use both methods together. Some use just one or the other. A narcotics dealer who wishes to generate a substantial amount of income to support a lavish lifestyle, may only overstate revenues. On the other hand, a money laundering front that hopes to evade taxes, would inflate only expenses.

Deposits of Cash

The third means for a legitimate business to launder money is to deposit cash proceeds generated from an illegal activity directly into business bank accounts without disguising the deposits as normal business receipts. This method cannot withstand the scrutiny of an investigator because any cash that goes into a business must come from somewhere; if not from revenues, then from loans, sales of business assets, or investments from the owners.

The deposits of cash method is used mainly to take advantage of the business's bank accounts to transfer illegal proceeds to the business transaction system. Checks can then be written on business accounts for personal living expenses, and purchase of personal assets, etc., thereby avoiding the arousal of suspicion that large amounts of currency would generate.

Indicators of Money Laundering Fronts

As you can see from our example involving Stage One Records and Video, the use of legitimate enterprises as fronts to conceal and commingle illicit dollars in a money laundering operation involves compromising accounting procedures. The illegal dollars are rarely physically mixed with the legitimate business receipts, rather, the accounting records are falsified to attribute more income or more expenses to the enterprise (and indirectly to the owners) than was actually earned or incurred.

Ideally, a money laundering store front operation would be one that:

- Deals primarily in currency
- Has relatively fixed costs
- Is exempt from bank currency reporting requirements

Historically, taverns, restaurants, movie theaters, and massage parlors have been used as "front operations" in money laundering schemes. These types of business operations provide a ready location for illicit sales and clandestine meetings. Depending on the sophistication and managerial talents of the persons involved, almost any business activity can be used for money laundering. However, businesses that are highly competitive or require substantial technical skills, are less likely to attract direct criminal involvement. The rationale for this is that it is difficult to run both a demanding business and a demanding criminal organization at the same time.

Independent indicators can be used to develop financial leads when money laundering is suspected. For example, if Stage One Records and Video had an inventory of 400 videotapes and the rental fee was $2 a day, then the monthly gross revenue should not exceed $24,000 ($400 x 2 x 30). If the store reports gross receipts of $35,000 per month, the investigator should deduce that $11,000 was coming from elsewhere. While small variations do not constitute adequate proof of fraud, large scale fraud is extremely hard to hide from this type of analysis.

The validity of certain types of expenses can be determined through the use of independent indicators. For example, the reported purchase of gasoline (a business expense) in amounts that are enough to keep a delivery service truck running for 24 hours a day all year long would obviously be suspect. The existence of fictitious employees may be independently verified by non-payroll sources of information (timecards, union records, unemployment compensation payments, and tax withholding records). Investigative findings revealing that certain sales never took place, employees on the payroll never existed, or reported inventory items are false, would provide strong indications of a money laundering operation. For the financial investigator, detection of money laundering is heavily dependent upon the quality of documentation. By using independent indicators to test the validity of reported revenue and expenses, the extent of the variation from true business-related activities can be determined.

Buy/Sell Transaction[3]

Besides using legitimate businesses as a way of moving money into the business transaction system, the manipulated buy/sell transaction can accomplish the same thing. Real estate or other types of personal property transactions can be manipulated to hide the flow of illegal proceeds and provide an apparent source of legitimate income to the financial criminal. Suppose you're buying a house that has a fair market value of $2 million. You and the seller agree that you will pay $1 million dollars for the house and pay the balance paid off the books (i.e. in currency, drugs). In this instance, the transfer from the cash transaction system to the business transaction system has been accomplished and money laundering has occurred. In principle, this type of money laundering can be used in any buy/sell transaction. Through independent appraisals or comparative sales data, the "real value" of a transaction can be discovered.

Off Shore Havens

Countries in various parts of the world have legal and/or economic climates exactly right for laundering of "dirty money." Historically, places such as the Cayman Islands, the Bahamas, Switzerland, Panama and the Netherland Antilles have been associated with hidden bank accounts, fictitious corporations, and money laundering. Even though there have been successful prosecutions, little is known about the actual operation of "laundering factories" in these "off shore" havens. Narcotics traffickers and other financial criminals frequently use financial institutions, legitimate businesses and/or front operations to move the proceeds of their illegal activity out of the country. Often, there is virtually no way to obtain documentation of these transactions once they leave the United States. Accordingly, in a money laundering investigation, it is incumbent upon the investigator to follow the flow of funds as they cross the border. The graphic on the next page highlights the common methods of moving cash into and out of the country during a money laundering operation. Each of these methods is discussed below.

Methods of Moving Money Out of the United States

- **Physical Transportation.** Illegally obtained currency is physically transported from the United States to an off shore haven in a briefcase, luggage, on a person, etc.

- **Wire Transfer.** Illegal proceeds are deposited into bank accounts in the United States in increments below $10,000, thus avoiding the filing of a Currency Transaction Report. After deposit, wire transfers are sent from the domestic bank to a bank account in an off-shore country.

- **Cashier's Check.** Currency is deposited into bank accounts (as described above) and cashier's checks are purchased. The cashier's checks are either mailed or physically transported off shore. Additionally, cashier's checks can be directly purchased in increments less than $10,000.

• **Attorneys, Accountants, and Money Managers.** Currency is given to a party such as an attorney, accountant, or money manager who deposits the currency into his or her trust account. A trust account is a bank account maintained by and under the custody and control of this party which is used for funds relating to the client's financial and/or business interests. The other party then transfers (i.e. wires, purchases cashier's checks, etc.) the funds off shore.

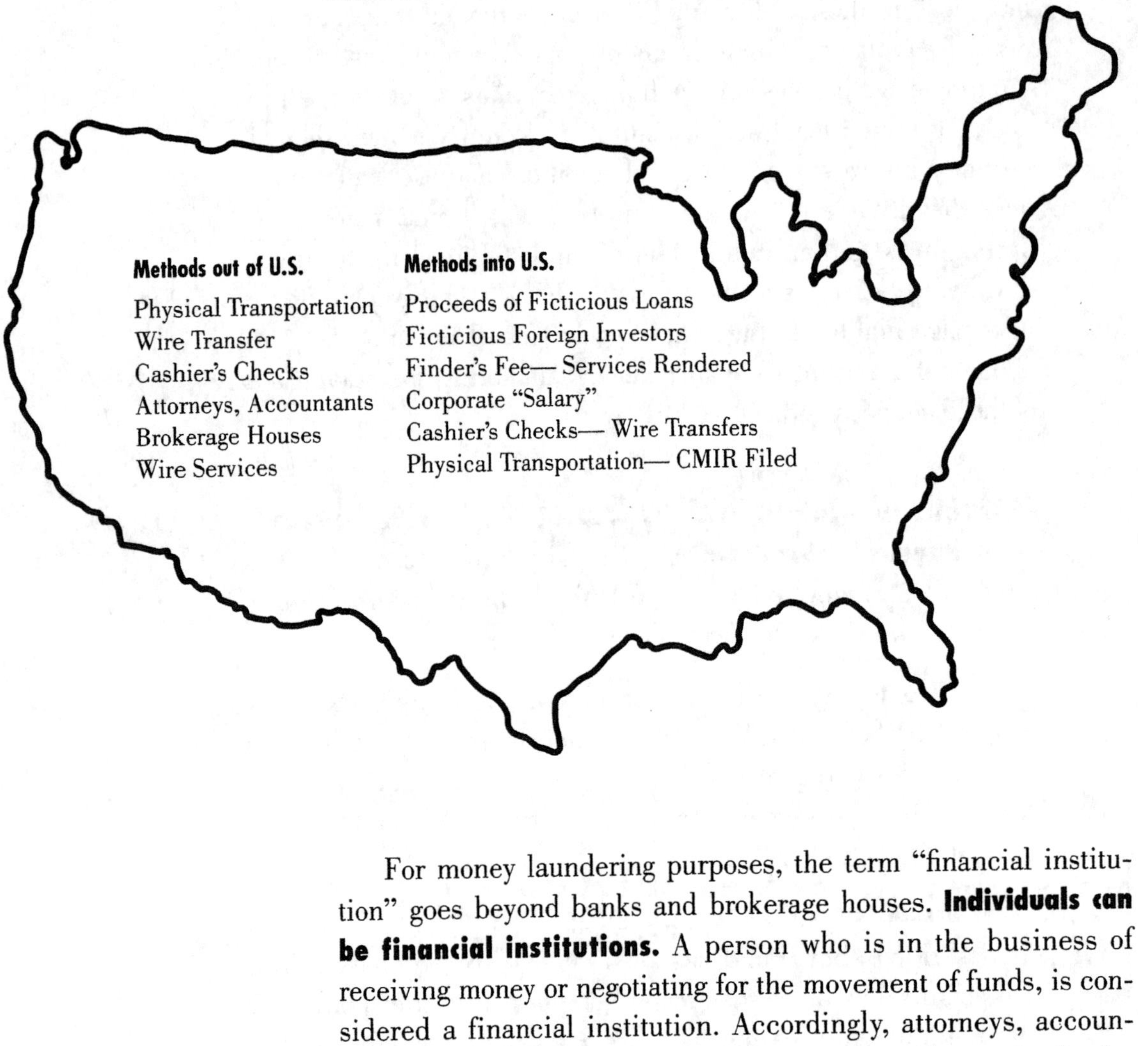

For money laundering purposes, the term "financial institution" goes beyond banks and brokerage houses. **Individuals can be financial institutions.** A person who is in the business of receiving money or negotiating for the movement of funds, is considered a financial institution. Accordingly, attorneys, accountants, money managers, and even couriers who assist in the movement of money can be considered financial institutions. As a financial institution, when currency is moved in increments of over $10,000 by an individual, he or she must file the required forms (Currency Transaction Reports, and Currency and Monetary Instrument Reports) to report the flow of funds.

- **Brokerage Accounts.** Currency, cashier's checks or fictitious business or personal checks are deposited into brokerage accounts. The subsequent withdrawals are mailed or physically transported off shore.

- **Wire Services.** Wire services (Western Union, American Express, etc.) are often used to domestically transfer funds, but can be used to move money off shore.

Western Union and other "wire service" transfers are no longer just point to point forwarding of funds. A "deposit" can be accessed by the receiving party at any domestic or foreign office of the wire service. Additionally, the sender is not required to produce identification and, by the use of passwords and/or false identification, the receiver can conceal his/her true identity. For example:

A local drug dealer, Perry Webster, needs to forward $30,000 to a supplier, Martin Sapata, in Phoenix, Arizona. Webster goes to a Western Union office, provides a fictitious name, and requests a $7,500 wire transfer to "Eddy Tucker" who will use the password "Ironwood" as an identifier. Webster goes to three other Western Union offices and repeats the procedure using different fictitious names and passwords at each office. Sapata then goes to the four different Western Union offices in Phoenix, provides the fictitious name and appropriate identifying password for each transfer and receives four drafts of $7,500 each.

Wire transfers can be difficult to trace, or even identify, and are available internationally.

Methods of Moving Money into the United States

- **Fictitious Loans.** Fictitious corporations can set up bank accounts in a foreign country. Checks are then mailed back to the United States as loans from these fictitious companies. Cashier's checks or wire transfers can also be used.

- **Fictitious Foreign Investors.** A legitimate business is formed in the United States, but fictitious "foreign investors" are used to provide capital to the enterprise. Business transaction system payments (cashier's checks, wire transfers, and business checks from fictitious companies or individuals) flow back into the country.

- **Finder's Fees.** Finder's fees or payments for services rendered are generated. These false transactions may be for locating investors for foreign businesses, negotiating real estate purchases, etc.

- **Corporate Salaries.** Corporate "salaries" are paid from fictitious off shore companies by way of corporate checks, wire transfers, or cashier's checks.

- **Cashier's Checks and Wire Transfers.** Cashier's checks and wire transfers are obtained from foreign banks and sent into the country.

- **Physical Transportation.** Physical transportation of large amounts of currency back into the United States with the appropriate Currency and Monetary Instrument Report (CMIR) being filed at the border. This isolates the incoming currency from the illegal activity that originally generated the currency.

Combinations of any of the before-mentioned methods, both going out and coming into the country, are often used in complex money laundering operations. For example, once the proceeds are in a bank account in the Cayman Islands, an electronic transfer can be made to a bank account held under a fictitious name in Panama by the Panamanian company that controls the Cayman account. From there a "loan" is made to a shell corporation in the Bahamas, which in turn "invests" in a real estate venture in the United States controlled by the financial criminal who in fact generated the illegal proceeds. Investigative problems arise when money laundering goes off shore, beyond the jurisdiction and resources of law enforcement. The key to detecting and resolving money laundering operations is documenting the flow of money prior to its leaving the United States.

Laundered funds may be left in a foreign country to be used by the criminal for foreign investments, trips abroad, or the purchase of assets. A secondary effect of international money laundering occurs when the funds are repatriated. They often come back in the form of "tax-free" sources of income. Loans, gifts and investments used to capitalize or start-up a business are nontaxable receipts and represent a nontaxable source of income to the alleged money launderer.

The investigator's most valuable asset in a money laundering investigation is information. Information is developed through informants or by the utilization of undercover and surveillance operations. Of particular importance is information concerning the movement of money through financial institutions. Once currency that is generated from an illegal activity enters the banking system, it loses its identity and becomes inseparable from other funds inside the bank. The transaction entry point (i.e. the teller window), is where currency moves into the business transaction system. It is here that the Currency Transaction Reports (Form 4789) are generated when more than $10,000 in currency is deposited, withdrawn, or exchanged. The information provided by these reports is used to detect money laundering activities. Similarly, Currency and Monetary Instrument Reports (Form 4790) are required to be filed with the U.S. Customs Service when more than $10,000 in currency or monetary instruments crosses an international border. The failure to file either of these reports is a criminal violation of the money laundering laws. Additionally, structuring transactions in such a way as to avoid the $10,000 benchmark for either the CTR or the CMIR, can be a prosecutable offense.

Money Laundering Statutes

Crimes involving money laundering made for big headlines in the 1980s and continue to do so in the 1990s. Over the years, federal statutes have been developed for use against those who launder money and/or those who assist them. Although the four money laundering statutes were listed and described in Chapter 2, it is appropriate that we revisit them here.

Title 18 U.S.C. § 1956. Laundering of Monetary Instruments

Title 18 U.S.C. § 1956 states that it is illegal to:

- Conduct or attempt to conduct a financial transaction if you know that the proceeds used in the transaction are from an illegal activity
- Take part in a transaction that is designed to conceal or disguise, in any manner, the proceeds of an illegal activity
- Transport, transmit, transfer, (or attempt to) money into or out of the United States with the intent to promote a specified unlawful activity or knowing that the money represents the proceeds of an unlawful activity
- Avoid a transaction reporting requirement or conduct a financial transaction involving property that law enforcement represents to be the proceeds of an unlawful activity

§ 1956. Laundering of monetary instruments

(a)(1) Whoever, knowing that the property involved in a financial transaction represents the proceeds of some form of unlawful activity, conducts or attempts to conduct such a financial transaction which in fact involves the proceeds of specified unlawful activity-

(A)(i) with the intent to promote the carrying on of specified unlawful activity; or

(ii) with the intent to engage in conduct constituting a violation of section 7201 or 7206 of the Internal Revenue Code of 1986; or

(B) knowing that the transaction is designed in whole or in part -

(i) to conceal or disguise the nature, the location, the sources, the ownership, or the control of the proceeds of specified unlawful activity; or

(ii) to avoid a transaction reporting requirement under State or Federal law, ...

shall be sentenced to a fine of not more than $500,000 or twice the *value of the property involved in the transaction, whichever is greater, or imprisonment for not more than twenty years or, both.*

(2) Whoever transports, transmits, or transfers, or attempts to transport, transmit, or transfer a monetary instrument or funds from a place in the United States to or through a place outside the United States or to a place in the United States from or through a place outside the United States —

(A) with the intent to promote the carrying on of specified unlawful activity; or

(B) knowing that the monetary instrument or funds involved in the transportation represent the proceeds of some form of unlawful activity and knowing that such transportation is designed in whole or in part—

(i) to conceal or disguise the nature, the location, the source, the ownership, or the control of the proceeds of specified unlawful activity; or

(ii) to avoid a transaction reporting requirement under State or Federal law...

shall be sentenced to a fine of $500,000 or twice the value of the monetary instrument or funds involved in the transportation, whichever is greater, or imprisonment for not more than twenty years, or both...

(3) Whoever, with the intent —

(A) to promote the carrying on of specified unlawful activity;

(B) to conceal or disguise the nature, location, source, ownership, or control of property believed to be the proceeds of specified unlawful activity; or

(C) to avoid a transaction reporting requirement under State or Federal law, conducts or attempts to conduct a financial transaction involving property represented by a law enforcement officer to be the proceeds of specified unlawful activity, or property used to conduct or facilitate specified unlawful activity, shall be fined under this title or imprisoned for not more than 20 years, or both.

Title 18 U.S.C. § 1957. Engaging in Monetary Transactions in Property Derived from Specified Unlawful Activity

Title 18 U.S.C. § 1957 states that it is unlawful to take part in, or attempt to take part in, monetary transactions involving criminally derived property that is of a value greater than $10,000 and is derived from a specified unlawful activity.

§ 1957. Engaging in monetary transactions in property derived from specified unlawful activity

(a) Whoever, in any of the circumstances set forth in subsection (d), knowingly engages or attempts to engage in a monetary transaction in criminally derived property that is of a value greater than $10,000 and is derived from specified unlawful activity, shall be punished as provided in subsection (b).

(b)(1) Except as provided in paragraph (2), the punishment for an offense under this section is a fine under title 18, United States Code, or imprisonment for not more than ten years or both.

Title 31 U.S.C § 5313. Reports on Domestic Coins and Currency Transactions

Financial transactions in excess of $10,000 must be reported on a Currency Transaction Report (CTR). Title 31 U.S.C. § 5313 requires that financial institutions file this report. If a person takes actions to falsely or fraudulently stop a financial institution from filing the report with the federal government, a violation of criminal law has occurred.

§ 5313. Reports on Domestic Coins and Currency Transactions

(a) When a domestic financial institution is involved in a transaction for the payment, receipt, or transfer of United States coins or currency (or other monetary instruments the Secretary of the Treasury prescribes), in an amount, denomination, or amount and denomination, or under circumstances the Secretary prescribes by regulation, the institution and any other participant in the transaction the Secretary may prescribe shall file a report on the transac-

tion at the time and in the way the Secretary prescribes. A participant acting for another person shall make the report as the agent or bailee of the person and identify the person for whom the transaction is being made...

(c)(1) A person (except a domestic financial institution designated under subsection (b) of this section) required to file a report under this section shall file the report —

(A) with the institution involved in the transaction if the institution was designated;

(B) in the way the Secretary prescribes when the institution was not designated; or

(C) with the Secretary.

(2) The Secretary shall prescribe —

(A) the filing procedure for a domestic financial institution designated under subsection (b) of this section; and

(B) the way the institution shall submit reports filed with it.

Title 31 U.S.C. § 5324. Structuring Transactions to Evade Reporting Requirement Prohibited

Title 31 U.S.C. § 5324 makes it unlawful to structure a single cache of currency over $10,000 into increments of $10,000 or less and conduct multiple transactions for the purpose of evading the CTR reporting requirements. The multiple transactions take forms such as depositing money:

- Several times at the same bank branch on the same day
- At different branches of the same bank on the same day
- At different banks on the same day
- At the same bank on different days
- At different banks on different days

Note that if the structuring occurs at the same bank on the same business day, then the bank must file a CTR if the bank has knowledge of the multiple transactions aggregating more than $10,000. If the bank files a CTR, then the launderer may still be guilty of an attempt.

§ 5324. Structuring transactions to evade reporting requirement prohibited

No person shall for the purpose of evading the reporting requirements of section 5313(a) with respect to such transaction —

(1) cause or attempt to cause a domestic financial institution to fail to file a report required under section 5313(a);

(2) cause or attempt to cause a domestic financial institution to file a report required under section 5313(a) that contains a material omission or misstatement of fact; or

(3) structure or assist in structuring, or attempt to structure or assist in structuring, any transaction with one or more domestic financial institutions.

Asset Forfeitures

The money criminals make from their financial crimes is often put toward their personal benefit. They buy cars, boats, property, clothing, etc. Fortunately for law enforcement, new and stronger laws provide the means to divest criminals of their illegal gains. This means is commonly referred to as **"forfeiture."** A forfeiture is a legal proceeding that the Government initiates against the proceeds of an illegal activity. The term **"proceeds"** is a flexible term that appears in many areas of the law and in virtually every context, the term means "whatever is received when an object is sold, exchanged, or otherwise disposed of." It does not necessarily mean just money. Each time proceeds are disposed of and exchanged for other property, the newly-acquired property becomes proceeds. In a sense, proceeds is a status that attaches to any property substituted for what was originally exchanged.

Criminal and Civil Forfeitures

In Chapter 2, you read that law can be divided into many categories. Two of these categories are criminal and civil law. Well, just like law, forfeitures can be either criminal or civil in nature. The government brings suit against the property or owner of the property and, if successful, gains right, title, and interest thereof. To initiate a forfeiture action, the government needs to show that **"probable cause"** exists. In this instance, probable cause is a belief that the property in question was either used illegally or represents the proceeds from unlawful activity. This probable cause standard is identical to the standard discussed in Chapter 9 for the issuance of search warrants.

Criminal forfeitures are imposed by Court order at the conclusion of a criminal trial or as a part of a guilty plea agreement. To impose a criminal forfeiture, *the government must prove beyond a reasonable doubt* that the property to be forfeited was either the proceeds of some illegal activity or was significantly connected to the illegal activity.

In a **civil forfeiture** proceeding, the government need only show that probable cause exists and that the property to be forfeited was involved in some illegal activity. No criminal conviction is necessary and it is up to *the individual with an interest in the property to prove,* through a preponderance of the evidence, that the government's contentions are incorrect. Should the claimant fail to present any evidence, the property is forfeited to the government. Because of this burden on the claimant rather than the government, in a civil forfeiture action the "discovery process" can be used to obtain information pertaining to the movement of money. The claimant may be deposed and the disclosure of his/her financial records compelled. Additionally, perjury and contempt sanctions are available for use by the government against untruthful or recalcitrant witnesses. These legal possibilities place the claimant in an awkward legal posture when criminal charges against him or her are pending. Asserting a Fifth Amendment Constitutional right against self-incrimination, may result in an adverse civil determination (forfeiture), while answering questions may have incriminating consequences in the criminal proceedings.

In Rem versus In Personam

The history of civil forfeiture goes back to Medieval England when in rem proceedings could be instituted against any property which had been involved in some type of wrongdoing. An **in rem** proceeding refers to a legal proceeding directed solely against property. The legal findings determine the proper ownership of the property in question. The defendant in an in rem proceeding is the object or property itself, and since in rem proceedings are limited to the determination of ownership, they do not impose personal obligations. In rem proceedings are totally independent of any criminal action against the owner.

Medieval England also had a form of criminal forfeiture. If an individual was convicted of a crime, the felon's property was forfeited to the king as a form of fine. The proceedings to establish the forfeiture action were **in personam,** against the felon, and success depended upon proving that the felon was criminally guilty. In 1790, the first Congress of the United States prohibited these "criminal" forfeitures and criminal forfeitures were unheard of in the United States for another 180 years. It wasn't until 1970 when Congress enacted the Racketeer Influenced and Corruption Organization Act (RICO) that the concept was resurrected.

Facilitation Versus Proceeds

Forfeiture laws distinguish between property which represents "proceeds" and property which "facilitates" a violation. To "facilitate" means to have a significant connection to. Federal law provides for the forfeiture of conveyances that facilitate the sale, receipt, possession, or concealment of illegal activity. Whether property can be seized and forfeited for facilitating an offense is determined by whether a significant connection exists to the prohibited activity. For example, an airplane used to move narcotics from Columbia to Chicago is closely connected to the illegal activity and could be seized and forfeited.

Federal Forfeiture Statutes

The key question in a forfeiture action, for both the investigator and the court, is not the good faith or guilty knowledge of the owner, but the <u>use</u> of the property in question and whether that use requires forfeiture under the statute. For instance, was the monetary instrument acquired in a financial transaction designed to conceal the ownership of proceeds of specific unlawful activity? Or, is a deposit in a financial institution traceable to coin or currency used in a transaction designed to evade or defeat the CTR filing requirements?

The following Federal statutes relate to forfeiture procedures:

- Title 18 U.S.C. § 981. Civil Forfeiture
- Title 18 U.S.C. § 982. Criminal Forfeiture
- Title 21 U.S.C. § 881. Forfeitures

Title 18 U.S.C. § 981. Civil Forfeiture

Title 18 U.S.C. § 981 states that the following property is subject to forfeiture:

- Property obtained, directly or indirectly, through violation of Title 18 U.S.C. § 1956 or § 1957

- Any property which represents the proceeds from the sale or distribution of a controlled substance

- Any coin, currency, or interest in property traceable to a transaction or attempted transaction in violation of Title 31 U.S.C. § 5313 or § 5324

§ 981. Civil Forfeiture

(a)(1)... the following property is subject to forfeiture to the United States:

(A) Any property, real or personal, involved in a transaction or attempted transaction in violation of section 5313(a) or 5324 of

Title 31, or of section 1956 or 1967 of this title, or any property traceable to such property.

(B) Any property within the jurisdiction of the United States, which represents the proceeds of an offense against the foreign national involving a manufacturer, "sale or distribution of a controlled substance..."

(C) Any coin and currency... or any interest in any other property, including any deposit in a financial institution, traceable to such coin or currency involved in a transaction or attempted transaction in violation of Sections 5313(a) or 5324 of Title 31 may be seized and forfeited to the United States government...

Title 18 U.S.C. § 982. Criminal Forfeiture

Title 18 U.S.C. § 982 states that a person convicted of money laundering is required to forfeit any property which resulted from the illegal activity.

§ 982. Criminal Forfeiture

(a) The Court, in imposing sentence on a person convicted of an offense under Section 1956 or 1957 (money laundering violations) of this title shall order that the person forfeit to the United States any property, real or personal, which represents the gross receipts the person obtained directly or indirectly, as a result of such offense, or which is traceable to such gross receipts.

Title 21 U.S.C. § 881. Forfeitures

Title 21 U.S.C. § 881 (see page 320) identifies items that are subject to forfeiture to the Unites States government. The items listed are associated with the manufacture and distribution of controlled substances.

Statutory Authority Versus Constitutional Standards

The authority granted by the language of a statute or the written opinions in a case law finding does not end the discussion on forfeiture proceedings. All case law and statutory authorizations must comply with Constitutional standards. A statute or legal opinion cannot authorize conduct which comes into conflict with protected Constitutional rights. Therefore, any seizure and/or subsequent forfeiture action must be in agreement with the reasonableness requirement of the Constitution's Fourth and Fifth Amendments.

For Constitutional purposes, a search results from an investigator's intrusion into an individual's "reasonable expectation of privacy" and a seizure occurs when an investigator's conduct "interferes with a person's ownership of property." The law has consistently preferred that a warrant be obtained prior to any search procedure. This legal preference for a warrant is not as great in seizure and subsequent forfeiture actions. The basis for this difference is that a seizure, the first step in a forfeiture action, when based upon probable cause is considered reasonable action under the Fourth Amendment. However, evidence obtained in violation of either Fourth Amendment or Fifth Amendment guarantees is not admissible in court. The seizure of property in "plain view" is presumed reasonable, assuming that the investigator can establish probable cause to associate the property with criminal activity.

The government's right to seize the proceeds of an illegal activity even though it interferes with the owner's Constitutional right of ownership was enacted by statute and upheld by the Supreme Court. The Supreme Court first enunciated this legal position, known as **The Doctrine of Relation,** in U. S. v. Stowell, 133 U.S. (1890).[4] In that decision, the Court indicated that when a statute provides for civil forfeiture, the forfeiture takes place at the moment the property is used or illegally generated, unless another statute provides otherwise. At that moment, all rights and legal title to the property vest in the government and any subsequent transfer is of no effect. In the eyes of the law, the subsequent judicial proceedings merely confirm a forfeiture that has, in theory, already taken place. Because the government's right to proceeds relates back to the time they are generated, it is legally entitled to all the gain thereafter accruing from the proceeds of the illegal activity.

§ 881. Forfeitures

(a) Subject property

The following shall be subject to forfeiture to the United States and no property right shall exist in them:

(1) All controlled substances which have been manufactured, distributed, dispensed, or acquired in violation of this subchapter.

(2) All raw materials, products, and equipment of any kind which are used, or intended for use, in manufacturing, compounding, processing, delivering, importing, or exporting any controlled substance in violation of this subchapter.

(3) All property which is used, or intended for use, as a container for property described in paragraph (1) or (2).

(4) All conveyances, including aircraft, vehicles, or vessels, which are used, or are intended for use, to transport, or in any manner to facilitate the transportation, sale, receipt, possession, or concealment of property described in paragraph (1) or (2), except that —

(A) no conveyance used by any person as a common carrier in the transaction of business as a common carrier shall be forfeited under the provisions of this section unless it shall appear that the owner or other person in charge of such conveyance was a consenting party or privy to a violation of this subchapter or subchapter II of this chapter; and

(B) no conveyance shall be forfeited under the provisions of this section by reason of any act or omission established by the owner thereof to have been committed or omitted by any person other than such owner while such conveyance was unlawfully in the possession of a person other than the owner in violation of the criminal laws of the United States, or of any State.

(5) All books, records, and research, including formulas, microfilm, tapes, and data which are used, or intended for use, in violation of this subchapter.

(6) All moneys, negotiable instruments, securities, or other things of value furnished or intended to be furnished by any person in exchange for a controlled substance in violation of this subchapter,

all proceeds traceable to such an exchange, and all moneys, negotiable instruments, and securities used or intended to be used to facilitate any violation of this subchapter, except that no property shall be forfeited under this paragraph, to the extent of the interest of an owner, by reason of any act or omission established by that owner to have been committed or omitted without the knowledge or consent of that owner.

(7) All real property, including any right, title, and interest in the whole of any lot of tract of land and any appurtenances or improvements, which is used, or intended to be used, in any manner or part, to commit, or to facilitate the commission of, a violation of this title punishable by more than one year's imprisonment, except that no property shall be forfeited under this paragraph, to the extent of an interest of an owner, by reason of any act or omission established by that owner to have been committed or omitted without the knowledge or consent of that owner.

(8) All controlled substances which have been possessed in violation of this subchapter.

Factors That Establish Probable Cause

The paper trail of financial events is the investigator's starting point in a forfeiture investigation. The investigator must be prepared to use techniques such as subpoenas, surveillance, and interviewing to secure financial records relative to the movement of money. The majority of forfeiture actions do not require complex document analysis. The basis for this in large part is due to the standard of proof (probable cause) necessary to start the forfeiture action and the judiciary's willingness to accept the fact that illegal activities generate illegal income. It follows then that the key to a forfeiture investigation is discovering factors that establish probable cause. The following are examples of court recognized situations that can be used by the financial investigator to establish probable cause in a forfeiture investigation.

• **Close proximity.** In situations where targeted forfeitable proceeds are found in close proximity to narcotics, probable cause can be established to support the forfeiture action. For example, in *The United States v. $33,000 United States Currency,* probable cause for forfeiture was satisfied by the following evidence:[5]

—Claimant's guilty plea to conspiracy to distribute marijuana and to evade taxes

—The seizure of $33,000 located in a brown paper bag in claimant's home

—The presence of drugs on the premises

—The claimant's lack of legitimate employment

Close proximity does not necessarily require direct physical proximity to the narcotics/contraband. In *The United States v. Brock,* the government sought forfeiture of jewelry valued at $120,000 which was found in a bag in the claimant's attic. Despite the absence of any direct evidence connecting the jewelry with the claimant's narcotic's activity, the Court of Appeals concluded probable cause was present and sufficient to support the forfeiture action. The court felt that[6] —

> *The circumstances were sufficient to warrant a conclusion that there was no other way that Brock could have acquired the jewelry other than... as proceeds of the alleged narcotics violation. The jewelry was found secreted in the same house as the narcotics and paraphernalia for distribution of narcotics. In addition, a large quantity of cash and a loaded revolver, further suggestive of ongoing narcotics activity, were seized at the house. These circumstances fairly lead to an inference that the jewelry was the proceeds of narcotics activity... circumstantial evidence and inferences therefrom are good grounds for a finding of probable cause in a forfeiture proceeding. . .*

• **Means of support.** In situations where there appear to be obvious discrepancies between the claimant's lifestyle and his or her apparent means of support, probable cause for a forfeiture action can be established. In particular, substantial currency expenditures, without apparent legitimate employment, has proven to be extremely probative (supplying evidence or proof).

- **Pre-trial statements.** Statements made to associates or to undercover agents during the investigative stages of a criminal prosecution can result in probable cause to establish a forfeiture action. For example, in *The United States v. A Single-Family Residence,* testimony from several co-conspirators established that the trafficker had told them narcotics proceeds had been used to buy the property.[7]

- **Narcotics records.** Records of narcotics sales can provide the basis for probable cause in a forfeiture investigation. By reporting the "profits earned," investigators can show the illegal proceeds generated from drug dealing. During the investigative process, the claimant's effort to conceal or commingle his or her illegal funds with legitimate sources of income and/or his or her evasive testimony can be important factors in the establishment of probable cause.

Summary

Money laundering is the process by which one conceals the existence, illegal source, or illegal application of income and then disguises that income to make it appear legitimate. There are two basic transaction systems money launderers work with: the cash transaction system and the business transaction system. The goal of the money launderer is to move from the cash transaction system to the business transaction system. The goal of the investigator is to spot this movement and halt the laundering operation.

There are three basic methods available to launder money: through legitimate businesses, buy/sell transactions, and off shore havens. Legitimate businesses launder money by overstating legitimate revenue and expenses, or by depositing currency into business accounts. Buy/sell transactions are manipulated financial transactions that use an apparent legitimate purchase or sale of an asset to transfer currency into the business transaction system. Off shore havens are used by criminals to hide their illegal proceeds.

Asset forfeiture continues to hold great potential for attacking large-scale financial crimes. By using the benefits of civil discovery and the lower burden of proof, law enforcement has an opportunity to strike at the profits generated by financial crimes. Existing case law demonstrates that forfeitures can be accomplished through modes of proof that are relatively straight forward when tracing the flow of funds from illegal activity. Even beyond that, indirect methods of tracing the movement of money may offer new means for reaching the proceeds of illegal activity and bankrupting complex financial criminal enterprises thereby putting them out of business.

Questions and Exercises

Answer the following questions and then check your responses with those provided at the back of the book.

1. What is the difference between the cash transaction system and the business transaction system?

2. List three characteristics of a business used for money laundering.

3. What affect does overstating its legitimate revenue have on a business? How is this affect counteracted?

4. Suppose you were going to purchase a $20,000 car from a friend. Explain how you could use a buy/sell transaction to launder money.

5. List three methods used to move U.S. currency into and three methods used to move currency out of the United States.

6. What is meant by "structuring" financial transactions? Identify three ways a criminal can structure transactions.

7. What are the "proceeds" of a crime?

8. Describe the burden of proof as it relates to civil and criminal forfeitures.

9. Explain what is meant by the following statement:

The car he owned "facilitated" his ability to sell narcotics; therefore, it is subject to forfeiture.

10. In Chapter 8, you read about the methods of indirect proof. What role would these methods play in establishing probable cause for forfeiture of assets?

Endnotes

1 "Laundering Drug Money: Whitewash— or Crackdown?", Economist, (Volume 310, Issue 7592, March 4, 1989), p. 76

2 President's Commission on Organized Crime, *The Cash Connection,* (U.S. Government Printing Office, October 1986), p. vii

3 Joseph T. Wells, W. Steve Albrecht, Jack Bologna, Gilbert Geis, and Jack Robertson, *Fraud Examiner's Manual,* (National Association of Certified Fraud Examiner's), 1989, Section 111, p. 69

4 U.S. v. Stowell, 133 U.S. (1890)

5 U.S. v. $33,000 United States Currency, 640 F. Supp. 899-900 (D.Md. 1986)

6 U.S. v. Brock, 747 F. 2d 761, 762-63 (D.C. Cir 1984)

7 U.S. v. A Single Family Residence, 803 F 2d 625 (11th Cir. 1986)

Responses to End-of-Chapter Questions

Chapter 2

1 Civil law deals with private conflicts and differences between individuals, whereas criminal law deals with public wrongs against the state. Remedies for violations of civil law are usually in the form of money damages or court-ordered actions to do, or refrain from doing, certain specific things. Remedies for violations of criminal law include fines, penalties, and/or incarceration.

2 A felony is a more serious crime than a misdemeanor. Felonies are punishable by incarceration of more than one year, a fine, and loss of certain civil rights. Misdemeanors are punishable by fines and/or incarceration of less than one year.

3 An offense that is "mala prohibita" is an offense made criminal by statute, whereas an offense that is "mala in se" is an offense that is evil in and of itself.

4 a. Jerry Wilson has conspired with a drug dealer to allow his clothing store to be used to launder drug money. The statutes violated and their corresponding elements are as follows:

1) Title 18 U.S.C. § 371. Conspiracy to commit offense or to defraud the United States

- The conspiracy was willfully formed
- The suspect willfully became a member of the conspiracy
- At least one of the conspirators knowingly committed at least one overt act in furtherance of the conspiracy

2) Title 18 U.S.C. § 1956. Laundering of monetary instruments

- The suspect must conduct or attempt to conduct a "financial transaction"
- The suspect must know that the property involved in the transaction represents the proceeds of some form of unlawful activity
- The transaction must involve property which, in fact, represents the proceeds of "specified unlawful activity"
- The suspect must engage in the transaction with either —

—the intent of promoting the carrying on of the "specified unlawful activity," or

—the intent to engage in conduct constituting tax evasion under Title 26 U.S.C. § 7201 or tax fraud under Title 26 U.S.C. § 7206, or

—knowledge that the purpose of the transaction, in whole or in part, was either to conceal or disguise the nature, location, source, ownership, or control of the proceeds of "specified unlawful activity;" or to avoid a transaction reporting requirement under State or Federal law

b. Troy Avery is using his position with the Navy to threaten another employee into doing something. Avery is committing extortion in violation of Title 18 U.S.C. § 872, extortion by officers or employees of the United States. Elements of the crime include the following:

- Intent
- The suspect is an officer or employee of United States government
- The suspect used his or her employment with government as part of the extortion scheme
- Extortion is committed or attempted

c. Since Jenny is using an 800 number to further her scheme to defraud, she is committing wire fraud in violation of Title 18

U.S.C. § 1343, fraud by wire, radio, or television. Elements of the crime include the following:

- Intent
- Scheme to defraud
- Use of interstate communications to further scheme

d. David Stevens is a bank employee who is using his position with the bank to commit embezzlement and bank fraud. The statutes violated and their corresponding elements are as follows:

1) Title 18 U.S.C. § 656. Theft, embezzlement, or misapplication by bank officer or employee

- Intent
- The suspect is a bank employee or officer
- The suspect attempted to defraud the bank

2) Title 18 U.S.C. § 1344. Bank fraud

- Intent
- Scheme to defraud a financial institution

e. Linda Carson is threatening to use the fact that her competitor is involved in a criminal activity to get that person to do something against his or her will. Linda is committing blackmail in violation of Title 18 U.S.C. § 873. Elements of the crime include the following:

- Intent
- The suspect made threats

f. Susan Tompkins is in violation of Title 26 U.S.C. § 7203, Willful failure to file return, supply information, or pay tax. Elements of the crime include the following:

- Duty to pay
- Failure to pay
- Willfulness

5 Lance Gordon is intentionally structuring his financial transactions so that the financial institutions he is dealing with do not file Currency Transaction Reports. The money involved happens to be from an illegal activity, therefore, Lance is in violation of Title 31 U.S.C. 5324, Structuring transactions to evade reporting requirement prohibited.

Chapter 3

1 a. 16 to 23 people "sit" on a federal grand jury.

b. It takes 12 jurors to return an indictment.

2 If a witness is granted transactional immunity, he or she cannot be prosecuted for any criminal offenses about which he or she testifies during grand jury proceedings. The witness could admit to murder and drug trafficking, and not be prosecuted for them.

If a witness is granted use immunity, the testimony that the witness provides cannot be used in prosecutions against the witness. For example, a witness testifies that she forged checks in order to get cash to buy drugs. If that witness is brought up on drug charges, that testimony cannot be used against her.

Transactional immunity is rarely used. If immunity is offered, it is more likely to be use immunity.

3 Evidence is anything that can make a person believe that a fact or proposition is true or false.

4 Proof is the result of evidence.

5 In criminal cases, the standard of proof is "beyond a reasonable doubt;" in most civil cases the standard is "preponderance of evidence." "Beyond a reasonable doubt" is a greater degree of proof than is "preponderance of evidence." To reach a conviction in a criminal case, each juror must have no doubt that, based on the evidence presented, the accused committed the crime. Verdicts in civil cases where the preponderance of evidence is the standard of proof, are reached by the jurors weighing the evidence presented and deciding who they believe, the plaintiff or the defendant.

6 Use of mails to further scheme— Direct evidence could be an item of mail received by a victim of the fraud that was sent by the suspect to perpetuate the fraud. Circumstantial evidence could be testimony from a postal employee who assisted the suspect in matters related to the mailing.

7 Judicial notice is when a judge allows a known fact to be admitted as evidence. Examples of judicial notice include: George Washington was our first president; May 2, 1993 falls on a Saturday; and a financial depression occurred in America in 1931.

8 According to Rule 401, evidence must be relevant and competent. A fact presented as evidence must, in some logical way, relate to proving the case. If you are trying to prove that the suspect committed bank fraud, you're not going to submit as evidence testimony stating that the suspect washed his car every Sunday morning. It's not relevant. And you've got to make sure that the relevant evidence is provided by a competent person. Testimony provided by a former spouse with an ax to grind may not come off as very convincing.

9 a. Kay White can, if she chooses to (she has testimonial privilege), provide the testimony because it is not a confidential communication since it occurred before she and Todd were married.

b. Again, Kay can, if she chooses, provide the testimony. In this instance she'd testify to something she saw, not something that was said.

c. This testimony is covered by the confidential communication privilege. Kay can provide it only if Todd consents to the testimony.

d. Joey can provide the testimony since there is no parent/child communications privilege.

e. Leon Norton can provide the testimony since the Federal courts do not recognize an accountant/client communications privilege.

f. Kent Parks can provide the testimony since it deals with an event rather than a communication.

10 Hearsay evidence is inadmissible because when one person repeats what another has said, there is room for distortion and misunderstanding.

11 The shop book rule allows that a person who currently is the "custodian" of a business's books can introduce the books and provide testimony about them even though that person did not make the original entries.

12 The terms "best evidence" and "secondary evidence" apply to documentary evidence. If evidence concerning a document is needed, the "best evidence" is the document itself. If the original has been destroyed or is not attainable even through the use of a search warrant or subpoena, an authenticated copy of the document can be used. "Secondary evidence" is used when an original of the document in question is unavailable. A witness can testify to the contents of the document or a copy of the document.

Chapter 4

1 According to the table in Appendix A, a social security number that begins with the numbers "421," is issued in the state of Alabama.

2 a. To discover if any complaints have been lodged against Base Ball, Inc., you should contact the Better Business Bureau that serves the area where the company is located.

b. To obtain a list of businesses in the Raleigh, North Carolina area, you should contact the Chamber of Commerce that serves the area.

3 a. If you want information concerning a suspect's use of his or her American Express Card, you can contact the American Express Company in New York City.

b. By analyzing a suspect's credit card activity you can find out all sorts of things. Has the suspect made any major purchases using the credit card? If the suspect used the card on a trip, you can track where the suspect went as well as what the suspect purchased. Did the suspect use the credit card to get a cash advance? How does the suspect pay off what he or she owes on the credit card? These are just some of the things that an investigator can discover about a suspect when analyzing the suspect's credit card activity.

4 The following factors come into play when selecting a suspect to target for investigation:

- Available law enforcement resources
- Probability of obtaining a conviction
- Jury appeal
- Judicial interpretations of the law

5 The best source of information concerning a suspect is the suspect. Suspects know what really happened and can easily provide, if they choose, information and documents to assist the investigator.

6 The Immigration and Naturalization Service and the U.S. District Court maintain information concerning aliens and naturalized citizens.

7 The U.S. Secret Service maintains records pertaining to forgery.

8 The FBI maintains the National Stolen Property Index.

Chapter 5

1 The check provides the following information:

- Owner of the account is Allison Henderson. She lives in Rockville, Maryland, at 923 Prospect Lane.
- The payee is Hankinson's Automotive. Apparently, Allison took her car in for a tune up and paid for it on June 8, 1992.

- Allison's checking account number is 084931121.
- The first part of the ABA transit number, "68," tells us that the Capital Bank and Trust is located in Virginia.
- The second part of the ABA transit number tells us that the code for the Capital Bank and Trust is "999."
- The number "561" is the check routing symbol. The "5" means that the Capital Bank and Trust is located in the fifth Federal Reserve district (Richmond). The "6" corresponds to the federal reserve facility that collected the check and the "1" indicates a deferred payment.

2 Check spread analysis is a useful investigative tool because it reveals a suspect's pattern of financial activity. A break in the pattern is cause for further investigation, for example, if a usual monthly payment (mortgage, rent, phone, electric, etc.) is absent, the investigator will want to see how the suspect made the payment.

3. A safe-deposit box rental agreement and entry log are available. The rental agreement will show who rented the box and on what date. The entry log shows the date and times of visits to the box and who made them. Bank records do not reveal the contents of the box.

4 Banks are required to retain the following records for 5 years:

- The signature card filled out when the account was opened
- Bank statements disclosing all deposits and withdrawals
- Copies of both sides of customer checks

5 It is difficult to trace currency-for-currency transactions because they seldom leave a paper trail inside the bank unless the transaction is in excess of $10,000. Transactions of $10,000 or more must be recorded on a Currency Transaction Report.

6 An investigator can ask suspects for their bank records or for permission to get them from the bank. If a suspect is uncooperative, it becomes a bit more difficult for the investigator

because the Bank Secrecy Act and the Right To Financial Privacy Provisions of Federal law cause banks to restrict access to a customer's records. However, banks can be legally compelled to provide records.

7 A haven country is a country that offers a legal and/or economic climate for laundering money or hiding illegally gotten profits. It is difficult for an investigator to gain access to information concerning money sent to a haven country via a wire transfer.

8 A loan application is good source of financial information because a suspect, wanting to get the loan approved, will identify assets and other accounts to impress the person who reviews to application.

9 The documentation surrounding a Western Union money order will identify who purchased the money order, who received it, and the money order's worth.

A casino can provide bank statements, loan applications, credit card applications, and other financial information. Casinos are also required to file reports on currency transactions in excess of $10,000.

10 a. Securities are stocks and bonds whereas commodities are produced goods, such as grain, livestock, gold, or timber.

b. A stock represents ownership in a corporation, that is a claim against the corporations assets and earnings. A bond is issued when a corporation or governmental unit wishes to borrow money for some period. Stockholders can sell their shares of stock at any time, and receive a profit or loss based on the relationship of the purchase price to the selling price. Bondholders can collect on their investment only at a specified time.

c. Common stock are units of ownership that allow owners to receive dividends on their holdings and vote on matters affecting the corporation in which they own stock. If a stockholder owns preferred stock, he or she will be paid dividends before common stockholders, however, preferred stock does not ordinarily carry voting rights. If a corporation is authorized to issue only one class of stock, it is common stock that is authorized.

d. Transfer agents keep a record of a corporation's outstanding stock certificates. A transfer agent is usually a commercial bank appointed by the corporation. A registrar double checks the actions of the transfer agent to prevent improper issue of stock or fraudulent transfer.

e. A corporate bond is a registered bond issued by a private corporation. A municipal bond is an obligation of a state, county, municipality or any agency thereof. All municipal bonds issued after July 1, 1983, are registered. The interest on a municipal bond is free from Federal taxes.

f. Treasury bills are short term securities with maturities of one year or less. They do not pay a fixed rate of interest and are issued and subsequently traded at a discount from face value. Treasury bills are issued in minimum denominations of $10,000, with $5,000 increments. Treasury bonds are long-term bonds with maturities of 10 years or longer. They carry a fixed interest rate and are issued and traded as a percentage of their face value. Their minimum denomination is $1,000.

g. Securities held in the name of the account holder simply reflect the name of the customer who maintains the account. Securities held in a street name are registered in the name of the owner's broker.

11 An investigator will probably want to pursue the following:

a. Check 183, written for $2000.

b. Check 187, written for $5,000. Both checks 183 and 184 are significantly higher than the next highest payment ($745).

c. The $5,000 deposit on June 10. All other deposits to the account are the same amount and deposited at the same time in each month.

d. No check was written in the amount of $745 in July. Mr. Davids has plenty of money to make the payment. Maybe he forgot. Maybe he paid in cash.

12 Both of the deposit slips show that currency was deposited. The total amount deposited equals $13,500. Had all of the currency been deposited into one account, the bank would have had to file a Currency Transaction Report (CTR). Since the deposits are into two different accounts owned by the same person, it looks like that person may have split the deposit to avoid having to have a CTR filed.

13 The brokerage account statement reveals that Nancy Garrity bought, sold, and received stock during July 1992. She made a $256.25 profit on her Lakewood, Inc. stock. Unless other account statements are available for analysis, an investigator cannot determine if Nancy's brokerage activities for July 1992 are unusual.

Chapter 6

1 In a proprietorship, the owner of the business is responsible for all debts incurred. In a partnership, the partners are personally responsible for the business's debts. Since a corporation is a legal entity in and of itself, it is responsible for its debts, not its owners (stockholders).

2 A corporation's Articles of Incorporation and a partnership's Articles of Partnership are important to the financial investigator because of the information they provide. Each of these documents provides personal and financial information relating to those involved in the start up of the business.

3 A liability is a claim on an asset by a creditor. An asset is something of value owned by a business and the owner's equity is the amount of capital furnished by a business's owner(s).

4 Based on the equation A = L + OE, and given that assets equals $675,325 and owner's equity is $276,580, it follows that liabilities equals $398,745.

5 Accounting is able to show, in summary form, the results of a business's financial transactions through financial records such as journals, ledgers, balances sheets, and income statements.

6 A balance sheet represents a business's condition at the moment the document is prepared. One prepared on Monday will differ from one prepared on Tuesday, etc. This is because Monday's transactions that affect balance sheet accounts will differ from Tuesday's transactions, and so on.

7 The following journal entry:

Cash	10,000	
Accounts Receivable		10,000

describes a financial transaction. An asset, cash, has increased by $10,000. Another asset, accounts receivable, has decreased accordingly. The journal entry indicates that $10,000 that was owed to a business through the extension of credit (accounts receivable) has been paid in cash.

8

Cash	
10,000	

Accounts Receivable	
	10,000

9

Collier Company
Balance sheet
December 18, 1992

Current Assets		**Current Liabilities**	
Cash	$ 1,000	Accounts Payable	$25,000
Inventory	40,000	Notes Payable	6,000
Total current assets	$41,000	Total Current Liabilities	$31,000
Fixed Assets		**Owner's Equity**	
Equipment	$15,000	Capital from stock	$25,000
Total assets	$56,000	Total Liabilities and Equity	$56,000

10

Gollier Company

General Journal

Date 1992	Accounts and Explanations	Ledger Folio	Debit	Credit
12/12	Cash		25,000	
	Capital			25,000
	Stock sale			
12/14	Equipment		12,000	
	Cash			6,000
	Notes payable			6,000
	Bought machine			
12/15	Inventory		40,000	
	Cash			15,000
	Accounts Payable			25,000
	Bought production materials			
12/16	Equipment		3,000	
	Cash			3,000
	Bought machine			

11

Cash

Date	Debit	Date	Credit
12/12	25,000	12/14	6,000
		12/15	15,000
		12/16	3,000

Capital

Date	Debit	Date	Credit
		12/12	25,000

Equipment

Date	Debit	Date	Credit
12/14	12,000		
12/16	3,000		

Inventory

Date	Debit	Date	Credit
12/14	40,000		

Accounts Payable

Date	Debit	Date	Credit
		12/15	25,000

Notes Payable

Date	Debit	Date	Credit
		12/14	6,000

12

Pratt, Inc.
Income statement
For the year ended December 31, 1992

Sales revenue		$155,000
Less: sales returns and allowances		5,000
Net sales		$150,000
Less: cost of goods sold		30,000
Gross profit		$120,000
Less: Administrative expenses	100,000	
Interest expense	10,000	
Selling expense	5,000	
Total operating expenses		115,000
Net income		5,000

13 A financial investigator can use accounting skills to evaluate the appropri-ateness of journal and ledger entries. By knowing how transactions are to be recorded and summarized, the financial investigator is better able to trace the impact of a transaction on a business.

Chapter 7

1 With the specific item method, the investigator tries to find a direct link between a suspect and a specific financial transaction involving the payment or receipt of illegal funds. Once discovered, this direct link is very difficult for the suspect to deny.

2 Bank account information is the type of information most useful in a fictitious payable scheme.

3 An investigator will want to look into an employee's travel expenses because travel expense reimbursements may be padded to generate illicit funds.

4 The following is in example of an overbilling scheme:

Company A buys a service from Company B for $2,500. Instead of writing Company B a check for $2,500, Company A writes a check for $3,500. Company B returns the extra $1,000, in cash, to Company A.

5 Illicit payments via currency are indicated by:

- Unexplained or unusual currency disbursements or withdrawals, particularly from a business which does not normally deal in currency
- Matching the payor's currency withdrawals to the recipient's corresponding currency deposits, expenditures, or visits to a safe deposit box
- The purchase of a cashier's check or a wire transfer made payable to the recipient at or shortly after cash withdrawals or disbursements by the payor

6 Each month, two checks are written to Lopez Electronics. In each instance, the second check is 10% of the first. This may indicate some type of kickback scheme.

7 Checks written to a business are usually deposited into an account at a financial institution. An investigator should become suspicious if too many checks are cashed out instead of being deposited.

8 Situations involving backup documentation that should make an investigator suspicious include the following:

- The absence of documentation to support a particular payment
- Discrepancies between the payment information and the backup documentation
- Coincidences in the backup documentation
- Unnumbered or sequentially unusual invoices
- Alterations or photocopies of backup documentation

Chapter 8

1 Indirect methods of proof are most useful when the suspect is taking currency or other payments that cannot be directly traced.

2 The base year becomes the point of comparison for subsequent years' net worth changes. If the base year findings come into question once the net worth analysis is complete, the entire analysis is in doubt and must be recalculated.

3 Looking at the expenditures method formula, it becomes clear that if the "known sources of funds" is understated, the "funds from unknown sources" will be overstated. For example, if "total expenditures" equals $50,000 and "known sources of funds" is $45,000, then "funds from unknown sources" equals $5,000. But if "total expenditures" equals $50,000 and "known sources of funds" is underestimated at $43,000, then "funds from unknown sources" becomes overstated at $7,000.

4 Both the net worth and expenditures methods look at a suspect's sources of funds, expenditures, assets, and liabilities. However, in the net worth method, the absolute amount of an item is considered whereas the expenditures method considers the net effect, not the absolute. For example, data shows that in the base year the suspect owned $500 worth of jewelry and in Year 1, she owned $1,000 worth. In the net worth analysis, the amount of jewelry owned in Year 1 would be listed as $1,000— the absolute amount owned. In the expenditures method, Year 1 would show $500 worth of jewelry— the difference between Year 1 and the base year. With the expenditures method, only the year-to-year increase and decreases in a suspect's assets and liabilities are considered.

5 With the specific item method, an investigator is looking for a specific financial transaction to link to a suspect. This link is a direct one— one to the point at issue— and cannot easily be denied by the suspect. The indirect methods, on the other hand, imply that a suspect's expenses exceed his or her known sources of income (funds). They cannot prove where the additional monies came from.

6. __E__ a. Suspect has a bank account balance of $1,300 on January 1, 1991, and $1,600 on December 31, 1991.

__E__ b. Suspect's mortgage decreased from $27,500 to $25,200 during the year.

__S__ c. Suspect's beginning inventory was $52,000 and ending inventory was $38,000.

__S__ d. Suspect sold stock costing $5,000 for $8,000.

__E__ e. Suspect paid $13,250 for a new car.

__S__ f. Suspect embezzled $40,000 from his employer.

__S__ g. Suspect took out a $50,000 loan to purchase a boat.

__E__ h. Suspect donated $10,000 to the University of Higher Education.

7 Net Worth Problem Solution

	1991	1992	1993
Assets			
Cash-on-hand	$ 1,000	$ 0	$ 0
Checking account	4,000	9,000	2,000
Jewelry	0	25,100	25,100
Mink coat	0	0	15,900
Car	25,000	25,000	25,000
Boat	0	0	24,000
Residence	130,000	130,000	130,000
Pool	0	20,000	20,000
Total assets	$160,000	$209,100	$242,000
Minus:			
Liabilities			
Loan- pool	$ 0	$ 7,000	$ 1,000
Mortgage- residence	98,000	96,500	94,500
Loan- finance company	5,000	5,000	5,000
Total liabilities	103,000	108,500	100,500
Equals: Net worth	$57,000	$100,600	$141,500
Minus: Prior year's net worth		57,000	100,600
Equals: Net worth increase		43,600	40,900
Plus: Known expenses			
Mortgage interest		10,500	10,000
Real estate taxes		1,500	1,500
Apartment rental		18,000	18,000
Lease payments - car		3,600	3,600
Vacation		0	12,000
Total known expenses		$77,200	$86,000
Minus: Funds from known sources			
Net Profit - flower shop		40,000	45,000
Equals: Funds from unknown sources		$37,200	$41,000

8 Expenditures Method Solution

	1992	1993
Expenditures		
Increase in bank account	$ 5,000	$ 0
Purchase of jewelry	25,100	0
Purchase of mink coat	0	15,900
Purchase of boat	0	24,000
Downpayment - pool	10,000	0
Pool loan repayments	3,000	6,000
Mortgage repayments	12,000	12,000
Real estate taxes	1,500	1,500
Apartment rental payments	18,000	18,000
Lease payments - car	3,600	3,600
Vacation	0	12,000
Total expenditures	$78,200	$93,000
Minus: Known sources of funds		
Cash-on-hand	$ 1,000	$ 0
Bank account decrease	0	7,000
Net profit - flower shop	40,000	45,000
Total known sources of funds	41,000	52,000
Equals: Funds from unknown sources	$37,200	$41,000

9 Bank Deposit Solution

		1992		1993
Total deposits		$30,000		$25,000
Minus: Transfers and redeposits		0		0
Equals: Net deposits		$30,000		$25,000
Outlays:				
Jewelry purchase	$25,100		$ 0	
Mink coat purchase	0		15,900	
Boat purchase	0		24,000	
Downpayment - pool	10,000		0	
Pool loan repayments	3,000		6,000	
Mortgage repayments	12,000		12,000	
Real estate taxes	1,500		1,500	
Apartment rental payments	18,000		18,000	
Lease payments— car	3,600		3,600	
Vacation	0		12,000	
Total outlays	$73,200		$93,000	
Minus: Net bank disbursements	25,000		32,000	
Equals: Cash expenditures	$48,200		$61,000	
Plus: Cash disbursements		48,200		61,000
Equals: Total receipts (income)		$78,200		$86,000
Minus: funds from known sources	1,000		0	
Cash-on-hand	40,000		45,000	
Net Profit— Flower shop total known sources	$41,000		$45,000	
Minus: Known sources		41,000		45,000
Equals: Funds from unknown sources		$37,200		$41,000

Chapter 9

1 A financial interview is conducted to obtain information and documentation from a witness. A financial interrogation is conducted for a different purpose. Its purpose is to elicit confessions or admissions of culpability from suspects or hostile witnesses.

2 Many investigative interviews focus on the recollection of witnesses. Questions such as "Do you remember seeing any suspicious cars in the neighborhood? or What color jacket was he wearing? are asked. Financial interviews go beyond recollection questions and deal with the specific details of financial transactions and the movement of money.

3 When planning interviews, an investigator should consider the following:

- Who should I interview?
- In what order should I interview the witnesses?
- What type of witness is this person going to be?
- Should I contact the suspect?
- When should I contact the suspect?
- What method of questioning should I use?

4 There are three general methods of questioning an investigator can use during a financial interview:

- The chronological method
- Questioning according to documents
- Questioning according to transactions or events

With the chronological method of questioning, a witness is questioned about the events in the order that they occurred, from beginning to end. With questioning according to documents, a particular document (financial statement, canceled check, tax return) is the focus of the interview. When questioning according to transaction or event, questions focus on a particular situation.

5 The introduction is critical as it sets the tone for the whole interview. Its primary objective is to put the witness at ease and get him or her to agree to answer questions.

6 To get hesitant witnesses to agree to cooperate, and investigator must avoid coming across as a threat. He or she should try to lead witnesses to believe that they will benefit from cooperating with the investigator.

7 An investigator must actively participate in the interview process. He or she must constantly analyze responses, and continually check for inconsistencies, inaccuracies, and incompleteness. Also, investigators must attend to what witnesses do during an interview. The visual and non-verbal aspects of an interview are very important.

8 The sentence is negatively phrased, and so long and complex that no one is going to understand it. Investigators should avoid asking complex and negatively phrased questions. All questions should be simple, to the point, and positively phrased.

9 The final question an investigator should ask is: "Is there anything else that you would like to say?" It gives the witness one final chance to say anything that he or she wishes.

10 The major advantage of the question and answer statement is that it contains all of the questions asked and answers provided during an interview. Of course, this could be viewed as a disadvantage also. The statement will be long, unedited, and could contain unnecessary material. On the other hand, the memorandum is more informal and it contains all pertinent testimony obtained during the interview. However, the testimony is recorded as the investigator recalls after refreshing his or her memory through informal notes. The memorandum does not contain the exact words of the witness. Both the memorandum and question and answer statement are good methods for recording an interview. The choice the investigator makes should be based on the complexity and investigative importance of the interview.

11 By allowing the affiant to create the affidavit, the investigator ensures that the affidavit will be in the affiant's own words and the credibility of the affidavit will increase because it is in the affiant's own handwriting. It would be difficult for the affiant to later deny the affidavit was his or hers.

Chapter 10

1 If an investigator seizes evidence from a suspect's home or office without first obtaining a search warrant, the evidence collected could be ruled inadmissible.

2 Probable cause means that, based on the facts presented and the experience of the investigator, a reasonable person would think that the evidence sought exists in the place to be searched. Probable cause is shown via an affidavit.

3 a. Affiant's experience

b. Detailed account of criminal activity

c. Description of place(s) to be searched

d. Financial evidence

e. Items to be seized

f. Conclusions based on the affiant's expertise*

4 The statement supports two types of information that must be in an affidavit. The statement— *While going through the trash left for garbage collection at 34 Tremont Avenue, I found an electric and phone bill addressed to John Winkler of that address*— shows that the suspect exercises dominion and control over 34 Tremont Avenue, the place you want to search. The second statement— *I also found a bill from Haggler's Electronic Store indicating that Winkler recently bought $2,435 worth of stereo and video recording equipment*— is financial evidence of a major expenditure and asset purchase.

5 A document examiner could perform handwriting analysis to determine the authenticity of the signatures on the contract, could determine whose typewriter was used to create the contract, and could analyze the paper to see if it's the same type of paper used in the creation of contracts in Mr. Friday's office.

6 Undercover operation objectives could include:

- Identifying persons on the basketball team and outside the team who may be involved in the point-shaving activities
- Obtaining probable cause for search and arrest warrants
- Gathering information and documents relative to the investigation
- Obtaining information and leads to purchases and expenditures made by members of the basketball team

7

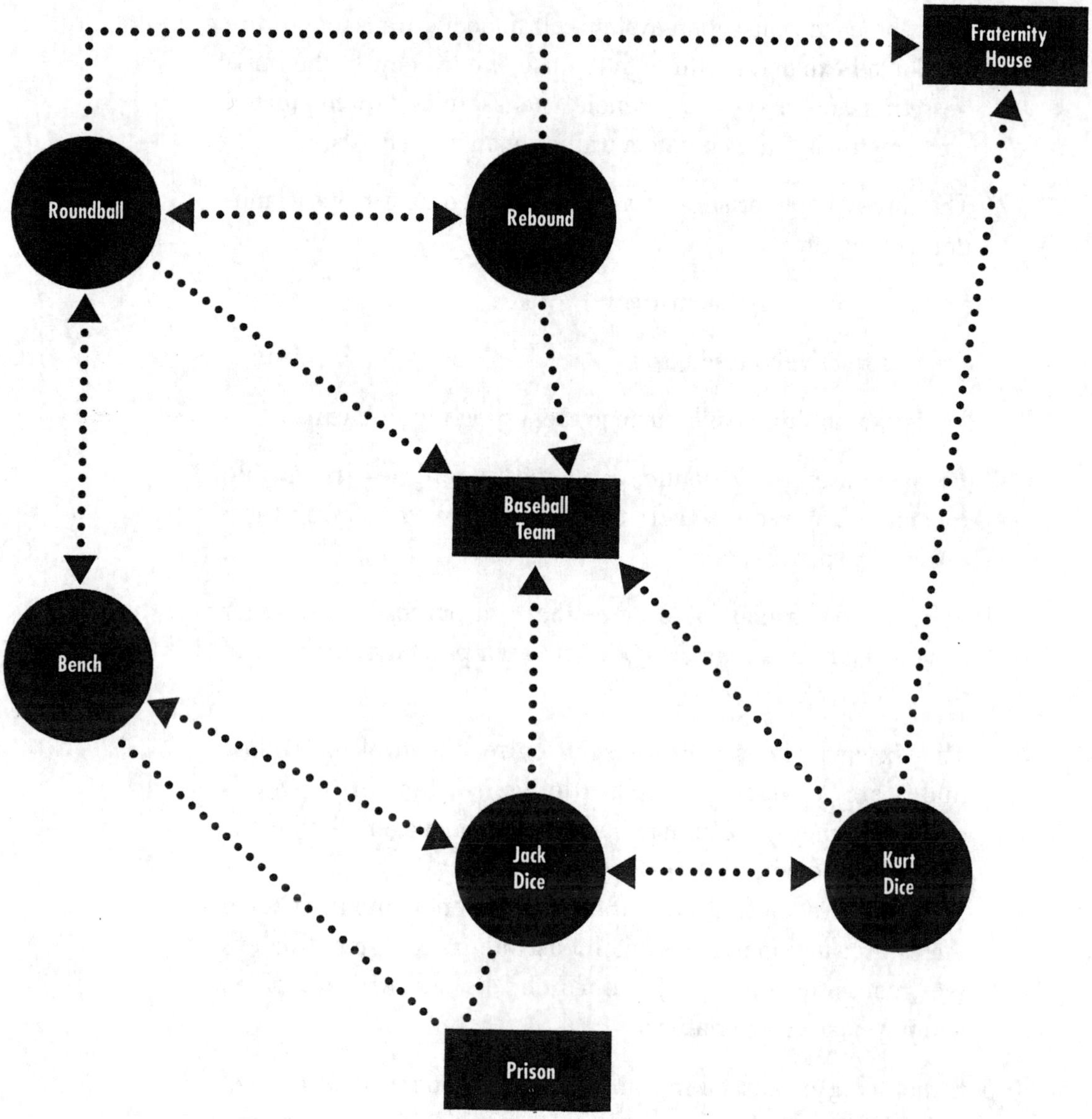

8 An informant could tell you many things including which basketball players are involved in point shaving, who on the outside directs the players to shave points, what past games were involved, what future games might be involved, and how the players are paid off.

Chapter 11

1 With the cash transaction system, all financial transactions are conducted exclusively through the use of currency. In the business transaction system, financial transactions are conducted using methods that generate a trail of financial records.

2 The three characteristics of a business used as a money laundering front are:

- Deals primarily in currency
- Has relatively fixed costs
- Is exempt from bank currency reporting requirements

3 By overstating its revenue, a business increases its taxable income. They reduce their tax liability by overstating their business expenses.

4 You and your friend could agree that you purchase the car for some amount less than $20,000 and then pay the remainder of the balance off the books.

5 The six methods used to transport currency out of the United States are: physical transportation; wire transfer; cashier's check; attorneys, accountants, and money managers; brokerage accounts; and wire services.

The six methods used to transport currency into the United States are: fictitious loans, fictitious foreign investors, finder's fees, corporate salaries, cashier's checks and wire transfers, and physical transportation.

6 Structuring means taking an amount of money in excess of $10,000, breaking it into increments of $10,000 or less, and then conducting multiple transactions for the purpose of evading the CTR reporting requirements. There are many ways money launderers can structure transactions. They can deposit money:

- Several times a day at the same bank branch
- At different branches of the same bank on the same day
- At different banks on the same day

- At the same bank on different days
- At different banks on different days

7 The proceeds of a crime are "whatever is received when an object is sold, exchanged, or otherwise disposed of." Money is not the only proceed that may result from a crime. Goods and services are also considered proceeds.

8 A major difference between the two types of forfeitures has to do with the burden of proof required and who that burden rests with. In a criminal forfeiture, the burden of proof is "beyond a reasonable doubt" and it rests with the government. In a civil forfeiture, the burden of proof is a "preponderance of evidence" and it rests with the claimant.

9 The car described assisted the criminal in performing a crime. It is subject to forfeiture.

10 The methods of indirect proof can be used to show that a suspect "lives beyond his or her means," and although they cannot pinpoint from where the suspect is receiving his or her additional funds, the methods of indirect proof can be used to strengthen the *means of support* or close proximity factors in establishing probable cause for forfeiture.

Glossary

This glossary contains terms presented in the text as well as terms which may be brought out in discussion.

Account
An accounting device used in recording the day-to-day changes in revenue, expense, asset, liability, and owner's equity items.

Account, nominal. Temporary account for an item appearing on an income statement and closed to a balance sheet account at the end of an accounting period.

Account, real. Account for an item appearing on a balance sheet.

Accounting
The system of recording and summarizing business and financial transactions in books and analyzing, verifying, and reporting the results.

Accounting, cost. The process of collecting material, labor, and overhead costs and attaching them to products.

Accounting Period
The period of time over which the transactions of a business are recorded and at the end of which a financial statement is prepared.

Account Payable
An obligation to pay an amount to a creditor.

Account Receivable
An amount that is owed to the business, usually by one of its customers, as a result of the ordinary extension of credit.

Account Transactions
Financial events that directly affect the movement of money through a bank account.

Accrual Basis of Accounting
Recording business revenues when they are earned, regardless of when they are collected,

and recording expenses when they are incurred, regardless of when cash was disbursed.

Accrued Expenses
Expenses incurred but not yet paid for.

Accrued Income
Income earned but not yet received.

Adjusting Entry
Recording the correction of an error, accruals, writeoffs, provisions for bad debts or depreciation, etc., expressed in the form of a simple journal entry.

Affiant
The person who prepares an affidavit.

Affidavit
A handwritten or typed declaration or statement of facts made voluntarily and confirmed by the oath or affirmation of the party making it before an officer having authority to administer such oath.

Alien Corporation
Corporation of another nationality operating in the United States.

Amortize
To write off a portion or all of the cost of an intangible asset.

Appraise
Cash or value established by systematic procedures that include physical examination, pricing, and often engineering estimates.

Asset
Property or resources owned by a business or individual.

Asset, current. An asset which is either currently in the form of cash or is expected to be converted into cash within a short period, usually one year.

Asset, fixed. Tangible property of relatively long life that generally is used in the production of goods and services.

Association Matrix
The graphic summary that results from link analysis.

Audit
A critical review of a business's accounting records.

Bad Debts
Accounts that are considered to be uncollectible.

Balance, Beginning
The amount in an account at the start of the accounting period.

Balance, New
The amount in an account at the end of the accounting

period, it is the difference between the beginning balance plus increases and minus decreases.

Balance Sheet
A financial statement that reports the assets, liabilities, and equities of a company as of a specified time.

Balance Sheet, consolidated. Aggregate accounts for the various categories of assets and liabilities of a corporate family (more than one corporation).

Bank Deposit Method
An indirect method of proving unknown sources of funds through an analysis of bank records and other financial transactions entered into by a suspect.

Bank Reconciliation
A comparison of the customer's records with the records of the bank, listing differences to bring balances into agreement.

Bank Statement
A document rendered by the bank to the depositor, usually monthly, which reflects deposits and checks which have cleared the bank.

Blackmail
A demand for money or other considerations under threat to do bodily harm, to injure property, to accuse of crime, or to expose disgraceful defects.

Bond
Any interest bearing or discounted government or corporate security that obligates the issuer to pay the bondholder a specified sum of money, usually at specific intervals, and to repay the amount of the loan at maturity.

Bond, corporate. A bond issued by a private corporation.

Bond, coupon. A bond that has coupons attached to the bond certificate, one coupon for each interest payment due during the life of the bond. The interest is payable to whoever turns in the coupon, whether or not that person initially bought the bond.

Bond, municipal. A bond issued by a state, county, municipality, or any agency thereof.

Bond, registered. A bond where the name of the owner appears on the bond certificate. Interest on the bond is paid by check directly to the registered holder.

Bond, registered coupon. A bond where the name of the owner appears on records maintained by a registrar and/or transfer agent. The interest coupons attached to the bond certificate do not contain the name of the owner and are payable to the bearer. Registered coupon bonds are registered for the principal only, not for interest.

Bribery
When money, goods, services, information, or anything else of value is offered with the intent to influence the actions, opinions, or decisions of the taker.

Bylaws
The rules adopted by the stockholders setting forth the general method by which the corporate functions are to be carried on subject to the corporate charter.

Case Law
The practice of judges and lawyers looking into decisions from past cases to determine the state of law for the case they are currently handling.

Cash Basis of Accounting
Recording business revenues when cash is received and business expenses when cash is paid.

Cash Flow
The cash flow calculation attempts to measure the actual cash receipts and cash expenses of a firm.

Cashier's Check
A check drawn by a bank on its own funds and issued by an authorized officer of the bank.

Certified Check
A check where the bank guarantees that there are sufficient funds on deposit for that particular check.

Chart of Accounts
A listing, in sequentially numbered order, of a business's accounts.

Civil Law
That body of law that deals with conflicts and differences between individuals.

Closed Corporation
Corporation owned by a few stockholders, not available for investment by public.

Codification
The process of collecting and arranging laws by subject.

Collateral
Something of value pledged as security for a loan.

Common Law
The system of law that originated in England and was the body of law carried by the earliest English settlers to the American colonies.

Contingency
A possible future event or condition arising from causes unknown or at present undeterminable.

Contra Account
One of two or more accounts which partially or wholly offset each other. On financial statements, they may either be merged or appear together, for example, an account receivable from and payable to the same individual.

Cooperative
A corporation in which profits are distributed to shareholders in proportion to the amount of business each shareholder does with the company.

Counterfeiting
Copying or imitating an item without having been authorized to do so and passing the copy off for the genuine or original item.

Corporation
An artificial being or business entity created under state or federal law which is legally separate from the persons who own it. Ownership is in the form of stock and the liability of the owners is limited to the amount of their investment in the company.

CR
Abbreviation of credit.

Credit Entry
An entry on the right-hand side of a T-account.

Creditor
One who lends money.

Criminal Law
That branch of law that deals with offenses of a public nature, that is, wrongs committed against the state.

Curtilage
The area inside the boundary of a person's residence or business location which has been marked off by man-made or naturally-occurring devices.

Debit Entry
A entry on the left-hand side of a T-account.

Debt
Current and non-current liabilities.

Defalcation
The embezzlement of money.

Depreciation
The expiration of an asset's "quality of usefulness."

Discount
Amount by which the face value of a financial instrument exceeds the sales price.

Dividend
Portion of a company's profits distributed to stockholders.

Dividend, cash. Dividend paid in the form of cash.

Dividend, property. Dividend paid in the form of stock from another corporation.

Dividend, stock. Dividend paid in the form of shares of stock in the issuing corporation.

Domestic Corporation
A corporation doing business in the state from which it received its charter.

Double-Entry Accounting
The type of accounting in which the two aspects of each financial event are recorded.

DR
Abbreviation of debit.

Draft
An order in writing directing the payment of money by one party (the drawee) to another party (the payee). A bank check is an example of a draft.

Electronics Fund Transfer
A transaction with a financial institution by means of a computer, telephone, or electronic instrument.

Elements of a Crime
Those constituent parts of a crime that must be proven to sustain a conviction.

Embezzlement
When one entrusted with money or property appropriates it for his or her own use and benefit.

Entry, Closing
An entry reducing one account to zero and offset by an entry increasing another account by the same amount. It is one step in transferring the balance of an account to another account.

Equity, Owner's
Claims against assets by the owner(s).

Evidence
Anything that can make a person believe that a fact or proposition is true or false.

Evidence, circumstantial. Evidence relating to a series of facts other than those at issue that tend, by inference, to establish the fact at issue.

Evidence, direct. Evidence precise to the point at issue.

Evidence, documentary. Evidence in the form of writings and documents.

Evidence, real. *Evidence that is tangible.*

Evidence, testimonial. *Evidence given by word of mouth.*

Exemplar
Non-testimonial identification evidence from a defendant, such as a blood or handwriting sample.

Expenditure
Payment for acquiring an asset or service.

Expenditures Method
An indirect method of determining unknown sources of funds by comparison of all known expenditures with all known receipts during a particular period of time.

Expense
Goods or services consumed in operating a business.

Expense, accrued. *A liability account arising from expenses that are incurred prior to the related expenditure, for example, accrued wages.*

Expense, prepaid. *An expense recognized after a relevant expenditure, for example, future benefits.*

Extortion
Illegally obtaining property from another by actual or threatened force, fear, or violence, or under cover of official right.

Felony
A serious crime punishable by incarceration for a period exceeding one year, a fine, and the loss of certain civil rights.

Financial Condition
The results conveyed by presenting the assets, liabilities, and capital of an enterprise in the form of a balance sheet. Sometimes called financial position.

Financial Interviewing
The systematic questioning of persons who have knowledge of events, those involved, and evidence surrounding a case under investigation.

Fiscal Year
An accounting period of twelve successive calendar months.

Foreign Corporation
A corporation with a charter from another state. A California corporation doing business in Nevada is a foreign corporation in Nevada.

Forensic Science
The application of scientific techniques to legal matters.

Forgery
Passing a false or worthless instrument, such as a check or counterfeit security, with the intent to defraud or injure the recipient.

Forfeiture
A legal proceeding that the Government initiates against the proceeds of an illegal activity.

Fraud
Falsely representing a fact to another in order to induce that person to surrender something of value.

General Partner
A partner personally liable for partnership debts.

Goodwill
An intangible asset representing the difference between the purchase price and the value of the tangible assets purchased.

Grand Jury
A jury who hears evidence obtained by the prosecution and then decides whether or not a trial ought to occur.

Guarantor
One who promises to make good if another fails to pay or otherwise perform an assigned or contractual task.

Hearsay
Evidence that does not come from the personal knowledge of the declarant but from the repetition of what the declarant has heard others say.

Hybrid Method
Method of accounting which is a combination of the cash and accrual methods.

Immunity
An investigative tool used by the grand jury that allows a witness to provide testimony or documents without fear of prosecution.

Income Statement
A financial statement showing revenues earned by a business, the expenses incurred in conducting business, and the resulting net income or net loss.

Income, Net
Excess of total revenues over total expenses in a given period.

Indictment
A formal written complaint of criminal charges.

Indirect Methods
Ways of proving unknown or illegal sources of funds which rely upon circumstantial evidence.

Informant
A person who has specific knowledge of a criminal event and provides that information to a law enforcement officer.

Insider Trading
Using "inside" or advance information to trade in shares of publicly held corporations.

Intangible Asset
Any nonphysical asset, such as goodwill or a patent, which has no physical existence. Its value is dependent on the rights that possession confers upon the owner.

Interest
Charge for the use of money.

Interrogation
Questioning of suspects and/or uncooperative witnesses for the purpose of obtaining testimony and evidence or proof of significant omissions.

Interview
A specialized form of face-to-face communication between people that is entered into for a specific task-related purpose associated with a particular subject matter.

Inventory
Goods being held for sale, and material and partly finished products, which upon completion, will be sold.

Investment Banker
A person or company in the business of marketing bonds and stocks for a corporation desiring to raise money.

Invoice
Bill for goods delivered or services rendered.

Journal
A book of original entry in which transactions are initially recorded before being posted to a ledger.

Judicial Notice
When a court recognizes the existence and truth of certain facts.

Kickback
When a person who sells an item pays back a portion of the purchase price to the buyer or public official.

Lapping
The substitution of checks for cash received. A term used in embezzlement schemes.

Larceny
Wrongfully taking another person's money or property with the intent to appropriate, convert, or steal it.

Law
A formal means of social control intended to guide or direct human behavior toward ends that satisfy the common good.

Ledger
An accounting device used to summarize journal entries by specific accounts.

Lessee
The person or company possessing and using a leased item.

Lessor
The person or company holding legal title to a leased item.

Letter of Credit
A document issued by a bank authorizing designated banks to make payments on demand to a specified individual up to a stated total amount.

Liability
A debt owed.

Liability, current. Obligation that becomes due within a short time, usually one year.

Liability, long-term. Obligation with maturity dates more than one year after the balance sheet date.

Line of Credit
A commitment by a bank to a borrower to lend money at a stated interest rate for a stated period.

Link Analysis
A technique for evaluating, integrating, and presenting complex information collected from various sources and putting them together to show patterns and meanings.

Liquidity
Ability to meet current obligations.

Loss, Net
Excess of total expenses over total revenue in a given period.

Mala In Se
Crimes that are said to be evil or immoral in and of themselves.

Mala Prohibita
Offenses that are made criminal by statute but in and of themselves are not necessarily immoral.

Maturity of Loan
The due date of a loan.

Memorandum
A written record of an interview embodying something that an investigator desires to fix in memory.

Mens Rea
A legal term meaning proof of criminal intent.

Misdemeanor
Crimes less serious than felonies that are punishable by incarceration for a period of less than one year and/or a fine.

Money Laundering
The process by which one conceals the existence, illegal source, or legal application of income and then disguises that income to make it appear legitimate.

Money Order
A negotiable instrument that serves as a substitute for a check.

Mutual Company
Type of corporation that has no stockholders, but is owned by its customers.

Net Worth
The excess of asset value over creditor claims; Assets - Liabilities = Net Worth (Equity).

Net Worth Method
An indirect method of proving unknown sources of funds by comparing net worth at the beginning and end of specified period of time.

Note
A written promise to repay a loan.

Note Receivable
A debt that is evidenced by a note or other written acknowledgment.

Open Corporation
A corporation whose stock is available for investment by the public.

Partner
One of the owners of an unincorporated business.

Par Value
A specified amount printed on the face of a stock certificate.

Partnership
A company created when two or more individuals agree to do business together.

Percentage Method
An indirect method of proving unknown sources of funds by using percentages or ratios considered typical of a business under investigation.

Physical Inventory, Taking of
Counting all merchandise on hand, usually at the end of an accounting period.

Posting
Transfer of an entry from a journal to a ledger account.

Probable Cause
All the facts and circumstances within the knowledge of an

investigator about a criminal activity that can be considered reasonable and trustworthy.

Proceeds
Whatever is received when an object is sold, exchanged, or otherwise disposed of.

Profit and Loss Account
A temporary account where revenue and expense accounts are transferred at the end of an accounting period.

Profit, Gross
Sales minus cost of goods sold.

Proof
The establishment of a fact by evidence.

Proprietor
The owner of an unincorporated business.

Proprietorship
A business owned by one person who is usually both the manager and the owner.

Prospectus
A summary of a corporation registration statement designed to inform a prospective purchaser of securities. It must contain a fairly extensive disclosure statement of essential facts pertinent to the security.

Question and Answer Statement
A complete transcript of the questions, answers, and statements made by each participant during an interview.

Questioned Document
A document that has been questioned in whole or in part in respect to its authenticity, identity, or origin.

Racketeering
Running an illegal business for personal profit.

Reasonable Doubt
The degree of certainty a person has in accomplishing or transacting the more important concerns in everyday life.

Registration Statement
A statement describing, in detail, the financial condition of a corporation, its business, and the reasons it proposes to offer an issue of stocks or bonds to the public.

Revenue
An increase in owner's equity arising from operations.

Search Warrant
A written order by a judge or magistrate, it describes the place to be searched as well as the items to be seized.

Security
A stock, bond, note, or other document that represents a share in a company or a debt owed by a company or government entity.

Shell Corporation
A corporation that has no assets or liabilities, simply a charter to do business.

Single-Entry Accounting
A system of accounting that makes no effort to balance accounts.

Silent Partner
A partner not liable for debts of the partnership beyond the amount of his or her investment in the partnership and who does not participate in management. Also known as a limited partner.

Stakeout
A common term for stationary surveillance.

Sting
A short-term undercover operation.

Stock
Ownership of a corporation represented by shares that are a claim on the corporation's assets and earnings.

Stock, capital. Stock that is authorized by a company's charter.

Stock, common. Units of ownership in a company that allow the owner to receive dividends on his or her holdings.

Stock, issued. The number of shares of stock actually sold or distributed by a corporation.

Stock, outstanding. Issued stock less treasury stock.

Stock, preferred. The class of stock entitled to preferential treatment with regard to dividends or with regard to the distribution of assets in the event of liquidation.

Stock, treasury. Shares of stock issued and subsequently reacquired by the corporation.

Stock Certificate
A document evidencing ownership in a corporation.

Stockholders
An owner of an incorporated business with the ownership being evidenced by stock certificates.

Stock Split
An exchange of the shares outstanding for two or more times their number.

Subpoena
A document that requires a witness to appear before a grand jury or requires the witness to produce records and documents for the grand jury.

Substantive Law
The body of law that creates, discovers, and defines the rights and obligations of each person in society.

Surplus, Capital
An increase in owner's equity not generated through the company's earnings.

Surveillance
The secretive and continuous observation of persons, places, and things to obtain information concerning the identity and activity of individuals suspected of violating criminal laws.

T-Account
An accounting device used for recording increases and decreases on either side of vertical line, with account title on the top.

Tax Evasion
Committing fraud in filing or paying taxes.

Torts
A terms used in civil law, it refers to the private wrongdoings between individuals.

Transaction
The exchange of goods and services.

Treasury Bill
A short-term security offered by the U.S. Government with maturities of 13 weeks, 36 weeks, and 52 weeks.

Treasury Bond
A long-term security offered by the U.S. Government with maturities of 10 years or longer.

Treasury Note
An intermediate-term security offered by the U.S. Government with maturities from one to ten years.

Trial Balance
A list of the account balances arranged in "balance sheet order" by debits and credits with adjustment columns for entries. Used as a basis summary for financial statements.

Undercover Operation
An investigative tool where law enforcement officers or private individuals assume an identity other than their own for the purpose of gathering information relating to criminal violations.

Underwriter
A person or firm guaranteeing and usually participating in the marketing of securities to the public. The guarantee states the dollar amount the underwriter guarantees that the corporation will receive from the sale.

Underwriting Syndicate
A group of underwriters formed for the purpose of guaranteeing the successful sale of a particular issue of securities.

Unit and Volume Method
An indirect method of proving unknown or illegal sources of funds by applying price or profit figures to the known quantity of business.

United States Code
A multi-volume publication of the text of statutes enacted by Congress.

Voucher System
A control system within a company for cash payment.

Worksheet
An accounting device used to organize accounting data.

Appendix A

This appendix contains a listing of selected sources of business information and government records available to the financial investigator.

Business Records

Abstract and Title Company Records

- Maps and tract books.
- Escrow index of purchasers and sellers of real estate (primary source of information)
- Escrow files (number obtained from index)
- Escrow file containing escrow instructions, agreements, and settlements
- Abstracts and title policies
- Special purpose newspapers published for use by attorneys, real estate brokers, insurance companies, and financial institutions. These newspapers contain complete reports on transfers of properties, locations of properties transferred, amounts of mortgages, and releases of mortgages.

Agriculture Records

- County veterinarians
- Commission merchants
- Insurance companies (insure shipments)
- Transportation companies
- Storage companies
- County and state fair boards
- County farm agents
- State cattle control boards (some states maintain records of all cattle brought in and taken out of state)

Automobile Manufacturer and Agency Record

- Franchise agreements
- Financial statements of dealers
- New car sales and deliveries (used car purchases, trade-ins, and sales)

- Service department (mileage, order, and delivery signature to indicate presence in area)

Bonding Company Records

- Investigative and other records on persons and firms bonded
- Financial statements and date
- Address of person on bond

Specialized Commercial Credit Organizations

- United Beverage Bureau
- National Fuel Credit Association
- Jewelers Board of Trade
- Lumbermen's Credit Association
- Produce Reporter Company
- Packer Produce Mercantile Agency
- Paper and Allied Trade Mercantile Agency
- Lyon Furniture Mercantile Agency
- American Monument Association

Credit Reporting Agencies

The Fair Credit Reporting Act of 1971 restricts the availability of information from credit reporting agencies to governmental investigative agencies. Credit reports may only be furnished:

—In response to the order of a court having the jurisdiction to issue such an order;

—Upon written request of the consumer; or

—To a person who has a legitimate business need for the information in regard to a business transaction involving the consumer, including but not limited to credit, insurance, and employment purposes.

There is no specific exception provided in the act that will allow law enforcement agencies to obtain credit reports for investigative purposes. The act provides criminal penalties for obtaining information under false pretenses and for unauthorized disclosures by officers or employees of consumer reporting agencies.

The identifying information which is available under the act is limited to a consumer's name, address, former addresses, place(s) of employment, and former place(s) of employment.

If identifying information is needed for investigative purposes the following credit reporting agencies can be checked:

- Local credit rating and collection agencies
- Local office of National Association of Retail Credit Men

—Insurance applicants

—American Service Bureau

—Hooper Holmes Agency

—Retail Credit Company

- Mortgage Loans

—Loan exchange (clearing house loan information)

—Retailer's Commercial Agency (performs credit investigations for credit cards, banking, and mortgages)

- Transportation

—TRINC (furnishes statistics on the trucking industry).

—Motor Carrier Directory (lists motor carriers with revenues totaling $50,000 or more).

- Manufacturers

—The "Census File of Manufacturers" contains a census of manufacturing plants in the United States.

- Marketing Services

—Dun and Bradstreet, Inc.

—Market Service Bureau

—Middle Market Director (business guide of firms with a net worth between $500,00 and $1,000,000)

—Million Dollar Directory (business guide firms with a net worth of $1,000,000 or more)

—Metal Working Directory (marketing director of metal working plants in the United States)

—Vendor Account Services (used by retail stores in processing accounts payable, buying, and merchandise control)

- International

—International Credit Reports (a division of Dun and Bradstreet which furnishes credit reports on overseas credit)

—International Market Guides (Middle and South America only)

—Continental Europe (lists European businesses in 39 countries)

—Guide to Key British Enterprises (lists prominent firms throughout the United Kingdom)

—Synopsis of Dun– Mexico

—Synopsis of Dun– Brazil

—Reference book– Argentina

—Bradstreet Register

International Mercantile Claims Division

Department Store Records

- Charge accounts
- Credit files

Detective Agency Records

- Investigative files

—Civil

—Criminal

—Commercial

—Industrial

- Character checks
- Fraud and blackmail investigations
- Divorce evidence
- Missing persons search
- Security patrols and guards
- Undercover agents
- Shadow work
- Lie detector tests
- Personnel screening and fingerprinting
- Service checking
- Restaurants
- Public transportation
- Stores

Distributors' Records

- Wholesale toiletry (cash rebates are paid by toiletry manufacturers). Details of available contracts which pay rebates to wholesale toiletry distributors are contained in publications issued by the Toiletry Merchandisers Association, Inc., 230 Park Avenue, New York, N.Y. 10017, and the Druggist Service Council, Inc., 1290 Avenue of the Americas, New York., N.Y. 10019
- Gambling equipment
- Wire service
- Factory, farm, home, office equipment, etc.

Drug Store Records

- Prescription records (name, address, date, and physician issuing prescription)

Fraternal, Veterans, Labor, Social, and Political Organization Records

- Membership and attendance records
- Dues, contributions, and payments
- Locations and history of members

Hospital Records

- Entry and release dates
- Payments made

Hotel Records

- Identity of guest
- Payments made by guest
- Credit record
- Forwarding address
- Reservations for travel (transportation companies and other hotels)
- Telephone calls made to and from room
- Freight shipments and luggage (in and out)

Insurance Company Records (Life, accident, fire, burglary, automobile, and annuity policies)

- Applications (background and financial information, insurance carried with other companies)
- Fur and jewelry floaters (appraised value and description)
- Customers' ledger cards
- Policy and mortgage loan accounts
- Dividend payment records
- Cash value and other net worth data
- Correspondence files
- Payment records on termination, losses, or refunds on cancellations
- Payments to doctors, lawyers, appraisers, and photographers hired directly by the insurance company to act for the company or as an independent expert

Laundry and Dry Cleaning Records

- Marks and tags (marks are sometimes invisible and are brought out by use of ultraviolet rays)
- Files of laundry marks

—Local or State police departments
—National Institute of Dry Cleaning, Inc., Washington, D.C.

Lenders Exchange or Consumer Loan Exchange

An organization known as the Consumer Loan Exchange or Lenders Exchange exists in all of the large cities in the United States, as well as in some of the smaller cities. It is a nonprofit organization supported by and for its members. Most the lending institutions are members of the exchange. It can supply information concerning open and closed loan accounts with member companies, and is a good source of general background information. These organizations are not listed in directories or telephone books. Their location in a city may be obtained through local lending agencies.

National Charge Plan Records

National agencies, such American Express, Diners Club, and Carte Blanche, which provide credit cards for use in charging travel, entertainment, goods and services, can determine whether an individual or business has an account from their central index files. If details of the account are needed, information requests should indicate whether only copies of the monthly statements or copies of both the statements and charge slips are desired, name, social security number, the time period to be covered, the subject's address, and the name and address of the subject's employer or business. Requests should be directed to:

American Express Company, 770 Broadway, New York, N.Y. 10003, and Diners Club/Carte Blanche, Adjustment Department, 180 Inverness Drive West, Englewood, CO 80111.

Newspaper Records (from a newspaper's morgue)

- Relatives, associates, and friends
- Previous places of employment (employee or company publications)
- Police and FBI files
- Schools (yearbooks, school papers, etc.)
- License bureaus (drivers, chauffeurs, taxis, etc.)
- Military departments
- Fraternal organizations
- Church groups
- Race tracks
- Nightclub or sidewalk photographers and photography studios

Public Utility Company Records

- Present and previous address of subscriber
- Payments made for service and "major" purchases

Publications

- *Who's Who in America* and various States
- Tax services
- City directories
- *Billboard* (amusements, coin-machines, burlesque, drive-ins, fairs, state, radio, TV, magic,

music machines, circuses, rinks, vending machines, movies, letter lists, and obituaries)

- *Variety* (literature, radio, TV, music, state, movies, obituaries, etc.)

- *American Racing Manual* (published by Triangle Publications, Inc., 10 Lake Drive, P.O. Box 1015, Highstown, New Jersey 08520). Records showing amounts paid to owners of winning horses by each race track in the United States, Canada, and Mexico

- Professional, trade, and agriculture directories and magazines

- *Moody's Investors Service Inc.*

- *Standard and Poor's Corporation*

Real Estate Agency or Savings and Loan Association Records

- Property transactions

- Financial statements

- Payments made and received (settlement sheets)

- Credit files

- Loan applications. These do not contain quite the same information as loan applications given to a bank. A savings and loan association depends primarily upon real estate security rather than upon other assets and liabilities of a borrower.

Telephone Company Records

- Local directories, library of "out of city" directories

- Message unit detail sheets (in some areas) which list numbers called by a particular telephone

- Investigative reports on telephones used for illegal purposes

- Payments for service

- Toll calls. Because of the existence of more than one long distance carrier, toll records of a local phone company may be an incomplete listing of such calls. There may be a second telephone bill from another company, such as GT&E or MCI.

Transportation Company Records

- Passenger lists, reservations

- Destinations

- Fares paid

- Freight carrier-shippers, destinations, and storage points

- Departure and arrival times

Government Records

State Police (Central Records Section)

- Criminal cases

- Criminal intelligence

• Inflammable liquid installations

• Firearms registrations

• Investigations conducted for other departments

• Traffic arrests and motor vehicle accident investigations

• Noncriminal and criminal fingerprint records

• "Rogues gallery"

• Investigation of aviation rules and non-carrier civilian aircraft accidents

• Police training school files

City Police

• Criminal identification

—Records of arrests, accidents, and general information

—Alphabetical indexes of every complainant or suspect

—"Aided" cards (citizen assistance)

—Gun permits or applications and registrations

—Lost or stolen articles

—Pawn shop files

—Towed or repossessed autos

—Ambulance files

—Business information files

—"Scofflaw files" (consistent violator of minor offense– primarily traffic)

• Other divisions

—Criminal division files

—Forgery squad (check squad)

—Juvenile division

—Morals or vice squad files

—Narcotics bureau

—Organized crime division

—Police force personal history files

—Public relations office (press file)

—Traffic division files

Small Town Police

• Criminal index cards

• Criminal arrest cards

• Accident reports

• Complaint forms

• Offense reports

County Police (Sheriff)

• Criminal records

—Crimes involving bodily violence

—Crimes involving theft

—Crimes involving worthless checks

—Personal history sheets on people connected with the crimes

—Juvenile division records

—County business owners

- Traffic records

—Name, address, license plate number, driver's license number, arrest number, date and place of birth, sex, color, age, occupation, height, weight, complexion, color of hair, eyes, marks, and facts of arrest

National Sheriffs Association Directory

- List of State institutions and their superintendents
- State and Federal enforcement agencies and territorial jurisdictions
- Associate members of National Sheriffs Association
- County sheriffs
- Address of National Auto Theft Bureau

Other State and Local Law Enforcement and Quasi-Law Enforcement Organizations

- Specialized police organizations
- Public, semi-public, and private organizations
- The industrial security officer
- International Association of Chiefs of Police
- The monthly police administration review list of police publications

State and Local Court Records

Typically, there are three levels of courts within the State system. There is a Trial Court, where most litigation begins, an Appellate Court, which is the first level of appeal, and Court of Final Appeal. Sometimes you will find a court below the Trial Court which works much like the magistrate does in the Federal system.

Most litigation, such as divorce or breach of contract, takes place in the State and local system. Documents submitted to the court in connection with a divorce are particularly helpful in financial investigations. It is not unusual for detailed asset and liability information to be present in a divorce file.

Probate records describing estates and distribution of estates are also found in the State and local court system. These may be particularly helpful in negating nontaxable sources of cash.

Anytime a person is involved in a civil action, whether it be for breach of contract or some type of negligence action, a wealth of background information on the individual is usually provided to the opposing party through the court. A record of this information will be kept in the case files of the court and is available to an investigator.

Federal Government Records

Bureau of Alcohol, Tobacco, and Firearms (ATF)

- Distillers, brewers, and persons or firms who manufacture or handle alcohol, as a sideline or main product
- Inventory or retail liquor dealers and names of suppliers as well as amounts of liquor purchased by brand
- Names and records of known bootleggers
- Names of subjects of investigations by ATF
- Processors, manufacturers, and wholesalers of tobacco products
- List of all Federal firearms license holders, including manufacturers, importers, and dealers
- List of all Federal explosives license holders, including manufacturers, importers and dealers
- For weapons manufactured or imported after 1986, capability of tracing any firearm from manufacturer or importer to retailer

Bureau of the Public Debt

- U.S. savings bonds purchased and redeemed
- Requests for information must be addressed to:

Bureau of the Public Debt
Division of Transactions and Rulings
200 Third Street
Parkersburg, West Virginia 26101

Federal Aviation Agency (FAA)

This agency maintains records which reflect the chain of ownership of all civil aircraft in the United States. These records include documents relative to their manufacture and sale (sales contracts, bills of sale, mortgages, liens, transfers, inspections, and modifications). They also maintain licensing and medical information on pilots.

Federal Aviation Administration
Civil Aviation Security Division
AAC– 90, P.O. Box 25082
Oklahoma City, Oklahoma 73125

Department of Agriculture

- Licensed meat packers and food canners
- Inspections made under Pure Food and Drug Act
- Transactions with individuals and businesses (subsidies and adjustments)

Department of Defense

The Department of Defense maintains data concerning pay, dependents, allotment accounts, deposits, withholding statements (Forms W-2), and any other financial information relative to military personnel. This information is available at one the following offices, depending upon the branch of the Armed Forces to which the individual was or is presently attached:

United States Army Finance Center
Indianapolis, Indiana 46249
Request must include the complete name and Army serial number

Air Force Finance Center
RPTP
Denver, Colorado 80279

Director, Bureau of Supplies and Accounts
Department of the Navy
13th and Euclid Streets
Cleveland, Ohio 44115

Department of the State

- Import and export licenses
- Foreign information
- Passport records (date and place of birth required). Recent data may be obtained from the local district court.

Drug Enforcement Administration (DEA)

- Licensed handlers of narcotics
- Criminal records of users, pushers, and suppliers of narcotics

Federal Bureau of Investigation (FBI)

- Criminal records and fingerprints
- Anonymous Letter Index
- National Stolen Property Index (stolen Government property, including military property)
- Nonrestricted information pertaining to criminal offenses and subversive activities
- National Fraudulent Check Index

U.S. Customs Service

- Record of importers and exporters
- Record of custom house brokers

• Record of custom house truckers (cartage licenses)

• List of suspects

• Records of persons who transport or cause to be transported currency of more than $10,000, or certain monetary instruments at one time into or out of the United States

U.S. Secret Service

• Records pertaining to counterfeit, forgery, and United States' security violation cases

• Records pertaining to anonymous letters and background files on persons who write "crank" letters

• Secret Service's central files in Washington, D.C., contain an estimated 100,000 handwriting specimens of known forgers. An electronic information retrieval system facilitates comparison of questioned handwriting with the specimens on file for identification purposes.

U.S. Postal Service

• Mail watch or cover

• Current or forwarding addresses of subjects and third parties

• Photostats of postal money orders. Requests for such records must be addressed to:

Money Order Division
Postal Data Center
P.O. Box 14965
St. Louis, Missouri 63182

• Addresses of post office box holders. These requests should be made only when efforts to obtain the information from other sources are unsuccessful. Information can be obtained from the Inspector-in-Charge or Postal Inspector. Check with the local post office to learn the identity of the inspector who can furnish the information.

Immigration and Naturalization Service (INS)

• Records of all immigrants and aliens

• Deportation proceedings

• Passenger manifests and declarations (ship, date, and point of entry required)

• Naturalization records (names of witnesses to naturalization proceedings and people who know the suspect)

• Lists of passengers and crews on vessels from foreign ports

• Financial statements of aliens and persons sponsoring their entry

Interstate Commerce Commission (ICC)

The ICC has information concerning individuals who are or have been officers of transportation firms engaged in interstate commerce. This information includes the officer's employment and financial affiliations.

In addition to the record information available from the ICC, most safety inspectors of the ICC are good sources of "reference" information because they have personal knowledge of supervisory employees of the various carriers in their region.

IRS National Computer Center
The National Computer Center is located in Martinsburg, West Virginia and it maintains the Master File, a tax record of all known taxpayers. The Master File is designed to accumulate all data pertaining to the tax liabilities of all taxpayers, regardless of location. The Master File is separated into several categories. Two of the categories are the Business Master File and the Individual Master File.

Securities and Exchange Commission (SEC)

- Records of corporate registrants of securities offered for public sale, which usually show:

—A description of registrant's properties and business

—A description of the significant provisions of the security to be offered for sale and its relationship to the registrant's other capital securities

—Information as to the management of the registrant

—Certified financial statements of the registrants

- Securities and Exchange Commission News Digest (a daily publication giving a brief summary of financial proposals files and the actions taken by the SEC)

- The SEC Bulletin is issued quarterly and contains information of official actions with respect to the preceding month. It also contains a supplement which lists the names of individuals reported as being wanted on charges of violations of the law in connection with securities transactions. It is available upon request at any of the SEC regional or branch offices in the following cities:

Atlanta, GA
Miami, FL
Boston, MA
New York, NY
Chicago, IL
Philadelphia, PA
Cleveland, OH
Salt Lake City, UT

Denver, CO
San Francisco, CA
Detroit, MI
Seattle, WA
Fort Worth, TX
St. Louis, MO
Los Angeles, CA
Washington, D.C.

- The SEC's Securities Violations Section maintains comprehensive files on individuals and firms who have been reported to the Commission as having violated Federal or State securities laws. The information pertains to official actions taken against such persons, including denials, refusals, suspensions, and revocations of registrations; injunctions, fraud orders, stop order, cease and desist orders; and arrests, indictments, convictions, sentences, and other official actions.

Social Security Administration

The Social Security Administration, headquartered in Baltimore, is responsible for the issuance of social security numbers. Records on social security paid by an individual or business are not available for review by the public.

If a social security number is known, it might lead to helpful information regarding the location in which the card was issued. Since many people apply for a social security number at a young age, this in turn can lead to locating the place of birth of an individual. There are nine digits in the social security number. With the exception of the 700 series, the first three digits reflect the state of issue. The last six digits are individual identifiers. The table on the next page contains a listing of the states of issue of the first three digits.

Initial Numbers	State of Issuance	Initial Numbers	State of Issuance
001 - 003	New Hampshire	449 - 467 627 - 645	Texas
004 - 007	Maine	468 - 477	Minnesota
008 - 009	Vermont	478 - 485	Iowa
010 - 034	Massachusetts	486 - 500	Missouri
035 - 039	Rhode Island	501 - 502	North Dakota
040 - 049	Connecticut	503 - 504	South Dakota
050 - 134	New York	505 - 508	Nebraska
135 - 158	New Jersey	509 - 515	Kansas
159 - 211	Pennsylvania	516 - 517	Montana
212 - 220	Maryland	518 - 519	Idaho
221 - 222	Delaware	520	Wyoming
223 - 231	Virginia	521 - 524	Colorado
232 - 236	West Virginia	525, 585, 648 - 649 allocated,not in use	New Mexico
237 - 246, 232 with middle digits 30	North Carolina	526 - 527 600 - 601	Arizona
247 - 251	South Carolina	528 - 529 646 - 647 allocated, not in use	Utah
252 - 260	Georgia	530	Nevada
261 - 267 589 - 595	Florida	531 - 539	Washington
268 - 302	Ohio	540 - 544	Oregon
303 - 317	Indiana	545 - 573 602 - 626	California
318 - 361	Illinois	574	Alaska
362 - 386	Michigan	575 - 576	Hawaii
387 - 399	Wisconsin	577 - 579	Washington, DC
400 - 407	Kentucky	580 groups 01 - 18	Virgin Islands
408 - 415	Tennessee	580 (groups above 20) - 584, 596 - 599	Puerto Rico
416 - 424	Alabama	586	Guam, American Samoa, Northern Mariana Islands, Philippine Islands
425 - 428, 587 588 allocated, not in use	Mississippi	700 - 728	Railroad employees with special retirement act
429 - 432	Arkansas		
433 - 439	Louisiana		
440 - 448	Oklahoma		

Veterans Administration (VA)

• Records of loans, tuition payments, insurance payments, and nonrestrictive medical data related to disability pensions are available at regional offices. This information, including photostats, may be obtained by writing the appropriate regional office. All requests should include a statement covering the need and intended use of the information. The veteran should be identified clearly and, if available, the following information should be furnished:

—VA claim number

—Date of birth

—Branch of service

—Dates of enlistment and discharge

Federal Reserve Bank (FRB)

• Records of issue of United States Treasury Bonds

United States Coast Guard

• Records of persons serving on United States ships in any capacity

• Records of vessels equipped with permanently installed motors

• Records of vessels over 16 feet long equipped with detachable motors

Treasurer of the United States

Checks paid by the U.S. Treasury are processed through the Office of the Treasurer of the United States. Photostats of the canceled checks may be obtained by initiating a request through the U.S. government agency which authorized the check.

National Crime Information Center (NCIC)

The National Crime Information Center is a repository of data relating to crime and criminals gathered by local, State, and Federal law enforcement agencies. The NCIC's computer equipment is located at FBI Headquarters in Washington, D.C. The present equipment is capable of accommodating nearly 2 million records on criminal activities. In a matter of seconds, stored information can be retrieved through equipment in the telecommunications network. Connecting terminals are located throughout the country in police departments, sheriff's offices, State police facilities, and Federal law enforcement agencies. Dispatchers can respond quickly to requests. NCIC, as well as operating statewide systems, furnishes computerized data in a matter of seconds to all agencies participating in the centralized State systems. The goal of NCIC is to serve as a national index to fifty statewide computer systems and heavily populated metropolitan area systems.

NCIC Headquarters might be compared to a large automated "file cabinet" with each file having its own label or classification. Such a cabinet of data contains information concerning:

Stolen, missing, or recovered guns

Stolen articles

Wanted persons

Stolen/wanted vehicles

Stolen license plates

Stolen/wanted boats

Stolen/embezzled/missing securities

National Law Enforcement Telecommunications System (NLETS)

NLETS is a computerized communication network linking State and local enforcement agencies in all 50 States. It can provide information such as criminal history, driver's licenses, and vehicle registration.

El Paso Intelligence Center (EPIC)

EPIC is a multi-agency operation that collects, processes, and disseminates information on narcotics traffickers, gun smugglers, and alien smugglers in support of ongoing field investigations.

If a suspect is or has been engaged in any of the previously mentioned activities, it is possible that EPIC will have intelligence information on him or her. This information might include the name of the individual, his or her known activities, significant events, associations among individuals or activities, aircraft or vessels used by the subject, observations of both foreign and domestic movements of the subject, and his or her associates and their aircraft or vessels. EPIC also provides the name, agency, and telephone number of each investigator having expressed an interest in or having data regarding a subject. EPIC records often contain substantial *financial* information relative to the subject.

International Criminal Police Organization (Interpol)

Interpol is an international police agency with bureaus set up in member countries. In the

United States, the National Central Bureau is under the direction and control of the Departments of Justice and Treasury.

The National Central Bureau can assist in such things as criminal history checks, license plate and driver's license checks, and the location of suspects, fugitives, and witnesses.

The Federal Courts

This system is basically a three step process. The first step is the U.S. District Court;, the second, the U.S. Court of Appeals; and the third, the U.S. Supreme Court. Since most court records are similar, we will only deal with the U.S. District Court in this appendix.

- U.S. District Courts

There are U.S. District Courts in every State (the larger States have several) and in the District of Columbia, Guam, Puerto Rico, the Canal Zone, and the Virgin Islands.

The U.S. District Court has exclusive jurisdiction in bankruptcy, maritime and admiralty, patents, copyright penalties, fines under Federal law, and proceedings against consul and vice consuls of foreign states. In addition, it has jurisdiction when the United States or a national bank is a party, and in cases where the law specifically states that the U.S. District Court has original jurisdiction.

The U.S. District Courts have concurrent jurisdictions with State courts on "Federal questions" when the dispute arises under the Constitution, laws, or treaties of the United States; disputes between citizens of different States; one U.S. citizen and one citizen of a foreign state; or a citizen and a foreign state.

The U.S. District Court has broad criminal jurisdiction over all offenses against the laws of the United States. When both Federal and State laws are violated by one committing a crime, the offender is subject to prosecution in both the Federal and State courts for the separate crimes.

The files of the clerk's office of a U.S. District Court are not as complex as those of a State court of original jurisdiction. For the investigator, **the most important records in the custody of a clerk of a U.S. District Court are the case records.** These records consist of the files (case papers), the minutes, and the dockets.

—The files consist of pleadings, processes, and written

orders and judgments of the court, and such other papers as pertain directly to the case.

—The minutes record, in summary form, of what happened during the proceedings. In some courts, the minutes are an integral part of the file.

—The docket sheet on each case is a chronological summary, not only of what takes place in court, but also of the papers in the file. The docket sheet can be very valuable to an investigator who is looking for only one item in a huge file. In most U.S. District Courts there are separate sets of dockets for bankruptcy, and civil and criminal cases. Some clerks have found it to their advantage to keep a set of miscellaneous dockets, and most clerks keep the docket sheets for closed cases in a separate area.

The clerk of a district court will have a record of banking institutions that have been designated as depositories for money of estates in bankruptcy.

The United States District Courts have jurisdiction to naturalize aliens and maintain copies of the certificates of naturalization as well as a name index of the individuals naturalized. If an alien elects to change his or her name at naturalization, both the old an new name appears in the index. In addition, a copy of the subject's Application to File Petition for Naturalization appears in the court records. This form (N-400) contains considerable information about the alien being naturalized.

- Other Federal Courts

To handle particular types of cases, Congress has established special courts. They are described in the *Guide to Court Systems* as follows:

—Court of Claims— The U.S. Government permits certain claims to be brought against itself in the U.S. Court of Claims.

—U.S. Customs Court— When certain merchandise is imported into the United States, customs duties have to be paid to the U.S. Government. Customs collectors at various ports in the United States classify merchandise and appraise it. When an importer complains on the rate, or that the merchandise was improperly excluded, the U.S. Customs Court is the court to which the case must be brought. Appeals from the U.S. Customs Courts are taken to the Court of Customs and Patent Appeals. This court also reviews certain decisions of the Patent Office and the U.S. Tariff Commission.

Appendix B

This appendix contains information regarding the American Bankers Association prefix numbers of cities and states and a listing of Federal Reserve Districts.

Federal Reserve Districts

1 - Boston
2 - New York
3 - Philadelphia
4 - Cleveland
5 - Richmond
6 - Atlanta
7 - Chicago
8 - St. Louis
9 - Minneapolis
10 - Kansas City
11 - Dallas
12 - San Francisco

American Bankers Association Prefix Numbers

THE NUMERICAL SYSTEM
of The American Bankers Association
Index to Prefix Numbers of Cities and States

Numbers 1 to 49 inclusive are Prefixes for Cities
Numbers 50 to 99 inclusive are Prefixes for States
Prefix Numbers 50 to 58 are Eastern States
Prefix Number 59 is Hawaii
Prefix Numbers 60 to 69 are Southeastern States
Prefix Numbers 70 to 79 are Central States
Prefix Numbers 80 to 88 are Southwestern States
Prefix Number 89 is Alaska

Prefix Numbers of Cities in Numerical Order

1 New York, N.Y.
2 Chicago, Il.
3 Philadelphia, Pa.
4 St Louis, Mo.
5 Boston, Mass.
6 Cleveland, Ohio
7 Baltimore, Md.
8 Pittsburgh, Pa.
9 Detroit, Mich.
10 Buffalo, N.Y.
11 San Francisco, Ca.
12 Milwaukee, Wis.
13 Cincinnati, Ohio
14 New Orleans, La.
15 Washington, D.C.
16 Los Angeles, Ca.
17 Minneapolis, Minn.
18 Kansas City, Mo.
19 Seattle, Wash.
20 Indianapolis, Ind.
21 Louisville, Ky.
22 St. Paul, Minn.
23 Denver, Colo.
24 Portland, Ore.
25 Columbus, Ohio
26 Memphis, Tenn.
27 Omaha, Neb.
28 Spokane, Wash.
29 Albany, N.Y.
30 San Antonio, Tx.
31 Salt Lake City, Ut
32 Dallas, Tx.
33 Des Moines, Iowa
34 Tacoma, Wash.
35 Houston, Tx.
36 St. Joseph, Mo.
37 Fort Worth, Tx.
38 Savannah, Ga.
39 Oklahoma City, Ok.
40 Wichita, Kan.
41 Sioux City, Iowa
42 Pueblo, Co.
43 Lincoln, Neb.
44 Topeka, Kan.
45 Dubuque, Iowa
46 Galveston, Tx.
47 Cedar Rapids, Iowa
48 Waco, Tx.
49 Muskogee, Ok.

Prefix Numbers of States in Numerical Order

50 New York
51 Connecticut
52 Maine
53 Massachusetts
54 New Hampshire
55 New Jersey
56 Ohio
57 Rhode Island
58 Vermont
59 Hawaii
60 Pennsylvania
61 Alabama
62 Delaware
63 Florida
64 Georgia
65 Maryland
66 North Carolina
67 South Carolina
68 Virginia
69 West Virginia
70 Illinois
71 Indiana
72 Iowa
73 Kentucky
74 Michigan
75 Minnesota
76 Nebraska
77 North Dakota
78 South Dakota
79 Wisconsin
80 Missouri
81 Arkansas
82 Colorado
83 Kansas
84 Louisiana
85 Mississippi
86 Oklahoma
87 Tennessee
88 Texas
89 Alaska
90 California
91 Arizona
92 Idaho
93 Montana
94 Nevada
95 New Mexico
96 Oregon
97 Utah
98 Washington
99 Wyoming
101 Territories

Index

C

D

E

U

V

W

☆ U. S. GOVERNMENT PRINTING OFFICE: 1998-441-325/90425